Race and Racism i

MW01610810

Racism has been endemic in the history of western societies, while the nature of race as a social category of difference is controversial and rigorously contested from scholarly and everyday perspectives today. This edited collection traces the history of considerations of the meaning and importance of race and racism in society and education through a deep dive into the contents of the archives of the journal *Educational Philosophy and Theory*.

Journal articles from the 1970s to today have been carefully selected throughout the text to showcase the trends and transformations in the field of educational philosophy over time. While historically western analytic philosophy of education did not focus particularly on race and racism, this changed in the 1990s, with the emergence of critical conversations about social justice that moved beyond liberal models. More recently, historical and theoretical accounts have sought to understand the processes of racialization in depth, as well as the intersectional nature of race privilege and discrimination across contemporary diverse societies worldwide. Taken together, the pieces in this book illustrate both the history of theorizing about race and racism in educational philosophy and theory as well as the breadth of present-day concerns.

This collection provides a foundation for developing a historical understanding of the position of race and racism in philosophy of education, while it also inspires new works in Critical Race Theory, Black and African Studies, critical pedagogy, and related areas. Additionally, it will inspire educators and scholars across diverse fields to further consider the significance of race and racism in education and in research in the present age.

Liz Jackson is Professor of Education at the Education University of Hong Kong. She is also President of the Philosophy of Education Society of Australasia and the former Director of the Comparative Education Research Centre at the University of Hong Kong. Her interests are in philosophy of education, moral philosophy, and global studies. She is the author of *Muslims and Islam in US Education: Reconsidering Multiculturalism* (2014), *Questioning Allegiance: Resituating Civic Education* (2019) and *Beyond Virtue: The Politics of Educating Emotions* (2020).

Michael A. Peters is Distinguished Professor of Education at Beijing Normal University and Emeritus Professor at the University of Illinois. He is the Executive Editor of the journal *Educational Philosophy and Theory*. His interests are in education, philosophy, and social policy, and he is the author of over 100 books, including *The Chinese Dream: Educating the Future* (2019), *Wittgenstein, Education and Rationality* (2020), and *Wittgenstein: Antifoundationalism, Technoscience and Education* (2020).

Educational Philosophy and Theory: Editor's Choice
Series editors: Michael A. Peters
Beijing Normal University, China

The EPAT Editor's Choice series comprises innovative and influential articles drawn from the *Educational Philosophy and Theory* journal archives, spanning 46 volumes, from 1969. Each volume represents a selection of important articles that respond to and focus on a particular theme, celebrating and emphasizing the heritage and history of the work, as well as the cutting edge contemporary contributions available. The series will create a rich vertical collection across five decades of seminal scholarship, contextualizing and elevating specific themes, scholars and their work. The EPAT Editor, Michael A. Peters, introduces each volume, the theme, and the work selected within that volume.

Titles in the series include:

The Methodology and Philosophy of Collective Writing
An Educational Philosophy and Theory Reader Volume X
Michael A. Peters, Tina Besley, Marek Tesar, Liz Jackson, Petar Jandric, Sonja Arndt and Sean Sturm

From Radical Marxism to Knowledge Socialism
An Educational Philosophy and Theory Economic and Liberal Studies Reader, Volume XI
Edited by Michael A. Peters and Liz Jackson

Marxism, Neoliberalism, and Intelligent Capitalism
An Educational Philosophy and Theory Economic and Liberal Studies Reader, Volume XII
Edited by Liz Jackson and Michael A. Peters

Race and Racism in Education
An Educational Philosophy and Theory Reader Volume XIII
Edited by Liz Jackson and Michael A. Peters

For more information about the series, please visit www.routledge.com/ Educational-Philosophy-and-Theory-Editors-Choice/book-series/EPAT

Race and Racism in Education

An Educational Philosophy and
Theory Reader Volume XIII

Edited by Liz Jackson and
Michael A. Peters

 Routledge
Taylor & Francis Group

LONDON AND NEW YORK

First published 2023
by Routledge
4 Park Square, Milton Park, Abingdon, Oxon OX14 4RN

and by Routledge
605 Third Avenue, New York, NY 10158

Routledge is an imprint of the Taylor & Francis Group, an informa business

© 2023 selection and editorial matter, Liz Jackson and Michael A.
Peters; individual chapters, the contributors

The right of Liz Jackson and Michael A. Peters to be identified as
the authors of the editorial material, and of the authors for their
individual chapters, has been asserted in accordance with sections
77 and 78 of the Copyright, Designs and Patents Act 1988.

All rights reserved. No part of this book may be reprinted or
reproduced or utilised in any form or by any electronic, mechanical,
or other means, now known or hereafter invented, including
photocopying and recording, or in any information storage or
retrieval system, without permission in writing from the publishers.

Trademark notice: Product or corporate names may be trademarks
or registered trademarks, and are used only for identification and
explanation without intent to infringe.

British Library Cataloguing-in-Publication Data
A catalogue record for this book is available from the British Library

Library of Congress Cataloging-in-Publication Data
Names: Jackson, Liz, 1980– editor. | Peters, Michael (Michael A.),
    1948– editor.
Title: Race and racism in education : an educational philosophy and
    theory reader. Volume XIII / edited by Liz Jackson and
    Michael A. Peters.
Description: New York : Routledge, 2023. | Series: Educational
    philosophy and theory: Editor's choice | Includes bibliographical
    references and index.
Identifiers: LCCN 2022029192 (print) | LCCN 2022029193 (ebook) |
    ISBN 9781032386515 (Hardback) | ISBN 9781032386546
    (Paperback) | ISBN 9781003346104 (eBook)
Subjects: LCSH: Racism in education—United States. | Education—
    United States—Philosophy—History.
Classification: LCC LC212.5 .R35 2023 (print) | LCC LC212.5 (ebook) |
    DDC 370.89—dc23/eng/20220713
LC record available at https://lccn.loc.gov/2022029192
LC ebook record available at https://lccn.loc.gov/2022029193

ISBN: 978-1-032-38651-5 (hbk)
ISBN: 978-1-032-38654-6 (pbk)
ISBN: 978-1-003-34610-4 (ebk)

DOI: 10.4324/9781003346104

Typeset in Galliard
by Apex CoVantage, LLC

Contents

Introduction

Liz Jackson and Michael A. Peters

Three of the most significant categories that divide people in societies and school systems are race, gender, and class (or socioeconomic status). However, within social and educational research, the three remain elusive concepts to work with (Jackson, 2019a; Jackson, 2014). To what extent they are 'natural', empirical, or socially constructed; whether and how they can be fixed or fluid; whether they 'really matter' and should retain our attention; or, alternatively, if they should be radically reconsidered or even discarded are all questions that have been debated by scholars and lay people throughout the last few centuries. Race, which is increasingly regarded as socially constructed, is particularly contentious, with many (e.g., political rightists) arguing that discussions about race and its existence are unnecessary or unhelpful when looking into the future (Leonardo, 2011).

Race, gender, and class have also been deliberated upon systematically for many decades in philosophy of education and in the journal *Educational Philosophy and Theory*. In past edited volumes in this series, we have examined the place of gender and feminist theory (Jackson & Peters, 2019a, 2019b) and Marxist, neoliberal, and other class and socioeconomic-related theory (Peters & Jackson, 2022; Jackson & Peters, 2022) in the history of philosophy of education and *Educational and Philosophy and Theory*. In this collection and in this introduction, we consider the role of race theorising in the field and the journal and its significance and development over time.

This introduction first gives a global picture about how race has been and is conceived in educational and other social theory, thus tracing a path in scholarship on race and racism in connection to other important global phenomena, such as ethnicity, colonialism, and nationalism. Given the journal's historical roots in Australian and New Zealand academia, it is also worthwhile here to identify how explorations of race and racism have been attended to in different ways around the world in recent decades, in relation to indigeneity and diverse communities' struggles for recognition, rights, and survival. Then we summarise the chapters that follow, analysing the place of race and race theory in *Educational Philosophy and Theory* over the years.

DOI: 10.4324/9781003346104-1

Understanding Race and Racism

Today, most articles in *Educational Philosophy and Theory* (among other journals) assume that the reader understands what is meant by the word 'race'. Indeed, as this collection shows, since the 2000s many articles that deal with race proceed with explanations about Critical Race Theory, anti-racist pedagogy, or other terms which include reference to race, dismissing the notion that race itself may also be subject to significant questioning or contestation (e.g., Leonardo, 2004; Lynn, 2004; Wun, 2014; Jahng, 2013). From a global, historical view, it is almost impossible to provide a general definition of race, however, or to describe its roots let alone its implications, while achieving a consensus view (Jackson, 2014). In relation, racism is also an empty signifier in a sense, given diverse meanings and connotations attached to race and its significance within and across societies.

At the heart of contemporary conundrums around race and racism is how race is ideological and constructed, while also being significant to people's lived, empirical experiences. Laurence Parker and David Stovall describe race primarily as 'a mythology that has been socially constructed for purposes of control, power and economic exploitation' (2004, p. 170). Here, the mythology of race is seen to have social force in the real world. George Yancy similarly defines race as a social construction, as a concept without a 'reference in the natural world' which has 'tremendous social ontological power', and whose roots lie in Western Europe (Peters, 2019, pp. 663–664).

Race and racism are frequently represented as problems from and of the western world, and particularly the United States (Peters, 2004, 2015; Parker & Stovall, 2004; Arday, 2021), given the history of African kidnapping and enslavement in the Americas and the ongoing legacy in the states today of stark inequity and anti-Black oppression and violence. This is manifested most recently in anti-Black rhetoric and violence in response to the Black Lives Matter movement and the 1619 Project (Peters, 2019). However, Zeus Leonardo (2011) also observes 'US imperialism' about what race is around the world 'at the level of theory' (p. 682). As Leonardo observes (2011), while in the states race has been conceptualised as primarily about skin colour, factors such as slenderness (in the case of the 'race war' of the Hutus and Tutsis in Rwanda) and social class (as in Brazil) complicate a homogeneous sense of what race is, and thus what racism is based upon, despite the continued pervasiveness and salience of skin colour-based racism in the western world.

Meanwhile, Chinese scholars will attest to the historical significance of notions akin to race that have divided and continue to frame different internal groups in (often violent) relations to one another in Chinese society, which do not appear to be particularly influenced by westerners or western thought (Dikötter, 2015; Yan, 2016; Jackson, 2021). In relation, despite the commonly assumed distinctiveness of race from ethnicity in western scholarship—assuming that race is ascribed and socially constructed in relation to skin colour and other physical markers, while ethnicity relates more closely to family ancestry and heritage—Rey

Chow argues that race and ethnicity are 'mutually implicated', both invoking 'biologism', a scientifically systematic, but in other ways questionable, approach to determining who people essentially, 'really' are (2002). Again, the slippery slope between race and ethnicity is particularly visible in China, which today contains numerous large-scale 'ethnic minority groups', all of which have been or are being absorbed within and assimilated (often by force, and not always effectively) to the 'Chinese race' (Jackson, 2019b; Lin & Jackson, 2021).

Nonetheless, most historical and contemporary scholarship on race and racism centres on western histories and experiences, and the situation in the United States, where Black lives continue to be in grave danger today given commonplace tolerated and legally sanctioned beatings and shootings of Black people by police and others, in the name of shallow, questionable constructions of 'law and order' (Peters, 2019; Arday, 2021; Jackson et al., 2022). In the states, the first society-wide discussions of the nature of race and race relations emerged alongside the development of a system of mass kidnapping of Africans and their subsequent enslavement in North America. (Related deliberations also unfolded with the project of westward expansion that was enabled through a genocidal political and military strategy against Native Americans.) Thus, much of the early scholarship on race and race relations grew in relation to fights since the time of enslavement for Black freedom. From W. E. B. Dubois in the nineteenth century, to the development of Black freedom movements throughout the twentieth (and now the twenty-first) century, Black/African Studies became widely recognised in the 1970s, with Black Legal Studies and Critical Legal Studies developing thereafter (Peters, 2015, 2019). Critical Race Theory (CRT) grew in influence in the 1990s, initially generated by legal scholars of colour to explore how legal and other social structures enable continued racialised experiences and racist discrimination in society despite various legal prohibitions against racism and other formal civil rights provisions (Lynn, 2004; Leonardo, 2004; Wun, 2014).

As varied, interrelated legacies of slavery and settler colonisation can still be seen (by those who want to look) across the vast majority of western societies among others, related conversations have emerged and developed over time in Australia and New Zealand, Canada, the United Kingdom (e.g., Arday, 2021), and Europe. Additionally, the related fields of multicultural education and anti-racist education, critical pedagogy, and whiteness studies have also been significantly influenced by Black/African Studies, and the work of diverse philosophers, social critics, and cultural theorists who have focused on race, such as Franz Fanon (1967), Charles Mills (2007), and Yancy, among others (Parker & Stovall, 2004; Jahng, 2013; Matias, 2016; Peters, 2019).

In the early twenty-first century, there have been two intersecting trends in western scholarship and popular thinking about race. First, regarding the latter there has been a recent backlash against the notion of 'ordinary' or 'everyday' racism—and thus against the major tenants of the fields of CRT and whiteness studies (i.e., studies of how people are impacted by experiences of being white), and the Black Lives Matter political protest movement. This backlash can be observed among politically rightist thinkers and ordinary people who suggest and believe that the human world has entered a 'post-racial' age. As Leonardo wrote in 2011, there was a sense particularly after the election of Barack Obama in the United States that racism was no longer a 'real problem' or issue, and that talking about race or racism any further was thus regressive. Yet that anti-Black racism nonetheless remains pervasive can be seen in the violence of this backlash as experienced by those who continue to emphasise that race is important to their own (and to others') lives (Peters, 2019).

As Yancy relates in his interview that is included in this collection, after publishing an essay, 'Dear White America' that invited white Americans 'to tarry with the concept of what it means for them to have inherited, even if unintentionally, white privilege', he received large quantities of hate mail that included 'threats of physical violence, death threats, and the use of unconscionable racist epithets' (Peters, 2019, p. 664). Since then, the Black Lives Matter movement against police (and other) violence against Black people in the states has been met with defensive 'All Lives Matter' rejoinders, effectively dismissing that Black people face disproportionate challenges to white people. At the same time, United States President Donald Trump refused to recognise, let alone take a stand against, recent clear cases of anti-Black brutality (Arday, 2021). Similarly, racism that paradoxically masquerades itself as a colour-blind dismissal of racism seems to be on the rise again elsewhere around the world, in relation to ethno-nationalist and other populist movements, in the United Kingdom, across Europe, and elsewhere (Jackson, 2019c). Academically, scholars of race and Black/African Studies and those who work with CRT and related theories and frameworks are now on the retreat, as teaching about CRT has been politicised by the political right and actually banned in several states and their schools and universities.

Second, relatedly, we see a flourishing of scholarship today highlighting the intersecting concerns of scholars around equality and equity and race, language, culture, religion, ethnicity, class, gender, and more. Kimberle Crenshaw's work on intersectionality is an important reference point here (2013) that undergirds a growing field of interdisciplinary theory and research that articulates how various social categories and markers interact in complex social and ideological spheres, matching a critical view of the nature of power in society with a holistic approach to understanding how people continue to have significantly divergent experiences even if they identify as 'Black', 'white', etc. in society and education (e.g., Maybee, 2011; Ibrahim, 2011). Many of the articles in this collection highlight this intersectionality of power and oppression in lived experience, also bringing in diverse interdisciplinary scholarly reference points to bear on elaborating distinctive experiences in varied educational contexts around the globe.

While intersectional theory is somewhat recent, the reality of intertwined identities is nothing new. Although there is less of a focus on race and racism historically in scholarship from New Zealand and Australia in comparison with the United States, a rich tradition has developed there (and in other Pacific societies) focused on the historical legacy of colonialism and imperialism, indigenous and settler relations, and indigenous rights (e.g., Smith, 1999; Connell, 2007). Important work on these areas continues, in the Pacific and elsewhere, in indigenous philosophy and indigenous philosophy of education and related topics (e.g., Mika, 2017; Stewart et al., 2022). In these areas, race theory has not been central in relation to other concepts, however, such as nationalism, colonialism, and imperialism. Thus, in this collection, essays that have been published in *Educational Philosophy and Theory* focused primarily on indigenous philosophy or anti-indigenous racism are not included, although racism, racialisation, and whiteness studies are pertinent across areas, and despite the significance of indigenous perspectives within the philosophy of education and in the journal (e.g., Rigney & Hemming, 2014; Stewart et al., 2022).

In the next section, we turn to discussions of race and race theory in the field of philosophy of education and in the journal *Educational Philosophy and Theory* and summarise the contents of the chapters that follow.

Race and Racism in *Educational Philosophy and Theory*

Owing to the analytical style that pervaded English-language scholarship in philosophy of education in the mid- to late-twentieth century and its concern with some generalised or universal sense of logical understanding of educational phenomena (as well as the prevalent influence of liberal political theory—see Griffiths, 1998), and likely owing as well to the stark lack of diversity in academia including education before quite recently, philosophy of education did not consider or focus on race or racism as particularly significant until the last few decades.

In relation, in the first two decades of publication of *Educational Philosophy and Theory* (1969–1989), few articles even mention race or racism. J. J. Smolicz (1970), in the second volume of the journal acknowledged the view that 'young people of different race [should] get acquainted with each other' (p. 43) and that some 'primitive communities' were less brutal or aggressive than others, including western civilisation, in his essay on 'aggression in man' (see also Jackson & Peters, 2019b). Kevin Harris noted in a 1974 essay that literature could be used to develop 'new and valuable understanding' and 'take on a more favourable outlook towards people of different races', or alternatively, to support racial intolerance (p. 37). And David Carr in 1979 considered whether 'some other race or culture might regard education as something other than the initiation of individuals into knowledge and understanding, rather like supposing that there might be a race who believed that 2 + 2 = 5?', in exemplary analytic form (p. 49). Such essays may reference the idea of race, but they do not examine it or its importance in any depth.

The first article included in this collection, which was published in 1981, showcases one of the clearest attempts in the early history of the journal to consider race. Joseph Diorio's 'Desire, Reason and Distributive Justice' focuses on the argument that people should be rewarded based on natural 'endowments', efforts, and desire, rather than socially or environmentally determined factors, related to 'sex, race, wealth or whatever' (1981, p. 18). Diorio argues in contrast that desire is not inborn, and that educators should therefore encourage student reflection on their desires, as part of 'the equalization of social and environmental influences through education' (p. 28). While race itself does not figure centrally here, this essay is significant for challenging naturalistic arguments in vogue with liberal theorists at the time, which could have negative impacts on racial minorities, among others, given the presumption of desire as natural or individually produced rather than socially shaped within schools and society (see also Diorio, 1976).

Apart from Diorio's article, the rest of the essays included in this collection were originally published in the last 25 years. Some of the reasons why race and racism were not central to philosophy of education before then are explained in the 1998 essay included in this collection by Morwenna Griffiths, 'Towards a Theoretical Framework for Understanding Social Justice in Educational Practice'. In this essay, Griffiths explores how educational theorists have pursued themes of equality and social justice over time but have been largely inadequate in their approach, in connection to the work of real-world educators. As Griffiths points out, a key problem has been the influence of liberal perspectives. In such framings, the individual and their rights loom large. However, when this work is applied in education, challenges arise. As Griffiths notes, diverse students who are taught, shaped, and developed through education are not the independent, fully formed individuals central to liberal views (as Diorio also elaborates in his essay). In this case, the problems educators face in terms of treating students equally and the just distribution of resources are simplified. Thus, Griffiths argues that new theories are needed that focus on complex and particular challenges of schools. While Griffiths writes from the perspective of British philosophy of education and in the context of the problems of English schools, these points are salient in relation to the field more generally. The article thus provides an important snapshot of historical limitations in educational philosophy and theory when it comes to understanding and responding to issues related to race and racism and education.

The landscape for discussing race and racism in philosophy of education changed dramatically in the 2000s. In 2004, *Educational Philosophy and Theory* dedicated a special issue to *Critical Pedagogies and Race Theories*, edited by Leonardo and prefaced by journal Editor-in-Chief Michael A. Peters. Two essays from the special issue are included in this collection, which reflect on the introduction of CRT into educational philosophy and theory: (1) Marvin Lynn's 'Inserting the "Race" into Critical Pedagogy: An Analysis of "Race-Based Epistemologies"' and (2) Parker and Stovall's previously cited 'Actions Following Words: Critical Race Theory Connects to Critical Pedagogy'.

Lynn's essay is included in this collection, because of its excellent introduction to CRT and Afrocentricity as they relate to critical theory and critical pedagogy. After spelling out the major insights and aspects of CRT, Lynn summarises its contributions to educational thought, before going on to examine Afrocentricity and its main features and importance. Lynn argues that both frameworks have helped to provide for what he describes as a Kuhnian-style paradigm shift, towards new 'epistemologies of transformation and liberation', while Lynn additionally considers how both uncover the need for more culturally sensitive research and race-based critiques of white supremacy in society and education (2004, p. 162). This essay provides a strong foundation to understand the direction of later essays in the field which take for granted some of the central tenets of CRT.

The 2004 essay by Parker and Stovall also zooms in on the relationship between CRT and critical pedagogy, but from a different starting point. Parker and Stovall begin their essay by discussing the racial educational politics confronting them as professors in Illinois. As they describe, while they both teach classes on CRT, evidence surrounds them in the region of students facing racism at an everyday level in public schools. As CRT and critical pedagogy both are aimed towards positive social action and change, the students in their classes felt compelled to engage in marches and protests related to racism in schools, as a local issue and a broader civic rights problem. This experience prompted the authors to consider the inter-relations between critical pedagogy, which has traditionally emphasised Marxist class-based analysis, and CRT, which highlights race and racism. In particular, the authors observe how CRT recognises the pervasiveness of colour-blind rhetoric in critical pedagogies of justice and emancipation, while many challenges faced by different identity groups (such as women, Native Americans, Latinos and Latinas, and Asian Americans and Pacific Islanders) are not adequately considered within a Marxist lens. Giving a rich view of the contemporary literature related to race, racism, racialisation, and related phenomena in (United States) education, this article provides a comprehensive account of concerns in the fields of CRT and critical pedagogy in the early 2000s, while ultimately arguing for both as means towards creating more successful schools for all, and particularly for children of colour.

As we approach the last decade, increasing numbers of papers published in philosophy of education and other educational research have focused on race and racism. This can be seen in the wide array of papers published in *Educational Philosophy and Theory* since 2010 that theorise race and racism in a variety of social, methodological, and disciplinary contexts. Leonardo's aforementioned mentioned 2011 essay, 'After the Glow: Race Ambivalence and Other Educational Prognoses', offers a great overview of the different topics and issues faced in the field and in the world related to race and racism in the early twenty-first century. As Leonardo notes, after the election of Obama in 2008, many expressed criticisms of the concept of race and suggested that it was no longer important. This led to broader reckoning regarding the value of race-based discourse. Those on the right question the salience of race and consider the merits of colour-blind, non-racialised discourse. However, while critics on the left also recognise the incoherence of race as a concept, they still identify an ongoing pernicious impact of racialisation on racialised people's lives. Thus, ambivalence about race marks the so-called 'post-racial' era, where race arguably cannot be ignored while any account of it must confront its theoretical inadequacy. This is a powerful essay that engages various debates about what race and racism have been and may look like in the future.

Another leading thinker when it comes to race matters in educational philosophy, Awad Ibrahim discusses race in relation to language and post-coloniality in Canada in his 2011 essay in *Educational Philosophy and Theory* (included here), 'Will They Ever Speak with Authority? Race, Post-Coloniality and the Symbolic Violence of Language'. In this essay, Ibrahim explores personal experiences with racialisation using ethnography to explore the challenges that African Parisian French-speaking youth face in a Canadian, Franco-Ontarian school. Theoretically, Ibrahim draws upon Jacques Derrida's discussion of language ownership to indicate how the students are racialised and treated as deficient and silenced by their white Franco-Ontarian teachers. While Parisian French is normally a marker of high social capital in Ontario, the African Parisian French-speaking students are treated with incredulity and astonishment by their teachers. Thus, the teachers' ignorance and prejudiced treatment of the African youth are normalised while the students' desires and interests and their tools of expression and power are muted. Here, Ibrahim notes that while teachers may have positive intentions, their day-to-day interactions are 'psychically painful' for the students. Furthermore, the teachers harm the students by tracking them into low-level classes and physical education and sports activities despite the students' expressed goals. This essay is exceptional for its intersecting of race, racialisation, and language, and its exploration of experiences often discussed simplistically as 'microaggressions' today (see also Ibrahim, 2004).

The next essay included in this collection, by Julie Maybee, focuses on teaching CRT and related topics in higher education (2011). In 'Audience Matters: Teaching Issues of Race and Racism for a Predominantly Minority Student Body', Maybee begins by framing her study as a kind of response to past research, by Leonardo and others, which focuses on teaching about white privilege to white students. As Maybee notes, Leonardo (2004) recommends a focus on white 'domination' rather than 'privilege', to centre the harms faced by people of colour, as 'privilege' sounds comparatively innocuous. However, this approach still foregrounds the needs of white students, while it also presumes that for students of colour white domination is an effective focal point. In this context, Maybee discusses her experiences as a white American woman teaching ethnic and racial minority students about CRT, race, and racism. As Maybee describes, CRT and related concepts are not intuitive to her students. This situation requires reflection on how race and racism are and are not experienced by Black and other racial and ethnic minority youth. Maybee observes that some of her students do not see themselves in racial stereotypes, but still accept those stereotypes, while they live in racial and ethnic enclaves which preclude their witnessing of racial exclusions. The essay thus foregrounds experiences of Black and ethnic minority youth in learning about race and racism, with implications for broader understanding of how these phenomena operate in relation to varied members of society.

As mentioned previously, over the years discussions of race in academia have expanded over time to consider the experiences of diverse groups in society not previously focused on in Black/African Studies, CRT, and related areas. Kyung Eun Jahng's 2013 essay included in this collection, 'Rethinking the History of Education for Asian-American Children in California in the Second Half of the Nineteenth Century', is one case in point. In the essay, Jahng uses CRT and Foucauldian theory to trace racism against Asian American children in the late-nineteenth century. While Asian Americans have been framed as 'model minorities', Jahng shows how such positive treatment does not extend to early American history. Instead, Asian Americans, described as 'Mongols' and 'Orientals', were framed as deficient, dangerous, unlawful, and infectious. Asian in the United States at that time were not provided citizenship rights given their apparently inferior and deviant racial status, and they were only educated, if at all, in segregated schools, so white students could be 'safe' and 'free' to develop apart from Asians (as well as Native American 'Indians' and Black children). This essay thus intertwines CRT with Foucauldian analysis of policy documents to trace historical racism faced by Asian Americans in society and schools.

Another policy analysis informed by CRT is provided in this collection by Connie Wun in her 2014 article, 'The Anti-Black Order of No Child Left Behind: Using Lacanian Psychoanalysis and Critical Race Theory to Examine NCLB'. In this essay, Wun explores the United States policy No Child Left Behind (NCLB) from the perspectives of Lacanian psychoanalysis and CRT. As Wun points out, Lacanian psychoanalysis demonstrates how people experience loss and anxiety as their cultivation of self depends on their use of external representations and symbols. As the symbolic and language exists within relationships, this means the subject is constituted in part through external language. Yet Wun observes here the deficiencies of this theory in relation to experiences of racism. As Wun notes, for Black children it is not only language and the symbolic that distorts the sense of self, but pervasive anti-Black racism which characterises them as deficient, abnormal, and transgressive. In connection with these theories, NCLB is on its surface 'colour-blind' or racially neutral. However, the disaggregation of student data by race for accountability purposes leads ultimately to a fixation on Black children as problematic. Lacking affirmative supports in relation to Black students' unequal outcomes, interventions are conducted by schools upon Black children themselves. These interventions do not necessarily benefit children academically, but instead facilitate stigmatisation, tracking and suspending of Black students, and shifting increasing numbers into special educational needs programs. Thus, Black bodies continue to be cast as in need of fixing or working against, given the social and ideological context of NCLB.

The next article in this collection is an interview by Michael A. Peters (2019), 'Interview with George Yancy, African-American philosopher of critical philosophy of race'. In this article, as previously mentioned, Yancy and Peters discuss

Yancy's experiences as a Black philosopher in the United States focused on race, racism, and whiteness, amidst the anti-Black backlash violence that has most recently led to the Black Lives Matter movement. In the interview, Yancy and Peters explore the nature of race relations in the United States and the difficulties speaking up and publishing research on racism at this historical moment, particularly as a person of colour. This interview is important for understanding a first-hand experience of what it is like for a person of colour to work in the field of Black/African Studies amidst a cultural backlash, and also showcases an innovative approach in contemporary academic publishing through its use of an interview approach to scholarly dialogue.

Like Maybee, Jane Chi Hyun Park and Sara Tomkins also explore teaching about race in their 2021 article, 'Teaching Whiteness: A Dialogue on Embodied and Affective Approaches'. However, in this case they write comparatively from their perspectives as two teachers, one Korean American and one white Anglo Australian, involved with a class 'Representing Race and Gender' at the University of Sydney. In the essay, Park and Tomkins focus on their pedagogy and practices and their implications, when they teach about whiteness. In particular, they consider the nature of embodiment during classroom discussions of white guilt, and the roles of various students, including students of colour, based on students' backgrounds, as well as who their teacher is. This article is noteworthy for taking an intersectional approach to the challenges faced in Australia related to race, ethnicity, gender, religion, and other issues, and for its strongly narrative style which creatively bends the rules for academic article publication, particularly through its use of a dialogical format.

The final essay included in this collection is a 2022 article by April-Louise M. O. O. Pennant, entitled 'My Journey into the "Heart of Whiteness" Whilst Remaining My Authentic (Black) Self'. In the essay, Pennant examines her educational experiences as a Black woman in England using analytic and critical autoethnography, interweaving her account with a more general review of the educational experiences of Black British women. While Pennant was encouraged by her parents to see herself as both British and shaped by the cultures of Nigeria and Jamaica, in the academically selective schools she attended she experienced a lack of diversity around her, as well as in the curriculum, where limited discussions of Black people focused on slavery and civil rights in the United States rather than the history of Black people in the United Kingdom. However, through engaging in extracurricular activities, Pennant was still able to cultivate her sense of self. In university, she was able to study Black feminism, Black British experience, and Black Caribbean women's experiences for the first time. From these foundations, Pennant pursued doctoral research on Black British women's education and the intersections of gender, race, and class. This article once more showcases the importance of intersectional theory while also highlighting the continued, distinctive challenges Black people (especially Black women) face in the United Kingdom to see themselves represented positively in society, education, and curricula (see also Arday, 2021).

Taken together, the pieces in this collection showcase both the history of theorising about race and racism in educational philosophy and theory, as well as the breadth of present-day concerns, as they intersect with ongoing societal issues with racism experienced around the world today. We hope this collection provides a foundation for developing historical understanding of the position of race and racism in philosophy of education, while it also inspires new works, historical and otherwise, in the vital scholarly fields of CRT, Black/African Studies, critical pedagogy, and related areas. Finally, we hope this collection inspires educators and scholars across diverse fields to further consider the significance of race and racism in education and in research, given their ongoing salience across diverse societies worldwide in the twenty-first century.

References

Arday, Jason (2021). Race, education and social mobility: We all need to dream the same dream and want the same thing, *Educational Philosophy and Theory*, 53:3, 227–232.

Carr, David (1979). Does 'education concerns the development of knowledge and understanding' express a necessary truth?, *Educational Philosophy and Theory*, 11:1, 35–50.

Chow, R. (2002). *The protestant ethnic and the spirit of capitalism.* New York, NY: Columbia University Press.

Connell, R. (2007). *Southern theory: The global dynamics of knowledge in social science.* Polity Press.

Crenshaw, Kimberle (2013). *On Intersectionality: Essential writings.* New York: New Press.

Dikötter, F. (2015). *The discourse of race in modern China.* Oxford: Oxford University Press.

Diorio, Joseph A. (1981). Desire, reason and distributive justice, educational, *Philosophy and Theory*, 13:2, 17–29.

Diorio, Joseph A. (1976). Cognitive universalism and cultural relativity in moral education, *Educational Philosophy and Theory*, 8:1, 33–53.

Fanon, F. (1967). *Black skin, white masks.* New York: Grove Press.

Griffiths, Morwenna (1998). Towards a theoretical framework for understanding social justice in educational practice, *Educational Philosophy and Theory*, 30:2, 175–192.

Harris, C. K. (1974). Empathy and the value of literary studies: A re-interpretation, *Educational Philosophy and Theory*, 6:2, 23–41.

Ibrahim, Awad (2011). Will they ever speak with authority? Race, post-coloniality and the symbolic violence of language, *Educational Philosophy and Theory*, 43:6, 619–635.

Ibrahim, Awad (2004). One is not born Black: Becoming and the phenomenon (ology) of race, *Philosophical Studies in Education* 35:1, 77–87.

Jackson, Liz (2021). *Contesting education and identity in Hong Kong.* London: Routledge.

Jackson, Liz (2019a). Becoming classy: In search of class theory in philosophy of education. In *Philosophy of Education 2018*, ed. Megan Laverty (pp. 315–328). Urbana: Philosophy of Education Society.

Jackson, Liz (2019b). Relations of blood? Racialization of civic identity in twenty-first century Hong Kong, *Discourse: Studies in the Cultural Politics of Education*, 40:6, 761–772.

Jackson, Liz (2019c). *Questioning allegiance: resituating civic education*. London: Routledge.

Jackson, Liz (2014). Comparing race, class and gender. In *Comparative education research: Approaches and methods*, 2nd ed., eds. Mark Bray, Bob Adamson & Mark Mason (pp. 195–220). Hong Kong, Springer/Comparative Education Research Centre.

Jackson, Liz, Kal Alston, Lauren Bialystok, Larry Blum, Nicholas C. Burbules, Ann Chinnery, David T. Hansen, Kathy Hytten, Cris Mayo, Trevor Norris, Sarah M. Stitzlein, Winston C. Thompson, Leonard Waks, Michael A. Peters & Marek Tesar (2022). Philosophy of education in a New Key: Snapshot 2020 from the United States and Canada, *Educational Philosophy and Theory*, 54:8, 1130–1146.

Jackson, Liz & Michael A. Peters (Eds.) (2022). *Marxism, neoliberalism, and intelligent capitalism: An educational philosophy and theory reader*, Volume XII. New York: Routledge.

Jackson, Liz & Michael A. Peters (Eds.) (2019a). *Feminist theory in diverse productive practices: An educational philosophy and theory gender and sexualities reader*, Volume VI. Oxon/London/New York: Routledge.

Jackson, Liz & Michael A. Peters (Eds.) (2019b). *From 'aggressive masculinity' to 'rape culture': An educational philosophy and theory gender and sexualities reader*, Volume V. Oxon/London/New York: Routledge (In paperback, 2020).

Jahng, Kyung Eun (2013). Rethinking the history of education for Asian-American children in California in the second half of the nineteenth century, *Educational Philosophy and Theory*, 45:3, 301–317.

Leonardo, Zeus (2011). After the glow: Race ambivalence and other educational prognoses, *Educational Philosophy and Theory*, 43:6, 675–698.

Leonardo, Zeus (2004). The color of supremacy: Beyond the discourse of 'white privilege', *Educational Philosophy and Theory*, 36: 137–152.

Lin, Cong & Liz Jackson (2021). Make China great again: The blood-based view of Chineseness in Hong Kong, *Educational Philosophy and Theory*, 53:9, 907–919.

Lynn, Marvin (2004). Inserting the 'race' into critical pedagogy: An analysis of 'race-based epistemologies', *Educational Philosophy and Theory*, 36:2, 153–165.

Matias, Cheryl E. (2016). White skin, black friend: A Fanonian application to theorize racial fetish in teacher education, *Educational Philosophy and Theory*, 48:3, 221–236.

Maybee, Julie E. (2011). Audience matters: Teaching issues of race and racism for a predominantly minority student body, *Educational Philosophy and Theory*, 43:8, 853–873.

Mika, C. (2017). *Indigenous education and the metaphysics of presence: A worlded philosophy*. London: Routledge.

Mills, C. W. (2007). White ignorance. In S. Sullivan & N. Tuana (Eds.), *Race and epistemologies of ignorance* (pp. 13–38). Albany: State University of New York Press.

Park, Jane Chi Hyun & Sara Tomkins (2021). Teaching whiteness: A dialogue on embodied and affective approaches, *Educational Philosophy and Theory*, 53:3, 288–297.

Parker, Laurence & David O. Stovall (2004). Actions following words: Critical race theory connects to critical pedagogy, *Educational Philosophy and Theory*, 36:2, 167–182.

Pennant, April-Louise M. O. O. (2022). My journey into the 'heart of whiteness' whilst remaining my authentic (black) self, *Educational Philosophy and Theory*, 53:3, 245–256.

Peters, Michael A. (2019). Interview with George Yancy, African-American philosopher of critical philosophy of race, *Educational Philosophy and Theory*, 51:7, 663–669.

Peters, Michael A. (2015). Why is my curriculum white?, *Educational Philosophy and Theory*, 47:7, 641–646.

Peters, Michael A. (2004). Critical race matters, *Educational Philosophy and Theory*, 36:2, 113–115.

Peters, Michael A. & Liz Jackson (Eds.) (2022). *From radical Marxism to knowledge socialism: An educational philosophy and theory studies reader*, Volume XI. New York: Routledge.

Rigney, Daryle & Steve Hemming (2014). Is 'closing the gap' enough? Ngarrindjeri ontologies, reconciliation and caring for country, *Educational Philosophy and Theory*, 46:5, 536–545.

Smith, L. T. (1999). *Decolonising methodologies: Research and indigenous peoples*. London: Zed.

Smolicz, J. J. (1970). Education and aggression, *Educational Philosophy and Theory*, 2:1, 37–52.

Stewart, Georgina Tuari, Liana MacDonald, Jacoba Matapo, David Taufui Mikato Fa'avae, Bruce Ka'imi Watson, Ryse Kahikuonalani Akiu, Brian Martin, Carl Mika & Sean Sturm (2022). Surviving academic whiteness: Perspectives from the Pacific, *Educational Philosophy and Theory*.

Wun, Connie (2014). The anti-black order of no child left behind: Using Lacanian psychoanalysis and critical race theory to examine NCLB, *Educational Philosophy and Theory*, 46:5, 462–474.

Yan, Hektor K. T. (2016). Learning from the barbarians? Reflections on Chinese identity and 'race' in the educational context, *Educational Philosophy and Theory*, 48:12, 1218–1232.

Chapter 1

Desire, Reason and Distributive Justice

Joseph A. Diorio

Editors' introduction

While not particularly focused on race, this 1981 essay by Joseph Diorio gives a glimpse into how philosophers of education in the 1970s and 1980s thought about diversity, inequality, and justice, and the analytical approach they generally took. The essay focuses on arguments from Alan Goldman's 1979 text *Justice and Reverse Discrimination*. According to Goldman, people in a free society should be rewarded based on their natural endowments rather than due to socially or environmentally determined factors related to (as he puts it), 'sex, race, wealth or whatever'. Among natural factors, Goldman emphasises abilities and talents as well as 'socially productive effort', conceptualised here as an indicator of individual 'desire'. This is a liberal and anti-egalitarian position, as Goldman specifies one should not impinge upon others' desires as 'natural' factors that, within his naturalistic schema, justify people's differential outcomes. Diorio dissects these arguments for their educational implications. While Goldman states we cannot expect students to make equal efforts in school, given different natural desires (and hence students should be treated differently based on effort and talent), Diorio contends desires are subject to rational assessment over time. In this case, the 'naturalistic recipe' sidesteps challenges educators face related to paternalism versus the possibility of encouraging student reflection about their desires as part of 'the equalization of social and environmental influences through education'. While race does not figure centrally here, this is one of few essays in *Educational Philosophy and Theory* before the 1990s that mentions race; and it is significant for challenging naturalistic arguments in vogue with liberal theorists at the time.

I

In *Justice and Reverse Discrimination*,[1] Alan H. Goldman has argued for a form of equality of opportunity in which socially and environmentally based differences and disadvantages among individuals are eliminated in order to allow free play for talented persons to be productive in socially beneficial ways and, through their demonstration of competence in responsible positions, to merit greater rewards than some of their fellows. The search for a just system for the distribution of differential rewards, for Goldman as for innumerable other writers on this subject, involves

DOI: 10.4324/9781003346104-2

making an accurate assessment of the relevant differences to be found among the various components and characteristics of the individual's identity. Though he does not construct a comprehensive theory of identity or personhood, Goldman provides us with only two categories into which aspects of individual identities relevant to questions of distributive justice can be placed. In one such category are those aspects of individuals which are socially or environmentally determined. In the other category fall aspects which, being free of social or environmental influences, are to be regarded as natural components inherent to the individual.

Goldman employs these two categories in describing the state of those initial actors in an original position, operating behind a Rawlsian veil of ignorance, upon whose presumed decisions the social structure of distributive justice is to depend. In his words:

> The contractors to which I *shall* appeal . . . can be defined as ignorant of their social positions, race and sex, but not necessarily of their natural endowments, such as intelligence or physical agility. My unwillingness to deny knowledge of the latter traits results from my uncertainty as to whether society has the right to nullify all natural differences among individuals, even those that are relevant to the performance of certain tasks and hence naturally useful to the individuals who possess them. If untalented or unintelligent people have no inherent claims upon the talents of others, and I do not see why they should, then it is not demanded, nor perhaps even permissible, that society nullify the distributive effects of these differences.[2]

While Goldman nowhere states explicitly that these two categories of the socially determined and the natural are sufficient for the comprehensive analysis of every person, all the human characteristics which he discusses in terms of distributive justice appear to fall into one or the other. Hence in any case where it is clear that some aspect or element of individual identity which he discusses does not belong in one of these categories we can presume that it falls into the other.

Goldman believes, contra Rawls, that natural differences among persons are the proper basis for differential distributive rewards, which is to say that in his view social justice lies in the closest possible correlation between social and economic differences on one hand and relevant natural differences among individuals on the other.[3] Goldman bases his rejection of egalitarian attempts to eliminate the social results of natural inequalities largely upon an appeal to the preeminence of liberty and particularly to the rights of individuals to maintain control over their own bodies. The right to dispose of one's own natural assets as one sees fit is taken as one such right required by liberty, and hence Goldman rejects attempts to nullify through social intervention the impact which appropriate natural differences have upon the construction and maintenance of a just hierarchical social order. In his words:

> the attack on social disadvantages is demanded by the moral priority of equality implied in the assumption of a moral point of view; when the right to an

equal opportunity is construed in this way, it cannot plausibly be overriden by other rights. Any real attempt to even out natural potentials . . . does come into conflict with other more important rights, which morally prevent its accomplishment. Literal redistribution of natural assets or attempts at natural equality through genetic tinkering are prohibited by the right of each person over his own body, a right which might well be the most fundamental of all . . . I can find no apparent reason why those naturally less well endowed have rights to contributions from those more intelligent, stronger, etc. . . . To consider the natural assets of the latter individuals simply as social assets appears to violate their rights over their own bodies (including their brains).[4]

Goldman sees differences based upon social and environmental factors as viola-tions of individual liberty, since extra-natural conditions imposed upon persons from outside themselves illegitimately restrict or unfairly enhance their capacities to dispose of the natural aspects of their own identities. Hence, differences in dis-tributive rewards which derive from social advantages, environmental deprivations or conditions contingently dependent upon sex, race, wealth or whatever, all are declared to be unjust. Differences in individual conditions based upon such fac-tors, therefore, are to be eliminated as far as possible, allowing those natural differ-ences concealed beneath the social and environmental patina to shine through and to give clear guidance to the determination of a just social arrangement.

In support of Goldman's view one might appeal to the very meaning of the concept of justice. As expressed recently by Antony Flew:

Justice . . . demands that everyone should have their own, their due: *suum cuique tribuere* . . . that this is what justice is I take to be a determination of the established usage of the term. Again, what facts about a person we ought to recognize as giving rise to what deserts and entitlements must be, by the same token, similarly moral and disputatious. But that all deserts and entitle-ments have to be grounded in some facts about the people so endowed is, I take it, a correspondingly conceptual point.[5]

By resting his argument for differential distributive justice on a foundation of nat-ural differences among individuals, Goldman would appear only to be following the tradition of inquiry into justice, as defined by Flew. Flew, however, does not restrict the facts about persons relevant to the concerns of justice to natural facts. One of the main thrusts of Goldman's argument is to reject the relevance of facts about persons which are dependent upon social and environmental conditions to the just differential distribution of rewards. Having offered this widely accepted argument, Goldman's search for justice is thrown back upon a naturalistic foundation.

Appeals to nature in the pursuit of justice generally involve the search for an argument-stopper; some natural factor which enjoys absolute status, which is not susceptible to rational control or human manipulation, and upon which hierarchi-cal differences in the quality and quantity of rewards provided to individuals can be based. The assumption behind such appeals is that nature in its pristine state is just, and that human action in the production of justice should be restricted to manipulations of contingent social and environmental factors until they reflect as closely as possible those natural differences identified as relevant to justice. Justice, essentially, is to be found and followed and is not to be produced or created through the use of human reason. The naturalistic persuasion sees the establishment and maintenance of a just social order largely as a matter of following a naturally provided recipe, placing all human agency in the construction of such an order in the role of midwife to nature. Hence education, in so far as it has a part to play in the pursuit of justice, has as its task the identification of relevant natural differences among persons and the enabling of those differences to develop and play themselves out so that they are reflected ultimately in the social hierarchy.

In order to serve their sought-after role in the production of social justice, natural differences among persons must be declared off-limits for intervention. Otherwise nature could be changed continually through human action, thereby negating its usefulness as a stable foundation for a just social order. Hence in order to do their job, whatever natural differences are accepted as standing properly at the base of the human hierarchy must be accepted as absolute and inviolable.

The over-riding difficulty facing the naturalist position is to isolate differentially shared common factors in individual identities which both can be accepted as relevant to the concerns of justice and can also be kept free of social and environmental influences. In trying to fulfill these two conditions, Goldman's argument encounters fatal difficulties.

II

Goldman acknowledges that it often can be difficult to determine whether a given difference among persons is environmentally induced or naturally founded, for he states that:

> the recent furor over IQ tests indicates that we may have no reliable means in practice of drawing the line between inequalities that are socially relative and those that are not . . . (hence) we may in practice have to attack both kinds of inequality to some degree.[6]

Despite his emphasis on rewarding ability on eliminating socially based obstacles to the demonstration of ability by competent individuals, however, Goldman does not regard ability as a sufficient condition for unequal rewards. Ability is to be coupled with desert as far as possible in determining who is to receive the greatest benefits. "The award of positions", he says:

> is not to be on the basis of a purely inborn trait like native intelligence but on the basis of actual competence, which will have resulted as well from socially productive effort.[7]

Goldman thus rejects intelligence, whether native or not, as a sufficient condition for greater rewards. Ability alone is not enough, but must be coupled with "socially productive effort". Goldman reflects Rachel's view that the expenditure of effort is the only basis of desert, and he defines socially useful effort as that which is productive or successful.[8] The granting of differential rewards, then, is to be justified on the dual grounds of ability plus desert on one hand and of social utility on the other. That is, it is advantageous to society to hire the most competent because the most competent do the best job, thereby contributing most to productivity and the provision of services which are in the interests of all. Likewise hiring the competent is a way of rewarding those whose abilities enable them to engage in socially useful effort which confers upon them the moral, quality of desert, and entitles them to a more satisfying life than their less productive fellows. Indeed, Goldman holds that those individuals who are most competent to perform a responsible job well—that is, those who are able to be most socially productive in a specific position at any given time and place—establish a *prima facie* right to that position.[9] These *prima facie* rights to positions, to be distributed justly, must rest as much as possible upon a combination of talent—whether natural or otherwise, effort or desert, and success, and as little as possible upon differential socially or environmentally based advantages.

Generally speaking, the relative importance of desert and of ability, or of effort and achievement, in establishing rights to differential distributive rewards is problematical. Effort does not necessarily meet with success, yet if effort confers desert upon an agent, that agent may be deserving of a responsible position and of the higher rewards which may go with it, without meriting that position through his achievements or his social productivity. If social utility is a primary reason for rewarding ability differentially, then the demands of social utility readily can be seen to be at odds with the moral concerns of desert in some cases.

Goldman offers a proposal which he believes provides a practically useful if not a perfectly accurate route through the potential conflicts between desert and ability. Desert may be present without ability, Goldman acknowledges, but by virtue of its nature it is far less likely, if not impossible, for specific abilities to be found without at least some degree of positive desert. This solution rests upon his definition of competence. Competence, for Goldman, can be exhibited either through demonstrated prowess in a position or through the acquisition of credentials such as medical or legal degrees which are acceptable as indicators of probable future ability to perform well. The demonstration of prowess and the acquisition of credentials ordinarily involve the expenditure of often considerable effort, Hence competence is to be taken not solely as a function of talent, but as a product of a mixture of talent with more or less hard work. Even the greatest of talents must be applied or exercised, thereby entailing the expenditure of at least some effort and the generation of at least some degree of positive desert.

Ability remains the more important notion in the establishment of a right to a desirable position, however, despite the at least partial coincidence of ability with desert. Though an individual may be highly deserving on the basis of having expended great effort, he still may fail to succeed. As long as his failure does not depend upon the intervention of irrelevant social or environmental factors but is due entirely to inherent inadequacies, he lacks competence and does not merit a desirable position. Goldman expresses this predominance of ability over desert in the following way.

> Where these two criteria might conflict . . . productivity itself should normally serve as the basis for differential rewards, while estimates of potential productivity would become the criterion for award of positions. The contractors' motivation for rewarding effort appealed to effort as a measure of desire . . . Given roughly equal natural abilities and correction for socially relative differences, however, productivity itself is some measure of effort and desire.[10]

This measure is admitted to be 'certainly not exact', but Goldman holds that more precise measures cannot be found or implemented effectively. Failure to reward ability is likely to be unjust, because it risks violating an individual's *prima facie* right to a position, which right was established most probably through his trying to develop competence and succeeding in doing so. Failure to reward desert which is not coupled with ability is not unjust, however, as long as the lack of success of the individual's efforts cannot be blamed upon correctable social or environmental disadvantages suffered by him. As long as no one prevents a person from trying to develop competence, however remotely, or places or allows to remain in place social or environmental disadvantages to his success, then his failure to achieve competence, if such be the outcome of his efforts, must be laid at the feet of his own nature. Since nature is to provide the foundations of justice, rewarding the incompetent hard worker as though he possessed ability would be unjust, as well as contrary to the demands of social utility.

From this we can see that both ability and desert are but intermediate steps in Goldman's progression from nature to justice. In the passage quoted immediately above, Goldman reveals the aspect of nature variations in which among individuals he intends to employ as the foundation for his hierarchical reward system. Productivity, he noted, is to be taken as a measure, even if slightly imperfect, of effort, but effort in turn is to be taken as a measure of *desire*. This is as far back as he pursues the sequence.

Desire is what is supposed to motivate effort and lead to desert. In most cases, effort leads to the development of competence and to productivity, thus establishing an individual's right to a desirable position. In a just society where unfair advantages attaching to initial social positions, race, sex or similar factors have been eliminated, individuals will come to possess "roughly equal natural abilities'. This being so, and given the fact that under just social conditions no one who desires greater benefits will be prevented from working for them or from receiving them if they are won, then unless there is some natural asymmetry between the possession of desire for greater benefits and the concomitant possession of what Rachels calls the 'willingness to work', those who desire greater benefits will work for them and, since all who work have roughly equal abilities, all who work should succeed and be rewarded.[11]

Hence while effort in itself does not confer any entitlement to rewards, the group of those who expend effort in the pursuit of greater satisfactions and benefits will correlate closely with the group that is socially productive and that receives differential rewards. Furthermore, since the expenditure of effort is to be taken as evidence of desire for rewards, those who do not receive greater rewards by and large will be those who do not want them. Which is to say that for the most part those who want greater rewards will be able to succeed in getting them, while those who do not get them can be presumed not to desire them.

Differential desires, then, stand at the foundation of the sequences of strivings and successes which are to result in the establishment of rights to positions carrying differential rewards. We have seen that Goldman wishes to free these sequences as much as possible from manipulable social and environmental influences. If such influences could be nullified totally we supposedly would be left with a social system in which all differences in rewards depended ultimately upon differences in the desires held by various individuals. Desires, then, along with similar notions to be encountered in a moment, are to be the touchstone of justice.

Not every desire is to be accepted *ipso facto* as a natural aspect of the person holding it, however. Sometimes desires can come under the control of social and environmental factors. When this happens, insofar as they set off sequences of effort and achievement which result in the acquisition of differential rewards, desires become the legitimate objects of intervention. Socially and environmentally based desires, like all advantages obtained through possession of factors influenced by outside forces, result in unjust distribution of rewards, as suggested by Goldman in the following passage:

> When we encounter differences in motivation among individuals of different social classes, when the upper or middle-class child is more highly motivated, we must give the underdog the benefit of the doubt and assume that the difference is socially caused, Where we find children of apparently similar social backgrounds differently motivated, on the other hand, we can justifiably give them only equal attention. We can not reasonably expect or demand all to make the same effort in school, if for no other reason than that to some individuals it may not appear worthwhile in terms of their ultimate goals.[12]

'Motivations' and 'ultimate goals' share many similarities with desires. Goldman's point is that a person's motives, goals and, by analogy, desires *may* be socially influenced. If they are, they become appropriate objects of attack in the name of justice. If they are not socially caused, however, they fall into the category of 'natural' and are to be left alone on pain of violating the liberty of the person holding them and of wrecking the justice of the distributive scheme to which they would lead.

Goldman apparently believes that individuals of the same 'class' have had such identical background experiences as to leave any differences in their motivations, etc., otherwise subject to social influences, due entirely to natural factors. Having acknowledged that motivations *can* be influenced by social factors, he provides no reason for assuming that differences in motives are not influenced in this manner in cases where persons with differing motives come from the same class.

We are given no way of knowing whether a person's motives are socially caused or natural except by comparing him with another person, determining whether his degree of motivation or the nature and level of his desires is the same as or different from those of the other person, and then checking to see whether his social background is similar. If his motivations are the same as those of the second individual but his social background is different, on Goldman's account we are to presume that his motives are due to his background and we are to try to change them if they are low. On the other hand, if his motives are different from the second person's but his background is the same, we presume that his motives are natural, and we leave them alone.

Consider here the case of A and B. A comes from a lower class background and exhibits poor motivation. B comes from a higher class background and exhibits high motivation. Applying Goldman's test, we compare A and B, identify A's motives as socially determined, and work to improve them. If, however, we compare A with C, who comes from the same lower class background but who exhibits high motivation, we would on Goldman's account have to acknowledge that these differences in motives were not socially caused and hence were not suitable objects for intervention. When compared with C, A's motives are natural (i.e., non-socially or environmentally caused) and should be left to stand. When compared with B, however, A's motives are socially determined and ought to be improved.

No single motive, goal or desire of a given individual may be both socially caused and natural at the same time, because such a coincidence would destroy the distinction upon which the determination of the justice of a distributive scheme is to be founded. In the case of A, however, the category into which his motives fall depends not upon an assessment of their origins but upon the motives of which of the two other persons they are compared with. If we compare A's motives simultaneously with those of B and C, then A's motives are simultaneously natural and socially caused. The distinction collapses, taking with it the superstructure of justice it is intended to support. We are left with a method of comparing the differences among the motives and goals of various individuals, which masquerades as a means of discovering the causal origins of those differences. Nothing is established as a result of such comparisons about the possible origins of different desires or motives.

Only socially caused differences in motivations and similar factors are accepted by Goldman as equalizable, though he provides no effective way of determining which differences are not socially caused and hence which are immune from intervention. Since we always potentially could find at least one person who had 'higher' motives than another, and since none of these differences in motives clearly could be identified as natural, all motivations would become subject, potentially, to intervention. Since none can be identified as natural, none are beyond attack. Furthermore, once all human motives and the like have been made the legitimate objects of intervention, all are potentially equalizable. This leads ultimately to egalitarianism, which is the very position which Goldman wishes to avoid.

Perhaps no such person as C exists, or at least he cannot be found, however. This would mean that in every case in which individuals exhibit differences in motivations, they also exhibit parallel differences in their social backgrounds. On the principle of granting the underdog the benefit of the doubt, we then would have to work to bring *all* cases of weak motives into line with stronger ones. This would entail, should our efforts succeed, that everybody then would have the same level of motives and goals. Given roughly equal natural abilities and a lack of any differential social or environmental advantages accruing to some but not to all individuals, this should result in the universal equalization of individual efforts. This, in turn, would lead to equalization of competencies and achievements. Everybody would be equally deserving, equally capable, equally productive, and hence would have a right to equal rewards. This would justify, not differential rewards, but egalitarianism.

III

Another problem lurking behind Goldman's proposals involves his belief that certain natural aspects of an individual are inviolable. Assume for the moment that he is correct in asserting that the predominance of the value of liberty prohibits equalizing individual differences based upon natural factors, and that violations of this prohibition constitutes violations of individuals' rights over their bodies. If my motives and desires are a part of my natural constitution, and if my rights over my body include rights to dispose of the elements of my constitution as I see fit, then no one else can alter my constitution, at the very least, without my consent. Is it possible for me, however, to consent to such an alteration, and is it permissible for me to carry out such an alteration myself? Does my right to dispose of my own desires and goals include the right to change them myself?

The naturalistic view holds that legitimate attempts by one person to influence another must be directed at aspects of that second person which are socially or environmentally derived only, and not at aspects which are natural. This implies that, if an individual were to change himself, in order for his action to be legitimate he would have to employ only his own natural aspects in bringing the change about, and the changes achieved must affect only socially or environmentally based components of his person. For an individual to change any part of his natural self on the basis of or through the use of aspects received from outside that self would be a violation of his own rights over his natural constitution in the same way as would the introduction of such changes by another person. If such a social versus natural dichotomy did exist within the person, all individuals would carry within themselves a sacred homuncule of essential elements which never could be brought under the direction of the individual's other components without introducing the control of natural factors by socially derivative ones and thereby violating the individual's own natural liberty.

Goldman's naturalism results in placing those desires, goals, motives, etc., which are not socially or environmentally derivative within such a homuncule. This means that if these factors can be changed at all, the sources of the changes would have to be within the homoncule itself. Which is to say that the sources of legitimate changes in a person's natural motives and desires themselves would have to be a part of that person's natural constitution. This, however, would mean that my nature was at odds with itself at least through part of my lifetime, which would undermine the ability of my nature to provide stable ultimate justification for the levels of differential rewards I am to receive. Different aspects of my nature at a given time could justify incompatible levels of rewards. If my nature is divided in this way, on the basis of which aspect of it should the determination of my just rewards depend?

In order for the just status of any given distribution of differential rewards to be maintained on the basis of natural desires, motives, and the like, these supposedly natural factors would have to endure. If an individual's motives, etc., change, then given the fact that there are to be no social or environmental barriers erected to prohibit individuals from pursuing their goals and desires freely, and assuming also that individuals when not faced with any such barriers *will* pursue their goals, the individual's efforts also will change, and with them his achievements, his rights, and the rewards to which he will be entitled. He will, in effect, become a different person from the point of view of distributive justice, and the distributive system will have to rate him differently. Hence if there is to be any stability in the level of rewards which an individual justly can claim and receive, there must be corresponding stability in that individual's desires and goals. Continually changing natural desires cannot provide a stable foundation for an enduring system of just differential distribution of benefits.

Goldman indeed does try to invest natural motives and desires with durability. He does not imply that this durability results from such factors being unchangeable. His position is, rather, that the durability of the natural components of a person is to be achieved through respecting the moral injunction based upon the principle of liberty, that such components should not be manipulated. Acceptance of this injunction leads to further difficulties, however. We have seen how outside interference in the natural motives of an individual constitutes an affront against liberty, and how each individual is bound by the same injunction against manipulating his own nature on pain of violating his own liberty. Thus every person is to have a built-in set of natural motives, goals and the like, upon which is to depend his efforts, achievements, rights and rewards, and which are to be kept free from intervention even by the individual himself by the moral injunction to respect liberty. Insofar as a person follows this injunction, the course of his life and the rewards which he justly should receive are pre-determined. Every individual thus would be confronted with a level of achievement and rewards determined for him in advance by his natural motives and goals. Such predetermination is not easily reconciled with an emphasis on liberty nor with free competition for differential satisfactions.[13]

IV

The most fundamental problem here is the naturalistic conception of desires and the like which stands at the base of Goldman's argument. The nature of desires, and of an extensive family of similar concepts such as motives, emotions, wants, goals etc., has been the subject of considerable recent philosophical debate. Much of this debate has centred around the question of the degree to which these notions fall within the domain of rational or cognitive deliberation. While this complex question cannot be discussed here in its own right, it can be noted that many opinions in the debate fall on a spectrum ranging from a greater to a lesser degree of commitment to the view that motives, wants, etc., either are equivalent to or are the products of cognitive processes and hence potentially are subject to rational control. Hence we can contrast views which see emotions and desires essentially as judgements which can, though perhaps do not necessarily, lead to action, with views which see desires and motives either as inherent elements of a personality or as occurrences which 'happen' to the person holding them and which can cause actions, but which are beyond his or her rational control.[14] If we adopt a position in keeping with the first type of view—which I believe generally to be correct—we will be enabled to avoid the deterministic eventualities of Goldman's naturalism, though of course this in itself does not constitute a reason for viewing desires, motives, and the like as part of or subject to rationality.

Reconsider an already quoted passage from Goldman's book:

> We cannot reasonably expect or demand all to make the same effort in school, if for no other reason than that to some individuals it may not appear worthwhile in terms of their ultimate goals.[15]

What provides the 'appearance of worthwhileness'? Is something to be accepted as worthwhile because it is illumined by the inner light of one's natural desires, or is it to be judged as such on the basis of a more-or-less rational assessment? The difference is between viewing goals as possessions which the individual has and must adhere to, versus seeing them as the results of choices—things which the individual can select and change, potentially at least on the basis of reasons.

Viewing desires and similar notions in the latter way places them within legitimate reach both of arguments originating outside the individual and of the person's own rationally self-directed manipulation. Individuals thereby would be entitled to change their motives, and other persons no longer would be prohibited *a priori* from arguing in favour of such changes. If they are susceptible to rational judgement, goals and the like must be subject to external influences. Reason may be practised internally by the individual, but it draws the grist for its mills from outside. Changes brought about in a person's desires, etc., will no longer necessarily constitute offences against liberty or ethics. Teaching people to make reasoned decisions about their goals and desires becomes a justifiable form of educational intervention in other people's lives, whereas it is forbidden by the naturalistic view. Hence we speak, both commonly and properly, of persons 'learning' to select reasonably appropriate goals, to hold rationally justifiable desires, and to be motivated in rationally defensible directions. This is different from being born with one's motives and desires, having them happen to one through some whimsy of fate, or having them conditioned into one by the environment.

As matters of judgement rather than products of nature, goals and desires suffer from all the uncertainties and ambiguities afflicting human judgements generally. Always subject potentially to further rational scrutiny and rectification, goals and desires can never be taken to be absolute or inviolable. Likewise, when understood as judgements they cannot be accepted *a priori* as ultimate justifications for distributive inequalities, without at the same time transmuting them into recondite elements in an individual homuncule sealed off from the outside world.

A further result of viewing desires, etc., as cognitive or rational factors would be to make the pursuits of liberty and justice more complicated than they are under naturalistic views. In views such as Goldman's, as long as each person's natural desires were allowed to play themselves out free of unequal social and environmental interference, liberty was being observed. If natural desires cashed out directly into distributive rewards, justice likewise was satisfied.

The naturalistic view holds, as we have seen, that once a motive or desire has been identified as natural it must be held inviolable on pain of affronting liberty and warping justice. This makes the pursuit of liberty and justice a matter of following a natural recipe. We are not to judge the worth of a person's goals and desires, but rather to provide equal opportunities for their fulfillment. Any moral problems involved in determining which goals individuals should be entitled to pursue are reduced to the concern to equalize social and environmental influences on goal formation. We are given no further tools for judging the worth of various natural goals, for we are presumed not to need them. The natural and the moral are assumed to be equivalent.

Once the naturalistic justification is removed from desires and goals, however, they become subject, like all human decisions, to rational reassessment. Any individual's goals are candidates for reassessment by others, opening the possibility that in some cases one person's claim to liberty to pursue his own goals may be at odds with the judgement of others. This conflict, when it arises, leads ultimately to the problem of paternalism—when is it proper, given the uncertainty of all judgements, for one individual to countermand the right of another to pursue his or her own self-stated goals? For that matter how do we know when goals which a person states for himself are really the result of reasoned deliberation, and when are they subject more to the irrational pressures of unexamined and uncontested social pressures—when, that is, are they the result of social indoctrination?

All of these problems are well known. They cannot be side-stepped in the pursuit of justice, however, by relying upon a naturalistic recipe for a just distribution of differential rewards based upon inherent differences in human motives and desires. True, the naturalistic approach makes the task of education in the pursuit of justice simpler than any rationalist alternative. However difficult the equalization of social and environmental influences through education and other means may be, if its success can be measured against some absolute naturalistic standard, however obscure, it is still easier than the pervasive uncertainty which afflicts the rationalist alternative. While it might be seen as unfortunate by some, however, this uncertainty cannot be dispelled by wishful reliance upon naturalistic countermeasures.

Notes

1 Goldman, A.H., *Justice and Reverse Discrimination*, Princeton University Press, New Jersey, 1979. (To be referred to henceforth as JRD).
2 *Ibid.*, p. 12.
3 Goldman rejects, in effect, Rawls' "difference principle". See John Rawls, *A Theory of Justice*. The Belknap Press of Harvard University Press, Cambridge, Mass. 1971, pp. 62, 75ff. For a discussion, see Kenneth J. Arrow, "Some Ordinalist-Utilitarian Notes on Rawls' Theory of Justice", *Journal of Philosophy*, Vol. LXX, No. 9, 1973, pp. 245–63.
4 *JRD*, pp. 179–81.
5 Flew, A., "Who Are the Equals?", *Philosophia*, Vol. 9, No. 2, 1980, p. 136.
6 *JRD*, p. 182.
7 *Ibid.*, p. 178.
8 See James Rachels, "What People Deserve", in John Arthur and William H. Shaw, eds., *Justice and Economic Distribution*, Prentice-Hall, Englewood Cliffs, New Jersey, 1978.
9 *JRD*, chapter two, *passim*.
10 *Ibid.*, pp. 30–31.
11 See Rachels, *op. cit.*, p. 158.
12 *JRD*, p. 182.
13 See Lloyd Thomas, D.A., "Competitive Equality of Opportunity", *Mind*, Vol. 86, 1977, pp. 394ff.
14 Much of the discussion of this topic stems from the problem of *akrasia* and involves the potential conflict between deliberative reasons and essential urges as roots of action. Of interest here are: R.S. Peters, "Emotions and the Category of Passivity". *Proceedings of the Aristotelian Society*, LXII, 1961–62, pp. 117–34; Raziel Abelson, "Because I Want To", *Mind*, LXXIV, 1965, pp. 540–53; A.O. Rorty, "Wants and JUSTIFICATIONS", *Journal of Philosophy*, LXIII, 1966, pp. 765–72; James Rachels, "Wants, Reasons and Justifications", *Philosophical Quarterly*, 18, 1968, pp. 299–309; Neil Cooper, "Oughts and Wants", *Proceedings of the Aristotelian Society*, Supplementary Vol. XLII, 1968, pp. 143–54; Robert C. Solomon, "Emotions and Choice", *Review of Metaphysics*, 27, 1973–74, pp. 20–41; E.J. Bond, "Reasons, Wants and Values", *Canadian Journal of Philosophy*, III, 1974, pp. 333–4 7; Don Locke, "Reasons, Wants and Causes", *American Philosophical Quarterly*, 11, 1974, pp. 169–79; William Lyons, "Emotions and Motives", *Canadian Journal of Philosophy*, VI, 1976, pp. 502–16; E.J. Bond, "Desire, Action and the Good", *American Philosophical Quarterly*, 16, 1979, pp. 53–59.
15 15 *JRD*, p. 182.

Chapter 2

Towards a Theoretical Framework for Understanding Social Justice in Educational Practice

Morwenna Griffiths

Editors' introduction

With one exception, all the essays included in this collection on race and racism in *Educational Philosophy and Theory* were originally published in the last 25 years. Some of the reasons why race and racism were not central to philosophy of education before relatively recently are explained in this 1998 essay by Morwenna Griffiths. In it, Griffiths explores the ways in which educational theorists have pursued the themes of equality and social justice over time, and their inadequacies in relation to real-world educational challenges. As Griffiths illustrates, a key problem has been the use of liberal perspectives in western societies. In such framings, as Griffiths shows in the case of England, the individual and their rights loom large. However, when this orientation is applied in education, serious challenges arise. As Griffiths notes, diverse students who are taught, shaped and developed through education are not the independent, fully-formed individuals central to liberal views of equality and justice. In this case, the problems educators face in terms of treating students equally and the just distribution of resources are simplified in unhelpful ways. Thus, Griffiths argues that new theories must focus more on the complex and particular challenges of schools in order to make values, liberal or otherwise, coherent with possibilities for practice. This article is commendable for its overview of the state of historical theorisation of equality and justice in education, its recognition of the importance of race and gender in relation to educational equality and its forecasting of emerging trends, such as the use of Critical Race Theory, which would come to dramatically transform the landscape for conceptualising race and racism among other key concepts in philosophy of education in the future.

Introduction

It is the argument of this paper[1] that a new kind of theoretical framework for social justice in education[2] is needed, and the suggestion is made that it will be one which is rooted in radically revisable theory developed in collaboration with practitioners. First, the discourses of equality in schools are becoming unhelpful, and are usefully becoming superseded by discourses of social justice. Second, theories of social justice rooted in liberalism have been based on considerations

DOI: 10.4324/9781003346104-3

of housing, health and welfare, and their categories do not readily or usefully apply to education. Third, liberal frameworks, themselves, have been brought seriously into doubt by theories such as those found in postmodernism, and this has implications for ways of theorising social justice. Finally, a suggestion is made for a way forward, building on the critiques of liberalism to develop a continuously revisable framework in place of the timeless universalism of current ones.

The shortcomings of old theories need to be shown before better ones can be developed: the construct will arise from the critique. In this paper there is space only to sketch the broad outlines of a new framework which would avoid some of the problems of the old ones. The argument is rooted in philosophy, but I also argue that philosophy as traditionally understood will not provide all the answers by itself. On the contrary: recent, convincing criticisms of traditional philosophy point to the need for a radically revisable theory, sensitive to difference and to historical specificities.[3] Thus in the particular case of philosophy in relation to education, theory will need to be a co-construction, made with the co-operation of, and in collaboration with, practitioners (Griffiths, 1997). Calling this process 'philosophy' constitutes a challenge to current, mainstream, English language philosophies, including philosophy of education.[4] Therefore, before beginning the main argument of the paper, I turn first, very briefly and schematically, to issues of epistemology and methodology.

Epistemological and Methodological Issues

This paper reports part of a larger educational research project, which I will refer to by the name, 'Fairer Schools'. In this project, philosophical research has formed part of a series of conversations with professionals who have a variety of institutional roles in education, with the aim of improving both the philosophy and the practice of social justice in education.[5] Thus it is a philosophical project located on the borderlands between established institutions of knowledge; or to use a different terminology—a different discourse—it is discursively positioned between mainstream discourses of academic and other educational knowledge. It is a philosophical/practical project which is too 'philosophical' to be standard 'educational research', but which is too 'empirical' to be standard 'philosophy of education'.

My methodological framework is rooted in the multi-disciplinary and plural approaches to be found in new developments in feminist epistemology and cultural studies which take account of epistemological standpoints, and dynamic models of identity underpinning them. Among the many examples of this approach, the papers in Lennon and Whitford's collection (1995) provide a recent and varied overview of feminist standpoint theory together with some discussions of the place of identity in epistemology. Other examples, focused on educational knowledge, are provided by Walkerdine (1990), Rattansi (1992), Weiner (1994), MacLure (1996), and Haywood & Mac An Ghaill (1997), all of whom explore the possibilities of developing knowledge based on dynamic models of the construction of identity.

Further, my framework is action-oriented, collective, and collaborative, depending on the difficult business of discovering the perspectives of others rather than assuming any universal subject or object of knowledge. In this it draws on recent philosophical discussions of the possibilities of open, focused interactions with concrete others in relation to their 'situated knowledges' (Spivak, 1990, 1992; Haraway, 1991; Benhabib, 1992; Dhanda, 1994). It also draws on the traditions of action-research and qualitative research, especially those versions of them which are collaborative, politically aware and reflective about ends, rather than those which are individual or technicist in motivation (Personal Narratives Group, 1989; Zeichner, 1993; Bryman & Burgess, 1994; Ladson-Billings, 1995).[6]

This methodological approach frames the 'Fairer Schools' project. Thus, first, the research is both philosophically and practically oriented. Second, it takes account of the situated perspectives of concrete others, without being relativist, but equally without aspiring to certainty. Third, it is collaborative, but does not depend on the collaborating group reaching a consensus. Fourth, it is iterative in that it depends on a cyclical process of explicit theorising and practical engagement. So this paper reports one stage in an iterative process. It presents a draft—but, necessarily in such a methodology of consultation and revision, so will all future reports.

The Fairer Schools project has been developed in collaboration with other professionals. Collaborative intentions are easy to state, but harder to carry out. The collaboration in this case is with deputy heads, with advisors from educational support services, and with representatives of groups set up by/for educationally disadvantaged groups in terms of race, special needs and sexuality (as well as in the more usual public forums of educational, philosophical and feminist research, such as academic conferences and journals). I regard these people as co-researchers; I do not regard myself as doing research on subjects of investigation. Conversations, interviews and conferences have been used as a means of testing and generating ideas; they were not intended as an information gathering exercise—as 'data' to be analysed. However, my place in the group is one which gives me peculiar powers and responsibilities for the particular bent of the project. Since I was given public resources for carrying out the research, I have a particular responsibility for delivering some useful results. It also means that I am the one who has decided parameters, with all the implications that has for 'stacking the deck' in relation to what can be known or done (Lather, 1991, p. xviii). There is another important difference: I have relatively easy access to educational theory and philosophy while most of the other participants have relatively easy access to current practical dilemmas in schools. The project is influenced (though not determined) by the way that I stacked the deck: in the choice of the focus on 'social justice' and in the uses of philosophical, social and political theory. Later developments of the project, some of which may have philosophical implications, were shaped by the work of everyone in the team. Collaboration requires that we each work from our strengths and acknowledge our powers and responsibilities in relation to them.

I began the research program with a critical investigation of a number of philosophical, educational and sociological theories of social justice as a basis for a draft theory of improving social justice in education. To do a critical investigation of theory in the field of philosophy is not to clear the ground for later investigation, as it is for other fields. Rather, it is to do a piece of philosophical investigation.

Talking of 'Social Justice' (Rather Than of Equal Opportunities)

The decks were stacked right at the start of the project by my describing it in terms of 'social justice', rather than talking of, say, 'equal opportunities', or 'equity'; or of some combination of 'anti-racism', 'feminism', 'inclusive education' and the like. I begin the argument of the paper by explaining the choice of the term. In this section I start by discussing its current usage in education and then go on to look at it from a broader perspective in social and political philosophy.

'Equality' Talk

History shows a long tradition of movements towards social justice, equality and 'equal opportunities' in education, occurring in England as in the rest of the world, over the last half century and more.[7] This movement started with a focus on social class, and was expressed in pushes towards meritocracy (for instance, in England, in the adoption of the supposedly neutral 11 + examinations) and towards egalitarian conceptions of education which would benefit children of all social classes (for instance in the establishment of community schools). It expanded in the 1970s and 1980s into a movement for race and sex equality in education—'equal opportunities' as it was usually known. This part of the expansion was so successful that race and gender issues have nearly eclipsed social class as a focus for attention. Meanwhile sexuality and disability are emerging as issues in equal opportunities alongside race and gender.

Some problems have been generated by the use of the term 'equal opportunities' itself, as was pointed out by E.P. Thompson as long ago as 1961. He argued that the rhetoric of 'equal opportunities' was used ambiguously, by both right and left wing political parties, such as the Conservative and Labour Parties in England. Moreover, he argued, using it had the effect of increasing the difficulty of articulating a broader vision of equality:

> 'Get on, get ahead, get up!' say the advertisers. 'The Opportunity State', says the Conservative Party. 'Equality of Opportunity', says the official Labour Party echo. In this orchestration of competitive values, how is incipient heresy to be heard at all? To say that our aim should be, not equality of opportunity within an acquisitive society, but a society of equals; that we need, not more ladders, but, more generous patterns of community life; to say these things is simply to proclaim one's political irrelevance. (Thompson, 1980, p. 2)

Thompson's misgivings were well founded. The history of the rhetoric of 'equal opportunities' in the intervening decades since he wrote this passage shows the way the term has been used by both right and left to argue for different versions of competitive values.

Other difficulties are with the term 'equality' itself. Philosophical difficulties with the idea of equality are well known. Bernard Williams expressed them elegantly in an article which is still a standard:

> It has only too often been pointed out that to say that all men are equal in all those characteristics in respect of which it makes sense to say that men are equal or unequal, is a patent falsehood. . . . Faced with this obvious objection the defender of the claim is likely to offer a weaker interpretation . . . it is their common humanity which constitutes their equality. . . . If all the statement docs is to remind us that men are men it does not do very much. . . . A similar discomfiture tends to overcome the practical maxim of equality. It cannot be the aim of this maxim that all men should be treated alike in all circumstances or even that they should be treated alike as much as possible. (Williams, 1973, pp. 230–231)

As Thompson and Williams point out between them, there are two discourses of equality which co-exist. There is, in the first place, a discourse of competition (as evidenced by Margaret Thatcher 'a soundbite: Equality to be unequal'); and, in the second place, a discourse of sameness (with the implication that equality is evidently wrong or evidently dreary). Thus there has been a move to *deride* aspirations for equality, for instance as the politics of envy,[8] while simultaneously *containing* such aspirations by identifying equality with equal competition in a market place governed by economic liberalism. Faced with this pincer movement, disadvantaged groups were able, as Cynthia Cockburn (1991) points out, to play on ambiguities in the meanings attached to 'equality' or 'equal opportunities', to generate coalitions between radicals, liberals and conservatives. But such coalitions are, necessarily, fragile.[9]

'Social Justice' Talk

Recently, a way forward has been found: using the term 'social justice' in preference to 'equality' or 'equal opportunities'. 'Social justice' is, itself, a term with a long history in philosophy and politics. It does not, of course, mean quite the same thing as 'equal opportunities'. The question of social justice was raised most influentially by Plato. In *The Republic*, Socrates posed the question of the possibility of there being a social system which would ensure 'the good', both for the city-state and also for the citizens in it. The arguments of *The Republic* focus on—and bring together—questions of individual morality and public justice: the question of why individuals should be just, with the question of what a just city-state would be like. In Part VI a reminder of the starting point is given (p. 192):

> We were concerned . . . to ensure the highest degree of happiness for the community as a whole without concentrating attention on the happiness of any particular section of it.

This is still a useful starting point.

Further progress was made by Aristotle, building on Plato's foundation. In his analysis, social justice is the justice that includes the law but which goes beyond it. The distinction between justice as following legal rules, and the wider sense of justice as the right distribution of benefits in a society ('distributive justice'), was first stated by Aristotle in the *Rhetoric*. He also discussed the tensions between justice for the individual and justice for the community in the *Politics* and *Nichomachean Ethics*. Aristotle's continuing influence can be seen in current formulations. Rawls, in his influential treatise on social justice, says that the principles of social justice provide a way of assigning rights and duties, and distributing the benefits and burdens of social co-operation (Rawls, 1972, p. 4).

This tradition of Western philosophy from Plato to Rawls has influenced what is now meant by the term 'social justice'. At its broadest, it still follows the conception of Plato as refined by Aristotle: the good of the community which respects the good of the individuals within it. It further follows a more implicit principle to be found in both Plato and Aristotle that the conception needs to be argued for and rationally accepted, rather than imposed, at least with respect to those members of society who are competent to make the laws. So it is one which must apply equally to all in the sense often described as 'the golden rule': treat others as you would like them to treat you under similar circumstances. Within this broad definition is a recognition that social justice concerns the distribution of resources (or of other desirable elements like status or power) and that this distribution is a principled one. This explains the close connection between issues of social justice and issues of equality, as evidenced, for instance, in the quotations from Thompson and Rawls.

The broad formulation leaves room for profound disagreements in different societies. David Miller usefully points this up in his historical analysis of different concepts of justice held by different societies. Using examples from feudal societies and market economies, he argues that (1976, p. 255):

> a man's idea of justice is strongly affected by the nature of the relationships which he enjoys with other men. The social structure of a particular society generates a certain type of interpersonal relationship, which in turn gives rise to a particular way of assessing and evaluating other men.

He talks of the 'evaluative overtones' of any concept of justice, stating: 'To describe a state of affairs as just or democratic is to pass a favourable judgement on it' (1976, p. 7). Even more profound a difficulty is posed by those who for one reason or another do not recognise the claims of society. Nietzsche gives some reasons for such a position. From another perspective, libertarians like Hayek say that there is no such thing as social justice, only individuals following their own fortunes. It has been pointed out, however, that such a position has its own contradictions since concepts like 'level playing field', are used by libertarians like Hayek, as defining criteria of a just society (Commission for Social Justice, 1993,

p. 4). For all these reasons, as Alasdair Macintyre has persuasively argued, at our own period of history there is as little agreement on what justice consists in, as there is on moral judgements, or on judgements of rationality (Macintyre, 1981, 1988). Nevertheless we still need to make judgements about justice in the same way that we need to make them about morality or rationality.[10]

I have been outlining a broad conception of social justice. It can be seen to apply to that particular bit of society represented by education. Education—a particular kind of teaching and learning—is only undertaken and given because of a widespread belief that it is good both for individuals and for communities. This good is precisely the kind of good aimed at in social justice, even though there are different ideas about what constitutes that 'good'. Therefore, social justice issues are recognised as important in education right across the political spectrum. Recent, widely publicised social justice concerns in education include: high levels of exclusion from school; under-achievement of boys; access to higher education and vocational training; parental choice; standards of literacy. They stem from a long history of concerns about the relationship of education to the good of society; about the use of education for the well being of the individual; and about equality. All of these are issues of social justice, because they all require judgements about how best to achieve both the good of individuals in the community and the good of the community itself. Many of them also concern the distribution of resources, status and power.

Social justice is never merely an optional concern either for teachers or for senior managers in education—whether or not they describe what they do in terms of social justice. Educational managers, in common with managers from other areas, sometimes deny that they are involved in anything evaluative: they claim that they are simply applying rational or scientific principles. This claim is false, as was persuasively argued by Macintyre (1981), and by many others since. An example from the world of education is provided by Padraig Hogan. In his analysis of Murgatroyd and Morgan's recent book on Total Quality Management, he focuses on their claim to be untainted by ideology. He shows up the fallacy in this assumption, by demonstrating how they promote a particular ideological conception of education as 'a customer-supplier relationship, governed primarily by the competitive practices of a market economy' (Hogan, 1995, p. 227).

Social justice issues continue to be vexed by the broad range of interpretations of goodness and justice which marks our fast-changing and increasingly plural and fragmented society—including the interpretation which refuses terms such as 'goodness' or 'justice' as relevant. They are further vexed because the questions are urgent: resources are limited, and many goods obtainable through education, such as status and power, are necessarily limited to a minority of individuals.

What if managers or teachers in the midst of all this change, plurality and fragmentation, faced as they are with competing demands, try to deal with the situation by turning to theory in the hope it will help them find some guiding principles? They will get little help. The theoretical underpinnings to which they could have turned are collapsing.

The Adequacy of Social and Political Theory, Especially These Days, in Education

Standard modern theories of social justice in education follow standard, ortho-dox political philosophy which is liberal in outlook and which is largely con-cerned with distribution of resources within a framework of individualism. Here I refer to liberalism in the context of political philosophy. Earlier I mentioned economic liberalism and referred to equality in the context of politics. These are conceptually separable meanings of 'liberalism', but they are, none the less, con-ceptually connected by a number of strands. The most significant of the strands which connect all the meanings of liberalism is the overriding importance given to individual liberty, understood as the preferences expressed by an individual, rational chooser. In this argument I continue to refer to political philosophy, but it is important to remember that the economic and purely political meanings also resonate within educational contexts—even though in their theoretically devel-oped forms they may be incoherent with each other (Jonathan, 1997).

Individual liberty depends on a number of assumptions and has been used in the development of particular political theories used in discussions of social jus-tice. The idea of an individual, rational chooser depends on the assumption of the 'unencumbered self'[11] (Griffiths, 1993). It also depends on the assumption that universal principles can be discovered which enable us to determine the right and the good. Utilitarian and Kantian rights-based liberalism remain the two most influential developments of these ideas in political philosophy. Kantian liberalism with its vocabulary of rights and entitlements is particularly firmly embedded in political discourse of justice. Miller provides a useful and succinct summary of the status of social justice from the perspective of rights-based liberalism (1995, pp. 1–2):

> Usually the theorist [of justice] will search for some fundamental principle or axiom which he or she believes lies behind all the more concrete beliefs and judgements that we express when we say that this or that action is a fair or just one. . . . We might suggest for instance that the fundamental principle of justice is that of *equal treatment . . . desert . . .* [or] respect of each person's inalienable *right*s. . . . We ask whether equal treatment requires that jobs be awarded strictly on the basis of personal merit, or whether belonging to a disadvantaged group gives you a fair claim to preferential consideration; and so on. [Italics in the original]

Miller is pointing out that rights-based liberal theory depends on making judge-ments based on merit (or desert), rights and/or needs. Rawls (1972), who was mentioned earlier as using the discourse of rights, is probably the most influential example of such a liberal political philosopher in the English speaking world.

In their current form these theories are largely inappropriate to educational decision making. Problems arise with the categories of 'merit', 'rights' and 'need' in the following ways: in assigning scarce educational resources; with the implicit idea of a person; and with the narrowness of the idea that meeting minimum standards is a central criterion for social justice. Firstly, the categories of merit, rights and needs are central to a liberal theory of social justice, but all of them are difficult to apply in educational contexts. This difficulty is related to a second problem in these theories: their implicit idea of an individual is a grown-up person who can argue rationally in the public forum and make contracts.[12] Thirdly, since the categories were worked out in the first place for housing, health and welfare rather than for education, minimum standards, but not competition for positional goods, are taken as central.

The central categories of the standard theories, 'merit', 'rights' and 'need', are very difficult to use when making decisions about assigning resources in education. First, individual 'merit' has little application as a basis for allocating educational resources to young children. It is hard even to agree on what counts as 'merit' in these circumstances: aptitude, effort or results. Second, using the category of 'rights' is not straightforward. Beyond a very few minimum rights, they are hard to rank Jonathan, 1997). Therefore, they provide little help in deciding between competing rights in conditions of limited resources. Special educational needs is one good example; private schools are another. Moreover, invoking 'rights' tends to level outcomes. A rights perspective is of little help in solving questions related to competition between individual students, once minimum standards have been met. (Minimum standards are discussed further, below.) Finally, the category of 'need' has proved difficult to apply even in the area of Special Educational Needs (Roaf & Bines, 1989). Like 'merit' it is difficult to agree on what counts as a 'need': in some formulations it is anything out of the ordinary, be that special talents or learning difficulties, while in others it is any obstacle to learning. Implicit definitions of 'need' can vary from 'anyone who is insufficiently supported and challenged' to 'those we feel sorry for'.

The second problem arises with the underlying conception of the person in liberal theory. Education is not confined to interactions or contracts between grown-up people. One aspect of this problem arises in relation to determining exactly which person (or group of persons) has the merits, rights and needs. Many of the interactions are between adults and very young children. Many others are between adults and young adults. Moreover, parents, the state and industry all claim to be stakeholders in the nature and outcome of these interactions. In these circumstances it is not a straightforward matter to determine whose merits are properly rewarded in a state system: those of an individual student or those of her parents, who can use their own talents and industry to help her 'get the edge' (Roker, 1993). Or the merits could be those of the school, whose staff can win a larger slice of available educational resources through their astuteness and hard work. Rights and needs are as difficult to work with. It is not clear whose rights and needs are being met: the student's or her parents'. Or it can be argued they are those of the state or industry, as the debates on Lifelong Learning show so clearly (Burgess, 1997).

Another aspect of the problem arises in relation to the assumptions about the capabilities of the person in liberal theory. In standard theory, this person is an individual rational chooser, and is assumed to be capable of making choices based on rational argument. Serious differences of viewpoint can be ironed out or agreed on through the process of such argument. However, any system which depends on its subjects engaging in public, rational debate must be a problem where small children are concerned. Within liberal philosophy of education the problem is often approached through questions of approaches to multicultural or multifaith communities. Feinberg (1995) uses the example of minority Japanese children in an American school to show how none of the children, Japanese or American, are able to debate their cultural differences or to make rational choices between them. There is only a possibility that cultural understanding may develop as a basis for further discussion. There is no possibility of this without the Americans demonstrating a prior acceptance of the Japanese children 'with their cultural identity reasonably intact' (1995, p. 210). To say this is to undermine liberal assumptions about the kinds of person subject to schooling. Macedo (I 995) takes a different approach in discussing how the American school system should accommodate fundamentalist and evangelical religious families who took issue with the reading books used in their Tennessee school district. He appears to assume that the rational discussion is conducted by the adults, 'parents and the local school district' for the sake of the children who must be educated into 'good liberal citizens' (1995, p. 227). However, as Feinberg's argument shows, even if Macedo is right, this approach is of little help in working out what kind of education would be able to produce such good, liberal citizens through liberal means.

The third problem is related to minimum standards, useful for assigning housing, health and welfare but less useful in education. Education is indeed partly about bringing all learners to a particular minimum standard, but a particular difficulty arises because of the inescapability of competition in education, given that educational achievement is used to obtain other, non-educational, goods: for example, jobs, power, status, spouses. Moreover, education is also partly about each individual achieving their potential, even if that does *not* conform to external notions of standards, as is often the case with learners with Special Needs. Furthermore, it is about producing, grading and ranking the future labour force. Finally, and most importantly, education is not just about teaching and learning. It always draws on and affects the personal identities of all concerned. School is a place where pupils—and teachers—form their individual identities and also their identities as members of communities. This is why self-esteem remains a central concern of educators (Griffiths, 1993).

In its published reports, the Commission on Social Justice (1994) (set up by the British Labour Party when it was in opposition) provided an example of ideas drawn from a consultative committee made up of philosophers, social theorists and political policy makers (though, oddly, not educationists). Using ideas of social justice and minimum standards taken from the relatively simpler cases of shelter, nutrition and healthcare, the Commission argues as if minimum standards were of primary interest in education, since the economy would benefit from a skilled labour force. It does not take into account the possibility that students might actively reject technological education and training which would benefit the current national economic strategy, in favour of the humanities and expressive arts, which might not. Finally, and in my view, perniciously, it takes no note of education as a highly personal and creative activity of teaching and learning.

These are arguments about the deficiency of liberal theories from the point of view of educational practice. More generally, liberal theories have been brought into doubt by arguments coming from a number of directions. Peculiarly persuasive, at the moment, are arguments stemming from postmodern and poststructuralist perspectives, which challenge what they tend to call 'humanism': universal theories based on individual, rational choosers. Other influential arguments stem from the perspective of communitarianism, which challenges basic tenets of liberalism in its relativistic arguments that individuals are not unencumbered selves because each individual is indissolubly part of the community in which she belongs. Thus, for communitarians, all human beings derive their rationality, morality and sense of justice in their particular communities, and these concepts are incommensurable between communities. The politics of identity has also been influential. These politics are underpinned by theories that identities are both formed and authenticated by race, class or gender; and thus, so are rationality, morality and a sense of justice. Such theories are critical not only of the liberal or humanist self but also of the unified communities of communitarianism. For the purposes of this paper, I will focus only on arguments that come from postmodern and poststructuralist perspectives.

There is, of course, no unified theory that can be labelled 'postmodern' or 'poststructuralist' although there are threads linking different theorists (Griffiths, 1995b). In this article, I shall refer to the whole range of them as 'postmodern'. Featuring strongly in many of them is the proclamation of the 'death of the subject'. This proclamation is based on an argument that there is no possibility of the existence of a central theoretical construct of the Enlightenment, the humanist subject: the bearer of the Rights of Man; the universal citizen with his equality of access to the public sphere, to rational discourse and to the fruits of education; and the holder of privileged knowledge of his own wants and beliefs. The death of the subject is a precursor to the introduction of a fragmented subjectivity constructed and re-constructed in a plurality of discourses.

The success of these arguments in academic circles has meant that old universal, humanist, liberal certainties of modernity have given way to analyses which are grounded in the plurality and fragmentation which characterise social groups. Within theories focusing on social justice, such as those found in feminist, antiracist or queer theory, this emphasis on plurality and fragmentation has resulted in it becoming increasingly obvious that social inclusions or exclusions cannot be simply described in terms of gender, or race, or class or sexuality: all inclusions and exclusions are non-additive combinations of all of these. Moreover, such inclusions and exclusions are themselves liable to change as they become the subject of reflexive discourse. Therefore, neither the exclusions nor the associated politics fit current theoretical categories. On the one hand, they are not constructed purely on the basis of individual political interests, as mainstream liberal modernity would have it. On the other, they do not arise solely on the basis of the simplicities of a political identity defined in terms of gender, race, class or sexuality.

Postmodern critique is increasingly found in educational theorising, and there are also signs of postmodern influences on the construction of theory and the development of practice, including practice related to the improvement of social justice. There are those who argue that postmodernism is inimical to any project of emancipation, while others try to incorporate aspects of it into their work while remaining critical. Burbules & Rice (1991) is one such example; Hargreaves (1994) is another. Certainly there is no shortage of suspicion expressed, especially by those coming from feminist or anti-racist perspectives, about the politics implicit in any kind of postmodernism. Some note how theorists trying to go beyond simple categories of identity are liable to oversimplify concepts such as 'empowerment' (Troyna, 1995); or to lose sight of a practical politics altogether (Phillips, 1993). Others work from a position that emancipatory politics shares concerns and perspectives with postmodernism. This is a continuing argument between different groups committed to emancipatory politics and postmodernists, as I have already detailed elsewhere (Griffiths, 1995b, 1998b)[13] It would be resolved if there were a clear demonstration of emancipatory use. In 1991, Lather was still commenting on the present limitations of postmodernism in answering the question of action (1991, 12). However, those influenced by postmodern perspectives, including Lather, continue to seek ways to work out the practical outcomes for education. By the end of the decade, there is clear evidence of possibilities opening up, for instance in the work of Weiner (1994), Sewell (1996), Weiner & Paechter (1996), Gore (1997) and Haw (1998). It is striking how many of these researchers are, in fact, committed to emancipatory politics of feminism and anti-racism. However this work is a long way from adding up to guiding principles for social justice issues, in general. Indeed 'adding up to' is not a postmodern possibility. Given the plural and fragmented nature of the postmodern turn, any principles would have to be sought elsewhere.

In summary: social justice is understood within an essentially liberal framework of universal ideals, individual freedom and rights-based morality. However, liberalism as it is currently developed, is of limited help in educational practice, especially in conditions of increasing plurality and fragmentation. Unfortunately, alternatives to liberalism are in an early stage of development, and none of them, as yet, is in a position to offer much help either (though it is hoped that this Fairer Schools project is part of the move to change this state of affairs). Meanwhile, social justice issues in schools remain as urgent as ever. Hard-pressed managers and teachers, themselves coping with ever changing conditions and turbulent times, would benefit from theories which addressed their urgent needs. They, like the children and students they teach, cannot wait until the theory is ready. In any case, the methodological framework within which I work indicates that reliable, useful knowledge is found if practitioners help guide the formulations of abstractions even as the abstractions help guide practice.

A New Framework?

In the last part of the paper I sketch how a new and better framework could be developed. As I said in my description of the methodological approach, this paper represents just one stage in an iterative process. There will be no finished product offered, though I will offer an outline of a provisional one. However, even a provisional framework needs to be of use in the educational search for social justice. I sketch its development in four stages. First, I argue that it is important to delve more deeply into the story of liberalism and its critique than does the story as I have told it. Doing this indicates, second, something of the way issues of justice are understood in practical educational situations. Third, from this position, it is useful to look at issues of justice in education in more detail, in order to measure up the generalities against particular cases. This involves looking both at underlying ethics and also at procedures (i.e. in philosophical terms, at both the good and the right). Finally, a suggested framework emerges. The purpose here is to understand issues of social justice in *education*. The critiques given in this article show that it is important to start with the context of education, rather than trying to develop a theory in isolation from it. I should note that it is possible that such an account could have implications beyond the world of education in political theory, for instance, though that is not the concern here.

The story, as I have told it, is an overly simple one—but it is an over-simplification which is widely believed. One reason that over-simple stories are told is the use of labels, which help to give a grasp on the debate, but which simultaneously obscure some of its interesting and significant complexities. For instance, I have talked about current theories in terms of labels like 'liberalism' and 'postmodernism'. But these are labels, which bring together a number of disparate views under the same name. It is common to put together Lyotard, Derrida, Irigaray, Foucault and Kristeva, for instance, as 'postmodern', but these are theorists with profound differences, and, often, with bitter disagreements among themselves. Similarly, I have described what is meant by liberalism for the purposes of this paper, but the lines between liberal and non-liberal are not at all clear, as adjustments are made to the assumptions of liberalism while trying to retain its broad framework. Walzer, for instance, appears as a critic of liberalism in Sandel's (1984) collection. However, Daniel Bell hails his (1983) book, *Spheres of Justice*, as 'the foundation of a new, emergent liberalism'.[14] Feinberg, discussed earlier, is committed to what he calls 'liberalism and democracy', but within the proviso that this 'liberalism' is an 'expanded liberal philosophy' (1995, p. 216). Similarly Jonathan remains committed to the 'liberal ideal' in education, in spite of many stringent criticisms of it, because she considers that an 'ethical interpretation adds to liberal theory' and is an improvement on neutralism of traditional liberalism Gonathan, 1997, p. 185).

It is worth re-examining the simple version of the story. In the simple version, there is a great deal of debate about the contradictions held to exist between different frameworks, especially with respect to justice. Indeed, as I said earlier, in some of the simple versions it is said that postmodern thinking is inimical to any project of emancipation and so also to social justice. However, as I have been arguing, justice and social justice are not ideas which appear only in versions of liberalism. On the contrary, they appeared in the philosophy of (non-liberal) ancient Greeks, and have continued to appear in various systems since, including, in various ways, in the texts of theorists labelled as 'postmodern'. The framework underpinning political philosophy of liberalism gives a way of interpreting them, which has been particularly influential for us in the West, but that does not mean it owns them. An analysis which includes the complexities enables us to see that apparently contradictory systems may be made up with threads which can be re-woven into new cloth.

It is possible to find the strands of different schools of thought in everyday, educational thinking about justice. In the world of education, liberal categories have an abiding influence. In schools and other places of learning, a concern with the merits, rights and needs of individuals remains strong. Similarly, some of the categories of communitarianism appear in both conservative and radical educational thinking. Community politics, meaning either the politics of ethnicity or of neighbourhood, is a powerful discourse in the everyday world of educational policy making. Less happily, in my view, community is invoked in the move back to the nostalgic ideas of 'nation' or 'Englishness' to be found in more conservative educational thinking. Meanwhile, most equal opportunity policies tend to assume that identity in the form of race and gender is the basis for intervention. These are assumptions taken from the politics of identity. Lastly, I would argue that postmodern ideas gain a purchase in everyday educational thinking, even though they are rarely labelled with such a term (Griffiths, 1995b).

All of these views can be subsumed under the broad understanding of social justice coherent with the views of Plato and Aristotle, but this is only a beginning. The broad understanding, as I stated it before, is that social justice is to be found in the good of the community which respects the good of the individuals within it. Within this broad definition is a recognition that social justice concerns the distribution of resources. This is only a beginning because serious differences emerge as the driving concepts are understood. Not only are our ideas in this regard very different from those of the Greeks, but they are also much more complex, influenced as we are by the range of understandings listed above, in conditions where that 'we' is much more diverse and fragmented than it was in the Greek city-states.

In the Fairer Schools project, we found that a useful way of proceeding was to discuss particular cases of injustice or of working for social justice. These were then used as a basis for reflection on how a coherent set of principles might be drawn up, which accommodated these intuitions. The examples were drawn from a number of threads. For instance, some of them related to equal treatment

(Nobody should run up the stairs or jump the dinner queue, not even teachers). Others related to the special concerns of gender, race or sexuality as they appear in school situations (giving children strategies for dealing with racism in school). Others again related to processes of resolving disagreements (who should be consulted and how the necessary trust could be built up). The resulting principles were not the result of the application of any kind of prior theory, liberal or other. On the contrary, threads of various theories might be discerned: in particular, an apparently liberal commitment to the individual and to discussion was obvious. However, the appearance of a commitment which would be acceptable to any one system was not taken as a signal to apply the rest of that system. Rather, the internal coherence of the set of principles itself was taken as success. This then opened the way to examine the set of principles for its epistemological and ethical commitments.

The final framework as we left it at the end of the project was a practical one. It was expressed as a series of guidelines for procedure. For instance, it starts:

> *A fair school is always a learning community of pupils, teachers, support staff, parents and neighbourhood.* 'Equality is not the end but the way.' The same is true for fairness.'

It expresses an ethical position but not a fixed one. Principles 5 and 6 are:

> *There is an in-built chance of learning leading to a complete change of direction (including of dearly held values and traditions).* A change of direction means wholeheartedly holding the new values. This cannot be undertaken lightly. The point is to acknowledge that people can change their minds when they learn.
>
> *Meanwhile it is important that both the leadership and also the rest of the school has a clear ethos and tries to act on it.* The core values must be the ones that create conditions for learning. The ethos must support this.

Each of these principles was worked out in response to sets of examples, which could be cited in explanation. The set as a whole can be described in abstract theoretical terms: a theoretical framework which underpins a movement for social justice in education. This framework includes: (1) both the good and the right; (2) a belief in and commitment to the good and the right; (3) an understanding that (1) and (2) are revisable. Further, in every case, attention is paid to particular cases of justice or injustice, which are measured up against abstract categories in an iterative process. Implicit in this process are attitudes (themselves revisable) which constitute the good and provide principled grounding for the procedures. They include, crucially: learning, consultation, commitment, humility, perseverance, love, respect and a desire for learning. This is a framework which allows progress to be made with improving itself, at the same time as giving guidance on how progress is to be made in improving social justice in educational practice.

This process has to be carried out, patiently, educational arena by educational arena. People working in each arena are likely to create their own versions, in formats useful to them. In the course of the Fairer Schools project this was done by people whose professional pre-occupations were at school rather than at classroom or policy levels, so we formulated a set of principles for use by any school manager (head or deputy) who wanted to work for a fairer school (see Griffiths, 1998a). Elsewhere I have used this framework to formulate a set of principles for educational research (Griffiths 1998b). This is work in progress, drawing on critiques and constructs drawn from liberalism and its critics, and which points to the possibility of finding ways of working for social justice in education, whichever part of our fast-changing, plural and fragmented world we inhabit.

Notes

1 The research on which this paper is based was funded by the ESRC senior research fellowship scheme, 1995–1996.
2 In 'education' I include tertiary and preschool education, non-school institutions like youth centres and careers guidance, and the institutional arrangements of 'lifelong learning'. However, I am mainly thinking of primary and secondary schools, since this is where my collaborating research partners work.
3 There is further discussion of the limitations of traditional philosophy in Griffiths (1995a).
4 LBCRC are exceptions. There are a few mainstream philosophers who consult with others and who consider the specificity of their own position. Walzer is one, and Foucault is another—in so far as either of them can now be called 'mainstream' in Britain.
5 The project is further described in Griffiths (1998b).
6 In my own recent work (e.g. Griffiths 1994, 1995a, b), I drew on these approaches and developed them.
7 This can be seen as the latest episode in what Raymond Williams has influentially described as a 'long revolution'.
8 For instance, see discussions by Kate Myers (1990) and Stephen Ball (1990).
9 A rhetoric of sameness or of competition continues to be pervasive in discussions of equality. The discussion between White (1994) and Norman (1995) points up the relative power of this discourse in relation to others which are to be preferred. In this, at least, both seem to be in agreement, though they disagree about whether the alternatives can properly be described as discourses of equality. See also the discussion by Leicester (1996) which draws attention to this peculiarity of the discourse.
10 In his 1995 inaugural lecture, Wilfred Carr (1997) points out that there seems to be decreasing agreement about what education is for or how it should be studied—but that we cannot do without it. Indeed it is more urgent than ever to speak 'for' education.
11 I say more about this in my article on the philosophical underpinnings of theories of self-esteem (Griffiths, 1993).
12 As Pateman (1988) has shown, the 'person' is in fact, an adult male, who makes a sexual contract with women. Hobbes is the only exception among social contract theorists here, according to Carole Pateman. This argument remains relevant because the legacy of the implicitly male person continues, living on in assumptions about the gendering of parents, work, childcare and the domains labelled private or public.

13 See also Lather (1991), hooks (1991), Flax (1993), Nicholson & Seidman (1995), Stronach & MacLure (1997).
14 In the blurb on the back of the book.

References

Ball, S. (1990) *Politics and Policy Making in Education* (London, Routledge).
Benhabib, S. (1992) *Situating the Self: Gender, Community and Postmodernism* (Cambridge, Polity).
Bryman, A. & Burgess, R. (1994) *Analyzing Qualitative Data* (London, Routledge).
Burbules, N. & Rice, S. (199 1) Dialogue across the differences; continuing the conversation, *Harvard Educational Review*, 61(3), pp. 93–416.
Burgess, R. (Ed.) (1997) *Beyond the First Degree: Graduate Education, Lifelong Learning and Careers* (Buckingham, Open University Press).
Carr, W. (1997) Professing education in a postmodern age, *Journal of Philosophy of Education*, 31(2), pp. 309–327.
Cockburn, C. (1991) *In the Way of Women: Men's Resistance to Sex Equality in Organisations* (London, Macmillan).
Commission for Social Justice (1993) *The Justice Gap* (London, Institute for Public Policy Research).
Commission for Social Justice (1994) *Social Justice: Strategies for National Renewal* (London, Institute for Public Policy Research).
Dhanda, M. (1994) Openness, Identity and Acknowledgement of Persons, in: K. Lennon & M. Whitford (Eds) *Knowing the Difference: Feminist Perspectives on Epistemology* (London, Routledge).
Feinberg, W. (1995) Liberalism and the aims of multicultural education, *Journal of Philosophy of Education*, 29(2), pp. 203–216.
Flax. (1993) *Disputed Subjects: Essays on Psychoanalysis, Politics and Philosophy* (New York, Routledge).
Gore, J. (1997) On the use of empirical research for the development of a theory of pedagogy, *Cambridge Journal of Education*, 27(2), pp. 211–221.
Griffiths, M. (1993) Self-identity and self-esteem: achieving equality in education, *Oxford Review of Education*, 19(3), pp. 301–317.
Griffiths, M. (1994) Autobiography, feminism and the practice of action research, *Educational Action Research*, 2(1), pp. 71–82.
Griffiths, M. (1995a) *Feminisms and the Self: The Web of Identity* (London, Routledge).
Griffiths, M. (1995b) Making the difference: feminism, postmodernism and the methodology of educational research, *British Educational Research Journal*, 21 (2), pp. 219–235.
Griffiths, M. (1997) Why teachers and philosophers need each other: philosophy and educational research, *Cambridge Journal of Education*, 27(2), pp. 191–202.
Griffiths, M. (1998a) The discourses of social justice in schools, *British Educational Research Journal*, 24(3).
Griffiths, M. (1998b) *Educational Research for Social Justice: Off the Fence* (Buckingham, Open University Press).
Haraway, D. (1991) *Simians, Cyborgs and Women: The Reinvention of Nature* (London, Free Association Books).
Hargreaves, A. (1994) *Changing Teachers, Changing Times: Teachers' Work and Culture in the Postmodern Age* (London, Cassell).

Haw, K. (1998) *Educating Muslim Girls: Shifting Discourses* (Buckingham, Open University Press).

Haywood, C. & Macangaill, M. (1997) Materialism and deconstructivism: education and the epistemology of identity, *Cambridge Journal of Education*, 27(2), pp. 261–272.

Hogan, P. (1995) *The Custody and Courtship of Experience: Western Education in Philosophical Perspective* (Dublin, The Columba Press).

Jonathan, R. (1997) Illusory freedoms: liberalism, education and the market, Special Issue, *Journal of Philosophy of Education*, 31(1).

Ladson-Billings, G. (1995) Special issue of *Theory into Practice: Culturally Relevant Pedagogy/Pedagogy for Diverse Learners*, 34(3) Summer.

Lather, P. (1991) *Getting Smart: Feminist Research and Pedagogy with/in the Post-modern* (London, Routledge).

Leicester, M. (1996) Equal opportunities in education: a coherent, rational and moral concern, *Journal of Philosophy of Education*, 30(2), pp. 277–287.

Lennon, K. & Whitford, M. (Eds) (1995) *Knowing the Difference: Feminist Perspectives on Epistemology* (London, Routledge).

Macedo, S. (1995) Mulitculturalism for the religious right? Defending liberal civic education, *Journal of Philosophy of Education*, 29(2), pp. 223–238.

Macintyre, A. (1981) *After Virtue: A Study in Moral Theory* (London, Duckworth).

Macintyre, A. (1988) *Whose Justice? Whose Rationality* (London, Duckworth).

Maclure, M. (1996) Telling transitions: boundary work in narratives of becoming an action researcher, *British Educational Research Journal*, 22(3), pp. 273–286.

Miller, D. (1976) *Social Justice* (Oxford, Clarendon).

Miller, D. (1995) Introduction, in: D Miller & M Walzer (Eds) *Pluralism, Justice and Equality* (Oxford, Oxford University Press).

Nicholson, L. & Seidman, S (Eds) (1995) *Social Postmodernism: Beyond Identity Politics* (Cambridge, Cambridge University Press).

Norman, R. (1995) No end to equality, *Journal of Philosophy of Education*, 29(3), pp. 421–431.

Pateman, C. (1988) *The Sexual Contract* (Cambridge, Polity).

Personal Narratives Group (Eds) (1989) *Interpreting Women's Lives: Feminist Theory and Personal Narratives* (Bloomington, Indiana University Press).

Phillips, A. (1993) *Democracy and Difference* (Cambridge, Polity).

Rattansi, A. (1992) Changing the subject? Racism, culture and education, in: J. Donald & A. Rattans! (Eds) *'Race', Culture and Difference* (London, Sage).

Rawls, J. (1972) *A Theory of Justice* (Oxford, Oxford University Press).

Roaf, C. & Bines, H. (1989) *Needs, Rights and Opportunities* (London, Palmer).

Roker, D. (1993) Gaining the edge, in: I. Bates & G. Rlseborough (Eds) *Youth and Inequality* (Buckingham, Open University Press).

Sandel, M. (Ed.) (1984) *Liberalism and Its Critics* (Oxford, Blackwell).

Sewell, C.A. (1996) *Black Boys and Schooling: How Black Boys Survive Modern Schooling* (Stoke-onTrent, Trentham).

Spivak, G. (1990) *The Post-colonial Critic: Interviews, Strategies, Dialogues*, S. Harasyn (Ed.) (London, Routledge).

Spivak, G. (1992) The politics of translation, in: M Barratt & A Phillips (Eds) *Destabilising Theory: Contemporary Feminist Debate* (Cambridge, Polity Press).

Stronach, S. & MacLure, M. (1997) *Educational Research Undone* (Buckingham, Open University Press).

Thompson, E.P. (1980) *Writing by Candlelight* (London, Merlin).

Troyna, B. (1995) Blind faith? 'Empowerment' and educational research, *International Studies in Sociology of Education*, 4, pp. 3–24.

Walkerdine, V. (1990) *Schoolgirl Fictions* (London, Verso).

Walzer, M. (1983) *Spheres of Justice: A Defense of Pluralism and Equality* (London, Basic Books).

Weiner, G. (1994) *Feminisms in Education* (Buckingham, Open University).

Weiner, G. & Paechter, C. (1996) Post-modernism and post-structuralism in educational research, Special Issue, *British Educational Research Journal*, 22(3).

White, J. (1994) The dishwasher's child: education and the end of egalitarianism, *Journal of Philosophy of Education*, 28(2), pp. 173–181.

Williams, B. (1973) The idea of equality, in: *Problems of the Self* (Cambridge, Cambridge University Press).

Zeichner, K. (1993) Connecting genuine teacher development to the struggle for social justice, *Journal of Education for Teaching*, 19(1), pp. 5–20.

Chapter 3

Inserting the 'Race' Into Critical Pedagogy

An Analysis of 'Race-based Epistemologies'

Marvin Lynn

Editors' introduction

In 2004, *Educational Philosophy and Theory* dedicated a special issue to *Critical Pedagogies and Race Theories*, edited by Zeus Leonardo and prefaced by journal Editor-in-Chief Michael A. Peters. Marvin Lynn's contribution to the special issue is distinctive for its introduction of critical race theory (CRT) and Afrocentricity as they relate to critical pedagogy. Lynn starts the article by elaborating on the concept of 'critical race pedagogy,' his term to describe emancipatory educational approaches for racially and culturally subordinated students. According to Lynn, this pedagogy is undergirded by both CRT and Afrocentricity. The remainder of the article examines key elements of CRT and Afrocentricity as fields of scholarship and as they relate to educational theory and practice. As Lynn sees it, CRT comes out of the legal tradition in the United States and considers how the legal system treats people of color unfairly while it fails to address racism which still manifests across society and its institutions. After spelling out major insights and aspects of CRT, Lynn summarizes its contributions to educational thought. Lynn then goes on to examine Afrocentricity as an African-centered critique of Eurocentrism and its features and educational importance. While noting some differences between the two frameworks and some limitations of each, Lynn argues that both indicate why race-based analysis remains important, providing for a Kuhnian-style paradigm shift as new 'epistemologies of transformation and liberation.' Additionally, Lynn observes that both uncover the need for culturally sensitive research and race-based critiques of white supremacy. This essay gives an excellent introduction to the importance of CRT and Afrocentricity in education and provides a strong foundation to understand the direction of later essays focused on race in philosophy of education.

Introduction

> *Enye sika nko ne ohia.* (Lack of money is not the only kind of poverty.)
> —Kofi Asare Opoku, *Hearing and Keeping: Akan Proverbs*, 1997

DOI: 10.4324/9781003346104-4

There has been some debate about whether 'critical pedagogy,' as a field of study, adequately incorporates issues of race and racism into its analysis of schooling and society (Gordon, 1995). Among other things, researchers have suggested that critical pedagogy, with its foundation in Marxist critiques of schooling and society, has privileged issues of social class over race or gender (Ellsworth, 1989; Gordon, 1995; McCarthy, 1988; Lynn, 1999). While critical pedagogy's racial blindspots have been illuminated by a number researchers, there have been very few efforts to examine the ways in which theories of race can and should be linked to teaching and learning in urban schools. In this article, I will extend previous work that aligns theories of race with notions of liberatory pedagogy and practice (Ladson-Billings, 1995; Lynn, 1999).

In the past decade, scholarship that examines the links between race, culture and schooling has proliferated (Irvine, 1990; Scheurich & Young, 1997). While some work in this area attempts to align the views and perceptions of African American teachers with race-based theory (Beauboeuf-Lafontant, 1999; Irvine, 1988; King, 1991), other work has explicitly drawn links between the pedagogical beliefs and practices of African American social justice teachers and critical race theory (Lynn, 1999; Morris, 2001) or African-centered thought and practice (Ladson-Billings, 1994, 1995). In doing so, scholars with interests in race and culture have literally begun to put the 'race' back into critical pedagogy by developing new ways of looking at the links between race, culture and pedagogy. For example, Ladson-Billings's (1994, 1995) groundbreaking work in developing a notion she refers to as 'culturally relevant teaching'—conjoining fundamental aspects of critical pedagogy with important elements of culture-centered teaching—has revolutionized the ways in which liberatory teaching is conceptualized and practiced. Extending Ladson-Billings's work (Ladson-Billings & Tate, 1995) and drawing from the work of critical pedagogists such as Kanpol (1988, 1992), Darder (1991, 1993), Freire (1973, 1993), and the scholarship on Black teachers (Foster, 1997; Henry, 1998; Irvine, 1988), Lynn (1999) has developed a notion referred to as 'critical race pedagogy' which explicitly connects African American teachers' liberatory practice with theories of race and racism in the law.

'Critical race pedagogy' could be defined as an analysis of racial, ethnic and gender subordination in education that relies mostly upon the perceptions, experiences and counter-hegemonic practices of educators of color. This approach necessarily leads to an articulation and broad interpretation of emancipatory pedagogical strategies and techniques proven to be successful with racially and culturally subordinated students. A critical race pedagogy is constructed via the reflections of African American practitioners/intellectuals who were strongly committed to the ideals and principles found in 'critical race theory' and/or Afrocentricity. For example, in conversations with Black social justice educators about their views on society and the nature of schooling, it was argued that critical race pedagogues seemed to be concerned with the following general issues: the persistence of racial discrimination in schools and in the wider society; the struggle to maintain and develop their own cultural identities, and the ways in which class interacts with race to make the lives of the Black poor even more miserable. They were also committed to understanding how to *practice a liberatory pedagogy* that involves: (1) teaching children about the importance of African culture; (2) dialogical engagement in the classroom; (3) engaging in daily acts of self-affirmation; and (4) resisting and challenging hegemonic administrators (Lynn, 1999). As such, the research did indicate that Black social justice teachers were committed to principles that could be found in more than one theoretical framework—namely critical race theory and Afrocentricity.

While it is important to have conversations about what a liberatory pedagogy looks like and how it is practiced by educators committed to the wholeness and wellness of racially subordinated youth in urban schools, it is also important to have deeper conversations about theory. Theories of race (Crenshaw *et al.*, 1995; Omi & Winant, 1994; West, 1993) and culture (Asante, 1987, 1988, 1991) are borne out by people's lived experiences with racial and cultural domination (Collins, 1991). To that end, a discussion about how critical race theory—as a field of study—came to life is, in many ways, a discussion about the development of a complex theory that both frames and contextualizes the historically situated narratives of racially subjugated peoples. In the same vein, an unveiling of the historicity of Afrocentricity as a cultural framework provides a telescopic lens through which we are able to view more fully the entire constellation of historical wrongs experienced by peoples uprooted from their homelands and forced to endure hundreds of years of cultural domination (Ani, 1994). In the next sections, I will explore both theories and then articulate their points of coherence and disjuncture. Then I will argue why they are both important for use in the continued development and articulation of a critical race pedagogy that rearticulates and re-centers race in the debates over schooling and liberatory praxis in urban schools.

Defining the Key Elements of Critical Race Theory

Critical race theory (CRT) has been defined by a number of scholars as a legal counter-discourse generated by legal scholars of color concerned about issues of racial oppression in the law and society. While this scholarship initially developed as a critique of critical legal studies—a Marxist analysis of the US legal system—critical race theorists are also concerned about creating and sustaining a politicized discourse that was by and about people of color. Critical race scholars argue that CRT, as an analytic framework for addressing issues of social inequity, can be utilized as a way in which to uncover the racism embedded within American social structures and practices. More importantly, critical race theorists seek to reveal the hidden curriculum of racial domination and talk about the ways in which it is central to the maintenance of white supremacy.

A number of CRT scholars argue that there are at least five tenets that guide their work. First, they believe that the legal system in the US is inherently unfair with regard to people of color and that it must be incessantly and systematically critiqued for its failure to address racism in the law. This criticism is most evident in the works of Derrick Bell (1992, 1995), who argued that the prevailing civil rights discourse in the law did little to acknowledge the extent of the problems faced by African Americans who continued to be subjected to unfair legal practices. To this extent, the work of critical race theorists is also meta-critical in the way that it offers a critique of existing critiques of the law—namely the Marxist and liberal critiques of the law which fail to account for, name, and critique the racial and/or racist dimensions of the law. For example, they suggest that CRT 'uncovers the ongoing dynamics of racialized power, and its embeddedness in practices and values which have been shorn of any explicit, formal manifestations of racism' (Crenshaw *et al.*, 1995, p. xxix).

Secondly, they recognize the centrality of race and intransigence of racism in contemporary American society. Derrick Bell (1995) has reiterated this argument most vociferously in his 'Racial Realism' thesis. He argues fervently that because racism is endemic to American culture and society, cultural workers and others attempting to liberate the oppressed must accept the permanence of racism and work toward improving conditions for such groups. Recognizing that race and racism are deeply rooted in American cultural and social practices, Crenshaw *et al.* (1995) suggest that 'Critical Race Theory aims to reexamine the terms by which race and racism have been negotiated in American consciousness, and to recover and revitalize the radical tradition of race consciousness among African Americans' (p. xiv). While critical race theorists agree that race is a socially constructed notion, they do not believe that limiting one's use of the term will increase the likelihood that racism will be eliminated as a social problem. Instead, they advocate a vigorous dialogical and pedagogical engagement with the term and the resultant privileging of certain racial groups over others.

Thirdly, critical race theorists reject West-European/Modernist claims of neutrality, objectivity, rationality, and universality. Charles Lawrence (1991) and Kendall Thomas (1995) argue that scholars of color should concern themselves with the way that the positivist paradigm in social science and the law has not only failed to address the subjective but has attempted to obliterate it completely from discussions of the law and history. These authors begin to call into question the notion that there exists an objective truth that remains unaffected and unsullied by the subjective nature of the human experience. In fact, they argue that emphasis must be placed on the subjective. In other words, those subjective components of experience should be relied upon heavily as a way in which to reconstruct the past and critique the law. This is also consistent with CRT's fourth principle, which is that it historicizes its critiques of the law by relying heavily upon the experiential, situated and 'subjugated' knowledge of people of color. This principle has implications for the ways in which theories of liberation that are grounded in the experiences of the oppressed can be constructed. Patricia Hill Collins, for example, has constructed a theory of 'Black feminist thought' that is grounded in the everyday experiences of Black women. Critical race theorists seek to do the same as regards people of color.

Finally, CRT is interdisciplinary, with deep roots in postmodern, Marxist, nationalist and feminist discourses. Clearly, much of the work of critical scholars is rooted in and sometimes in opposition to sociological, anthropological and historical scholarship on race and racism in the United States. Neil Gotanda, for example, bases his work on major anthropological work on race while articulating the ways that the concept of race has changed over time in the law. While the work is interdisciplinary, it also borrows from a number of epistemological traditions such as feminism. Likewise, Kimberle Creshaw's concept of 'intersectionality' is based on the notion that socially constructed categories such as gender and race are not and should not be considered mutually exclusive. In making such a claim, the author, like many others who work inside this tradition, inserts her identity as 'Blackwoman' race theorist who is equally committed to issues of gender and race oppression. To that extent, Crenshaw borrows heavily from the feminist tradition in order to craft a critique about the ways that women of color have suffered maltreatment and neglect in a society that does not favor Blacks or women. Furthermore, Cheryl Harris in her article 'Whiteness as Property' analyzes the relationships between white entitlement and the actual ownership of material assets that confirm the privileged status of the white dominant group. This is related, of course, to the last principle, which is that they seek to eliminate racial oppression in the US by linking to it other forms of oppression such as sexism and classism/elitism.

Critical Race Theory and Its Links to Education

Recently, a number of scholars in the field of education have applied critical race analyses to educational issues (Ladson-Billings, 1995, 1998; Solórzano, 1997, 1998; Solórzano & Villalpando, 1998; Solórzano & Yosso, 2000; Tate, 1997). Ladson-Billings (1998) argues that a critical race analysis in education would necessarily focus on 'curriculum, instruction, assessment, school funding, and desegregation as exemplars of the relationship that can exist between CRT and education' (p. 18), schools and the larger society. A major concern of a critical race analysis of education would be to look analytically at the failure of the educational system in the US to properly educate the majority of culturally and racially subordinated students. Even more importantly, a critical race analysis of education might begin to examine the ways that schools participate in explicit forms of racial sorting whereby students of color are not only tracked into lower academic tracks, but are over-represented in special education programs, and 'pushed out' of public urban schools. Considering that many of these students are then tracked into lower-paying jobs requiring few skills, or shipped off to jails in order to meet the growing demand for free prison labor, adds yet another analytical dimension. Moreover, the glaring absence of teachers of color from schools where the majority of students are Black or Latino speaks to yet another dimension of a critical race analysis of schooling (Darder, 1993; Irvine, 1988). In this case, the racial homogeneity of the teaching force is not viewed as a simple accident of history. It is viewed as a result of the systematic annihilation of Black and Brown students at every step of the educational pipeline from kindergarten to graduate school. While these issues and others that affect the ability of racially subordinated peoples to participate fully in democratic life are often framed primarily in terms of social class differences, it has also been suggested for some time there are very clear racial dimensions. The development of a critical race project in education can help to move us closer toward developing an understanding that considers strongly the race-effects of schools and schooling process. However, before we can begin this process, we must articulate clearly the nature of the paradigm we propose to employ.

According to Daniel Solórzano and Tara Yosso (2000) critical race theory in education is 'a framework or set of basic perspectives, methods, and pedagogy that seeks to identify, analyze, and transform those structural, cultural, and inter-personal aspects of education that maintain the subordination of Students of Color' (p. 42). In addition, they state that CRT in education 'asks such questions as: what roles do schools themselves, school processes, and school structures play in helping to maintain racial, ethnic and gender subordination?' (p. 40). They also argue that CRT can be utilized as a point from which to begin the dialogue about the possibilities for schools to engage in the transformation of society by putting forth the question: 'Can schools help *end* [my emphasis] racial, gen-der, and ethnic subordination?' Solórzano has created a theoretical starting point from which to begin to think directly on the possibilities which lie in connecting CRT to a broader discourse on pedagogy, particularly the emancipatory teaching practices of people of color attempting to utilize such liberatory strategies as a vehicle for counteracting the devaluation of racially oppressed students.

Afrocentricity

Afrocentricity is an African-centered critique of Eurocentrism that offers a detailed critique of European cultural and ideological domination. According to Molefi Asante (1988), 'Afrocentricity is the belief in the centrality of Africans in postmodern history' (p. 6). In other words, it is a call to reclaim African and African American history, philosophy and science and to begin the conversation about the ways in which these new discourses can be used for liberatory means. Afrocentricity is a way of seeing the world; a way of thinking that serves to affirm African people and delegitimize the myths of African inferiority. This body of knowledge operates in some ways as a counter-narrative to the ideology of white supremacy that constructs Blacks as inferior beings without an historical legacy to which they can lay claim. Afrocentricity could also be referred to as a movement toward Pan-African unity and collective consciousness building. To that extent, a major task of Afrocentrists is to talk specifically about the ways in which Africans around the globe share cultural, linguistic, and social links that have not been severed by the reign of European world domination.

According to Asante (1988), Afrocentricity traces its lineage back to the work of African American men such as: (a) W. E. B. Du Bois for its intellectual rigor and inces-sant demand that scholarship be done with activist intentions; (b) Marcus Garvey for its attention to the African condition and promotion of racial separation as solution to the problem of Black oppression in the United States; (c) Booker T. Washington for its arguing for the need for African American economic independence. The work of cultural nationalist Maulana Karenga is also used in many ways to ground this work philosophically. For example, Kawaida, an African American 'religion and ideology founded by Maulana Karenga in the 1960's' is also utilized as a foundation from which Asante builds a more unified theory of Afrocentricity.

Another important task is the re-Africanization of Africans who, many claim, have, for example, negated their own spiritual centers. For this reason, there is a focus on the relearning and reteaching of traditional African traditions, customs and ways of thinking. In this regard, Asante outlines what he calls 'levels of Afrocentric awareness.' According to Asante (1988):

> The first level is called skin recognition . . . The second level is environmental recognition . . . [where] a person sees the environment as indicating his or her blackness through discrimination and abuse. The third level is personality awareness . . . [where] a person . . . talks black, acts black, dances black, and eats black, but does not think black . . . The fourth level is interest-concern . . . [where one] tries to deal intelligently with the issues of African people . . . Afrocentric awareness . . . is when the person becomes committed to a conscious level of involvement in the struggle for his or her own mind liberation . . . [and is committed to struggling for] African liberation . . . [or making a] constant determined effort to repair any psychic, economic, physical, or cultural damage done to Africans. (p. 8)

There are elements of Afrocentric theory that could be characterized as psychosocial because there is an explicit focus on the ways in which the thinking and behavior of Africans either affirms or negates their African identity. Psychologists, not all of them Afrocentric, have developed instruments for measuring levels of Afrocentric awareness and racial identity development.

Because Afrocentric theorists believe that their work should be accessible to the majority of African people (most of whom are working-class and have not attended a four-year collegiate institution), a great deal of the work published in the United States is written for non-academic audiences. While this has caused the work to have a greater sphere of influence on Black popular culture, it has also provided non-Afrocentric scholars with reasons to claim that the work is not rigorous, in an academic sense, and is therefore lacking in analytic utility and application. I will revisit this and other critiques later. The work of anthropologist, Marimba Ani, however, is a strong counter-example.

In her widely read book entitled *Yurugu: An African-Centered Critique of European Cultural Thought and Behavior*, Ani (1994) develops an extensive critique and analysis of the ways in which Eurocentric ideological formations have impacted the very foundations of their culture and ways of seeing the world. Situating her work within the tradition of Wade Nobles' theory of culture, which emphasizes the ideological dimensions of culture, she develops a theory of the 'cultural structuring of thought' which involves an in-depth anthropological investigation of European customs and traditions—particularly as they regard epistemology, axiology and ontology. In general, this work serves as a way to deconstruct and decenter traditional western scholarship, especially in terms of the way in which it constructs Blacks. After a brief review of some of the key works in the field, I would suggest that there are three domains within which the majority of literature considered to be Afrocentric is written. For the purposes of this paper, I refer to them as (1) Historical Reconstructionist, (2) Cultural Analyst, and (3) Cultural Archeologist. Historical reconstructionists such as Cheik Anta Diop seek to retell African History from the African perspective (Karenga, 1993). Cultural analysts such as Marimba Ani (1994) engage in an extensive critique of European cultural practices and traditions, while cultural archeologists like Maulana Karenga have attempted, as others have, to engage in actual historical research as a way in which to recover lost elements of African culture, particularly Ancient Egyptian or Kemetic culture. Other more popular Afrocentric literature operates within and outside of many of these frames simultaneously, though they might more closely be associated with what I call the cultural analyst paradigm which has a tendency to argue that there exists a biological basis for European cultural practices that have disenfranchised others.

Afrocentric Education

Afrocentric or culture-centered educational theory existed long before the post-modern concept of Afrocentricity came into being. In fact, in the early twentieth century, noted author and scholar Carter G. Woodson (1998) vociferously addressed the cultural miseducation of African peoples in public schools. Others have suggested that schools for Africans, as they were conceptualized by white abolitionists, were not created with the intent of being spiritually, emotionally and intellectually emancipating. Rather they served as a way for whites to maintain control over the minds of newly freed slaves (Butchart, 1976; Woodson, 1998). Other African American scholars (Kunjufu, 1985; Lee, 1992; Shujaa, 1994) have continued the tradition of building sound arguments about the failure of schools to properly educate the vast majority of African Americans.

While Afrocentric scholars have consistently critiqued the US educational system for alienating African Americans from their cultural roots, a number of them have also worked to define the 'Afrocentric Idea in Education' (Asante, 1991). Carol D. Lee (1992), Mwalimu Shujaa (1994) and others have defined Afrocentric education in very specific ways. According to Lee,

> An effective African-centered pedagogy: legitimizes African stores of knowledge; positively exploits and scaffolds productive community and cultural practices; extends and builds upon the indigenous language; reinforces community ties and idealizes service to one's family, community, nation, race and world; promotes positive social relationships; imparts a world view that idealizes a positive, self-sufficient future for one's people without denying the self-worth and right to self-determination of others; and supports cultural continuity while promoting critical consciousness. (pp. 164 and 165)

In other words, a practice of teaching that is Afrocentric centralizes and normalizes the narratives of people of African descent within the context of community—taking into account historically rooted ways of being and knowing. More important, Afrocentric education—with its emphasis on the teaching of the history of African and African American peoples—helps students develop a commitment to community (Lee, 1992). As mentioned previously, 'culturally relevant' pedagogy (Ladson-Billings, 1995), 'culturally responsive' teaching (Gay, 2000; Irvine, 2000), and other culture-centered frameworks in education (King, 1995) are rooted in Afrocentric educational theory and practice with links to critical theory and pedagogy. With that in mind, it seems important to talk about the ways in which Afrocentricity as a body of knowledge is similar to or different from critical race theory as an emerging critical discourse on the law.

Critical Comparative Analysis of CRT and Afrocentricity

There is some suggestion, within the pages of the introduction to widely read compendia of leading articles on race and the law, that critical race theory has taken the position that racial essentialism (in my mind, a code word for Afrocentricity and/or cultural nationalism) is not consistent with what they imagine to be emancipatory or liberatory praxis (Crenshaw et al., 1995). They suggest that these discourses operate as totalizing metanarratives that are largely based on the experiences of Black men who rarely concern themselves with the ways that gender and class oppression interact with race oppression (Crenshaw, 1988). Crenshaw further elaborates on this notion in her discussion of intersectionality or the relationships between race and gender oppression. She cites specific examples of 'Afrocentric' literature that argue for the containment and control of the Black woman through physical abuse. She argues that work of this nature not only undermines the quest for social justice but also further delimits the agency of Black women. To that extent, critical race theorists, Crenshaw being chief among them, raise serious questions about the degree to which a politics of cultural consciousness can lead us toward a greater degree of freedom. Besides the critique of Afrocentric thought as gender-blind, some also see it as racial essentialism: the ascribing of specific qualities, albeit good ones, to any one race. Furthermore, while critical race theorists argue for the use of race in discussions of social inequality, they also contend that there are various forms of race. Gotanda (1995), for example, argues that there are biological, social, political, and cultural ways of understanding race that are appropriate given the particular context in which they are being utilized. To that extent, critical race theorists also argue that there are no fixed notions of race or racial/cultural identity and that racial and cultural identity, though they are important in helping one to develop a sense of consciousness about social inequality, are not to be judged, valued, or measured. To that end, most critical race theorists lean more heavily toward a constructionist view of race, arguing that race is primarily a construct which is made and remade for different purposes and for different uses (Lee, 1995).

There has been some discussion regarding the ways in which critical race theory, as a discourse on race in the law and education, fails to address issues of culture and language (Perea, 1997; Revilla & Asato, 2002). Critiques have asked questions like, 'Why aren't critical race theorists taking up the question of cultural domination as an integral part of racial subordination in a white supremacist context?' Moreover, as I suggested previously, one could seriously question CRT's silence on the question of culture and language (Perea, 1997). For example, while critical race theorists talk about the importance of experiential knowledge and the use of narratives as a way in which to more accurately tell the stories of oppressed people of color, there is no discussion regarding the source (other than experiences with oppression) of the experiential knowledge of the people of color. What does it mean to utilize the knowledge of the oppressed as grounding for theoretical construct-building when the oppressed are only defined in relation to their oppressors? What is it that makes the story of the oppressed valid anyways? Does it not have something to do with their pasts? Furthermore, while critical race theorists reject claims of objectivity and neutrality, they are not clear about which claims they do, in fact, embrace. The Afrocentric would ask, for example, do they embrace Kemetic ontological, epistemological or axiological claims? This also leads us to ask: Is it enough to simply reject prevailing modes of thought or does one have a responsibility to be explicit about one's epistemological underpinnings?

Afrocentric theorists might also argue that CRT's commitment to racial equality is little more than a pipe dream, given the fact that white power in the United States has become so entrenched. While Derrick Bell does argue that racial equality is an unrealistic goal for African Americans, his suggestions for improved conditions do not argue for complete social transformation or separation of the races, as many Afrocentrists might advocate. For many Afrocentrists, the only solution is to divest totally from mainstream American culture and begin the process of nation building (Akoto, 1992). While some critical race theorists might see this as a worthy goal, others would frown upon the Afrocentrists' tendency toward a separatist politics, which, they would argue, remains somewhat blind to the fact that there must be action behind our words; that we must strongly resist racism in all its variegated manifestations. So, while Afrocentric theorists might critique CRT for not addressing the culture question, and presuming that racial equality in a white society is possible, critical race theorists have argued, on some level, that the Afrocentrists practice an essentialist politics that gives women little or no voice. However, as I will show in the next section, the points of agreement between these paradigms is far greater than the sum of their differences.

Conclusion: Exploring the Connections

In an article about the deep-rooted racist nature of social science research methodology, Sheurich and Young (1997) refer to both Afrocentricity and critical race theory as 'race-based epistemologies' (p. 10) that offer important alternatives to Eurocentric ways of knowing and theorizing about the world. While this categorization of these and other transformative epistemologies can be viewed as a form of ghettoization of research and theory that addresses the needs of racially subordinated peoples, I find it useful for the purposes of helping me to better understand the points of connection between two paradigms that have similar aims. For example, while many Afrocentric theorists would not refer to their work as race-based, they would probably agree with critical race theorists who argue that race and its progeny, racism, must be utilized as tools through which we can theorize about the ways in which people of color are oppressed. To that extent, they both level rather harsh critiques at Marxist, liberal and conservative demagogues who attempt to assert that race-consciousness is but a mere game of identity politics (Asante, 1987, 1988; Ani, 1994; Crenshaw *et al.*, 1995; Gordon, 1995).

What do CRT and Afrocentricity have in common? Both offer new discourses about the ways that people of color have been historically marginalized and oppressed in a race-obsessed society that privileges white over Black. In this sense, it could be argued that both theoretical paradigms have eventuated in an epistemological revolution or, to use Khunian terms, a major paradigm shift. To that extent, both could be referred to as *epistemologies of transformation and liberation.* CRT and Afrocentricity also attempt to operate from the vantage point of oppressed people or people of color. In doing so, Mari Matsuda (1987) and Molefi Asante (1988) both argue, in slightly different ways, that people of color can and should be placed at the center of the analysis and not at the margins. Both epistemologies offer implications for the way that research can and should be conducted in communities of color. In other words, they offer valuable ideas about the way that *culturally sensitive and attuned research* can be done.

Finally, both areas of study offer extensive critiques of the ways that Blacks have been constructed by whites in this context of white supremacy. This is exemplified through a comparison of the work of Kimberlé Crenshaw and Marimba Ani. In an article which explores the ways that Blacks are constructed in a white supremacist context, Crenshaw argues that the ideology of racism has constructed Blacks as 'lazy, unintelligent, immoral, ignorant . . . criminal, shiftless, [and] lascivious' (p. 113). She further argues that as races were constructed, specific characteristics were tied to certain races. Marimba Ani (1994) has written extensively about how Blacks have been otherized in western societies. In her chapter on Europeans' 'image of others,' she argues that while Europeans tend to view 'others' as 'irrational, noncritical, illogical, uncivilized, primitive, unlawful, unruly, lazy, passive, apathetic' they tend to view themselves as the direct antithesis of this (p. 307). These analyses of the ways that Blacks are constructed provide a well-developed *critique of white supremacy.* This analysis critiques the ways that racism as an ideological formation dictates that whites and even Blacks learn to believe a certain kind of story about Black people, what it means to be Black and what it means to not be Black.

In sum, both frameworks could be referred to as: (1) epistemologies of transformation and liberation; (2) theoretical constructs that help us to do empirical research that is culturally sensitive; and (3) race-based critiques of white racial and cultural supremacy in the United States and in the world. These three common-alities, of course, cannot begin to account for the complexity of both theories. However, this new framing of the issue does suggest the importance of 'digging out' what's good and utilizing it for liberatory means. In that sense, I do not find it a useful exercise to write excessively about the deficiencies of these two theo-ries. Instead, I have tried to take from them what I find to be useful in helping me to frame the nature of Black teachers' emancipatory practice. It is my hope that other critical pedagogists, with perhaps less of a vested interest in these issues, will begin the work of excavating the literature and looking at the ways that it can enhance their own work as we continue to explore the role of theory in the development of pedagogy and praxis that helps make the world whole.

References

Akoto, K. A. (1992) *Nationbuilding: Theory & Practice in Afrikan Centered Educa-tion* (Washington, DC, Pan Afrikan World Institute).

Ani, M. (1994) *Yurugu: An African-Centered critique of European Cultural Thought and Behavior* (Trenton, Africa World Press, Inc.).

Asante, M. K. (1987) *The Afrocentric Idea* (Philadelphia, Temple University Press).

Asante, M. K. (1988) *Afrocentricity* (Trenton, NJ, Africa World Press).

Asante, M. K. (1991) The Afrocentric Idea in Education, *Journal of Negro Education*, 60:2, pp. 170–180.

Beauboeuf-Lafontant, T. (1999) A Movement Against and Beyond Boundaries: 'Politically Relevant Teaching' among African American Teachers, *Teachers College Record*, 100:4, pp. 702–723.

Bell, D. (1992) *Faces at the Bottom of the Well: The Permanence of Racism* (New York, Basic Books).

Bell, D. (1995) The Racism Is Permanent Thesis: Courageous Revelations or Uncon-scious Denial of Racial Genocide, *Capital University Law Review*, 22, pp. 571–578.

Butchart, R. E. (1976) Educating for Freedom: Northern Whites and the Origins of Black Education in the South, 1862–1875 (unpublished doctoral diss., State Uni-versity of New York, Binghamton).

Collins, P. H. (1991) *Black Feminist Thought: Knowledge, Consciousness, and the Poli-tics of Empowerment* (New York, Routledge).

Crenshaw, K. W. (1988) Race, Reform, and Retrenchment: Transformation and legitimation in antidiscrimination law, *Harvard Law Review*, 101, pp. 1331–1387.

Crenshaw, K., Gotanda, N., Peller, G. & Thomas, K. (eds) (1995) *Critical Race Theory: Key Writings that Formed the Movement* (New York, New Press).

Darder, A. (1991) *Culture and Power in the Classroom: A Critical Foundation for Bicultural Education* (Westport, CT, Bergin & Garvey).

Darder, A. (1993) How Does the Culture of the Teacher Shape the Classroom Expe-rience of Latino Students?: The Unexamined Question in Critical Pedagogy, in: S. Rothstein (ed.), *Handbook of Schooling in Urban America* (Westport, CT, Greenwood Press).

Ellsworth, E. (1989) Why Doesn't This Feel Empowering? Working Through the Repressive Myths of Critical Pedagogy, *Harvard Educational Review*, 59:3, pp. 297–324.

Foster, M. (1997) *Black Teachers on Teaching* (New York, New Press).

Freire, P. (1973) *Education for Critical Consciousness* (New York, Seabury Press).

Freire, P. (1993) *Pedagogy of the Oppressed*, 20th-anniversary edition (New York, Continuum).

Gay, G. (2000) *Culturally Responsive Teaching: Theory, Research and Practice* (New York, Teachers College Press).

Gordon, B. M. (1995) Knowledge Construction, Competing Critical Theories, and Education, in: J. A. Banks & C. A. McGee Banks (eds), *Handbook of Research on Multicultural Education* (New York, Macmillan).

Gotanda, N. (1995) A Critique of 'Our Constitution is Color-Blind', in: K. Crenshaw, N. Gotanda, G. Peller & K. Thomas (eds), *Critical Race Theory: Key Writings that Formed the Movement* (New York, New Press).

Henry, A. (1998) *Taking Back Control: African Canadian women Teachers' Lives and Practice* (Albany, NY, SUNY Press).

Irvine, J. J. (1988) An Analysis of the Problem of Disappearing Black Educators, *Elementary School Journal*, 88:5, pp. 503–513.

Irvine, J. J. (1990) *Black Students and School Failure: Policies, Practices, and Prescriptions* (Westport, CT, Greenwood Press).

Irvine, J. J. (2000) DeWitt Wallace—Reader's Digest Distinguished Lecture, paper presented at the Annual meeting of the American Educational Research Association, New Orleans.

Kanpol, B. (1988) Teacher Work Tasks as Forms of Resistance and Accommodation to Structural Factors of Schooling, *Urban Education*, 23:2, pp. 173–187.

Kanpol, B. (1992) *Towards a Theory and Practice of Teacher Cultural Politics: Continuing the Postmodern Debate* (Norwood, NJ, Ablex).

Karenga, M. (1993) *Introduction to Black Studies*, 2nd edn (Los Angeles, CA, University of Sankore Press).

King, J. E. (1991) Unfinished Business: Black Student's Alienation and Black Teachers' Pedagogy, in: M. Foster (ed.), *Readings on Equal Education: Qualitative Investigations in Schools and Schooling* (New York, AMS Press).

King, J. E. (1995) Culture-Centered Knowledge: Black Studies, Curriculum Transformation, and Social Action, in: J. A. Banks & C. A. McGee Banks (eds), *Handbook of Research on Multicultural Education* (New York, Macmillan).

Kunjufu, J. (1985) *Countering the Conspiracy to Destroy Black Boys* (Chicago, African-American Images).

Ladson-Billings, G. (1994) *The Dream Keepers: Successful Teachers of African-American Children* (San Francisco, Jossey-Bass Publishers).

Ladson-Billings, G. (1995) Toward a Theory of Culturally Relevant Teaching, *American Educational Research Journal*, 32:3, pp. 465–491.

Ladson-Billings, G. (1998) Just What Is Critical Race Theory and What's It Doing in a *Nice* Field Like Education?, *International Journal of Qualitative Studies in Education*, 11:1, pp. 7–24.

Ladson-Billings, G. & Tate, W. F. (1995) Toward a Critical Race Theory of Education, *Teachers College Record*, 97:1, pp. 47–68.

Lawrence, C. (1991) The Word and the River: Pedagogy as Scholarship and Struggle, *Southern California Law Review*, 65, pp. 2231–2298.

Lee, C. D. (1992) Profile of an Independent Black Institution: African-Centered Education at Work, *Journal of Negro Education*, 61:2, pp. 160–177.

Lee, J. (1995) Navigating the Topology of Race, in: K. Crenshaw, N. Gotanda, G. Peller & K. Thomas (eds), *Critical Race Theory: Key Writings that Formed the Movement* (New York, New Press).

Lynn, M. (1999) Toward a Critical Race Pedagogy: A Research Note, *Urban Education*, 33:5, pp. 606–626.

Matsuda, M. (1987) Looking to the Bottom: Critical Legal Studies and Reparations, *Harvard Civil Rights—Civil Liberties Law Review*, 22, pp. 323–399.

McCarthy, C. (1988) Rethinking Liberal and Radical Perspectives on Racial Inequality in Schooling: Making the Case for Nonsynchrony, *Harvard Educational Review*, 58:3, pp. 265–279.

Morris, J. E. (2001) Forgotten Voices of Black Educators: Critical Race Perspectives on the Implementation of a Desegregation Plan, *Educational Policy*, 15:4, pp. 575–600.

Omi, M. & Winant, H. (1994) *Racial Formation in the United States: From the 1960's to the 1990's*, 2nd edn (New York, Routledge).

Opoku, K. A. (1997) *Hearing and Keeping: Akan Proverbs* (Accra, Ghana, Asempa Publishers).

Perea, J. F. (1997) The Black/White Binary Paradigm of Race: The 'Normal Science' of American Racial Thought, *California Law Review*, 85, pp. 1213–1258.

Revilla, A. T. & Asato, J. (2002) The Implementation of 227 in California Schools: A Critical Analysis of the Effect of Proposition 227 on Teacher Beliefs and Classroom Practices, *Equity and Excellence in Education Journal*, 35:2.

Scheurich, J. J. & Young, M. D. (1997) Coloring Epistemologies: Are Our Research Epistemologies Racially Biased?, *Educational Researcher*, 26:4, pp. 4–16.

Shujaa, M. J. (ed.) (1994) *Too Much Schooling, Too Little Education: A Paradox of Black Life in White Societies* (Trenton, NJ, Africa World Press).

Solórzano, D. (1997) Images and Words that Wound: Critical Race Theory, Racial Stereotyping, and Teacher Education, *Teacher Education Quarterly*, 24, pp. 5–19.

Solórzano, D. (1998) Critical Race Theory, Racial Microaggressions, and the Experiences of Chicana and Chicano Scholars, *International Journal of Qualitative Studies in Education*, 11:1, pp. 7–24.

Solórzano, D. & Villalpando, O. (1998) Critical Race Theory, Marginality, and the Experience of Minority Students in Higher Education, in: C. Torres & T. Mitchell (eds), *Emerging Issues in the Sociology of Education: Comparative perspectives* (New York, SUNY Press).

Solórzano, D. & Yosso, T. (2000) Toward a Critical Race Theory of Chicana and Chicano Education, in: C. Tejeda, C. Martinez & Z. Leonardo (eds), *Charting New Terrains of Chicana(o)/Latina(o) Education* (Cresskill, NJ, Hampton Press).

Tate, W. F. (1997) Critical Race Theory and Education: History, Theory and Implications, *Review of Research in Education*, 22, pp. 195–247.

Thomas, K. (1995) Rouge et Noir Reread: A Popular Constitutional History of the Angelo Herndon case, in: K. Crenshaw, N. Gotanda, G. Peller & K. Thomas (eds), *Critical Race Theory: Key Writings that Formed the Movement* (New York, New Press).

West, C. (1993) *Race Matters* (Boston, Beacon).

Woodson, C. G. (1998) *The Miseducation of the Negro*, 10th edn (Trenton, Africa World Press).

Chapter 4

Actions Following Words
Critical Race Theory Connects to Critical Pedagogy[1]

Laurence Parker and David O. Stovall

Editors' introduction

This essay by Laurence Parker and David Stovall, which is part of a special issue of *Educational Philosophy and Theory* on critical pedagogies and race (2004), zooms in on what has become an enduring question in philosophy of education: the relationship between critical race theory (CRT) and critical pedagogy. Parker and Stovall begin their essay by discussing the racial educational politics confronting them as professors in Illinois. While they both teach classes on CRT, evidence surrounds them in the region of students facing racism at an everyday level in public schools. As CRT is oriented toward positive social action and change, their students felt compelled in this case to engage in marches and protests related to racism in the schools, as a local issue and a broader civic rights problem. This experience prompted the authors to consider the interrelations between critical pedagogy, which has traditionally emphasized Marxist class-based analysis, and CRT, which highlights race and racism as distinctive features of the social landscape. The essay thus considers the limitations of critical pedagogy for facing racism given its focus on political economy, before considering how CRT coheres and conflicts with critical pedagogy. In particular, the authors observe how CRT recognizes the pervasiveness of color-blind rhetoric in critical pedagogies of emancipation, while different groups (such as women, Native Americans, Latinos and Latinas, and Asian Americans and Pacific Islanders) face predicaments not adequately provided for by a Marxist lens. Giving a rich view of the contemporary literature related to race, racism, and related phenomena in United States education, this article provides an in-depth account, ultimately arguing for the need for both CRT and critical pedagogy as means toward creating more successful schools for all and particularly for children of color.

Critical Race Theory Class Narrative

On September 17, 1999, six African American students were involved in a melee at a high school football game in Decatur, IL. After that incident, the Decatur school board gave all of them two-year expulsions from school. Since these events took place, a firestorm of controversy has erupted surrounding issues related to school violence, race, social class, and the implementation of school district rules over

DOI: 10.4324/9781003346104-5

student behavior and discipline. When this incident took place in the fall semester (1999), a number of students in my critical race theory class www.ed.uiuc.edu/EPS/people/Parker_490E.html discussed some type of response to this action in support of the African American residents in Decatur and the young men to protest the 'zero-tolerance' violence policy action by the Decatur school board. As we were reading the 'theory' of race, the students decided to take action in connection with this critical race theory. The disparate impact of the data related to race and African American student discipline also told a 'narrative' according to some of the students in class, as we not only read Kimberlé Crenshaw, Richard Delgado, Derrick Bell and other CRT founders, but critically asked questions from these CRT positions and their own personal experiences with racism, as to why we saw such high rates of disciplinary actions against African American youth in our own area?

For example the 1998–9 figures from the three neighboring towns near Decatur were illustrative of the problem of percentages of African Americans over-represented in school disciplinary actions. In the Champaign district white enrollment is at 63% and the white suspension is 36%, while the African American enrollment is at 31% and the comparable suspension rate of African Americans is at 62% for the same district. In the Urbana district the white enrollment is at 62% while the white suspension is 47%. The African American enrollment in Urbana is 28% but their suspension rate is 49%. For the Danville district, the white enrollment is 61% while the suspension rate is 47%, but the comparable figures for African Americans are 33% and 49% respectively (Puch, 2000).

From the discussions of the CRT readings in the class, the data as narrative, the personal experiences of some of the students in the class with racism in schools and their own individual efforts to deal with it, the students decided to get involved in marches and protests because they saw it not as a local concern, but a broader civil rights problem that needed to be addressed within the national conservative 'colorblind' context of race relations and policy implementation that has had a disproportionate impact on African American students. These students felt that it was their responsibility to put the theory (i.e., class readings on the politics of race in education) into action by attending the marches and lending their effort and support to the protests. The students met and discussed their thoughts and feelings about the issues involved in the Decatur situation in the formal class sessions after the various marches, and the informal meetings and focus groups that they had on their own. Some of them also organized and participated in their own marches and vigils on campus and to the Urbana, IL, Federal District court where the law suit was filed claiming that the school board violated the due process rights of the six African American Decatur students. As an instructor, a piece of me will argue, 'students should come to class and be prepared to do the seminar work and assignments.' But the Decatur incident created an 'interest convergence' in the graduate level seminar, as theory was linked to protest by students by challenging racism in school discipline policy and overall equity for African Americans in the Decatur and Champaign-Urbana schools, and the students in the Decatur, IL, incident.

The purpose of this opening narrative is to illustrate the importance of critical race studies in education with respect to discussing race, racialism, racism, and its connection to the larger sociopolitical context and ideological forces of domination, and how critical theories of race can be linked to educational praxis and critical pedagogy. It has been noted that a major problem with critical race theory is that it reinforces a racialized politics of identity and representation that ignores the imperatives of capitalist accumulation in a globalized economy and class divisions within racialized communities (McLaren, 1998). The post-Marxist critics of CRT in particular have forcefully argued that it fails to provide a systemic analysis of global capitalism and its effect on communities. This strand of critical pedagogy argues that emphasis on race-based identity politics ignores the overwhelming tendency of capitalism to homogenize rather than diversify the human experience (Darder & Torres, 2002).

Furthermore, others position critical pedagogy as connected to social justice and multicultural education, with an emphasis on teaching values of genuine concern about students from all racial, linguistic and social class backgrounds, as opposed to just focusing on race and the black–white binary (Banks & McGee, 1997). This type of critical pedagogy is rooted in holistic curriculum reform through the detection of bias in texts and instruction, and developing a classroom climate that focuses on student achievement through a more critical educational process. Critical pedagogy calls for educators to be agents working for social change and equity in schools and communities.

The aforementioned problems with CRT specifically, and critical theories of race in general, are indeed noted shortcomings when one initially considers it in conjunction with critical pedagogy. These criticisms have merit, yet they have also been discussed in other ways in terms of noting CRT's limitations with respect to providing answers to a host of social class and feminist issues, from lack of proper child care for single mothers on college campuses, to homophobia (see Parker, 1998). However, more recent discussions about critical race theory from a Latino/Latina perspective have emerged as the LatCrit movement and have engaged in challenging theoretical and practice-based discussions related to the growth of global capitalism and exploitation that has had a profound impact on Latino–Latina populations not only in the US but in Central and South America regarding immigration, language, gay, lesbian and transgendered identity, wealth disparities and political power relations between Latinos–Latinas and other racialized groups (Igleias & Valdez, 1998; Valdez *et al.*, 2002). But the continual question is, can someone committed to critical pedagogy also find merit in CRT and/or critical studies of race as well? Another question that arises is, how useful is a critical theory of race, when there is an overemphasis on racial identity politics, rather than on attacking capitalism and social class disparities through democratic social justice for all racialized groups?

In this essay we will discuss some of the ways that CRT could be linked to critical pedagogy in order to provide a more comprehensive analytical framework to analyze the role of race–class dynamics. This approach will attempt to address some of the gaps and silences that critical pedagogy has had regarding critical theoretical positions on race and racism and the operation of white supremacy in education. However, we will also point out some of the problems and raise more issues of concern related to critical pedagogy and race in educational research and practice. Handel Wright (2002) articulated insightfully the problems within North American critical pedagogy in terms of its evolution to a rigid dogmatic binary of positions within itself: on the one hand, postmodernist, poststructuralists and feminists argue for a post-critical pedagogy, while post-colonial and neo-Marxist critical pedagogy supporters, on the other hand, argue strongly for the merits of their arguments rooted in class analysis. For the most part, this binary has left race out of the theoretical discussion. More specifically, Wright questions 'where is the black representation in the discussion of the future of critical pedagogy?' (p. 1). This question is important because of the African American/Black ambivalence toward critical pedagogy. Part of the unease and trepidation stems from the fact that although issues such as racism against African American/Black students have been addressed within critical pedagogy, and African American, African Caribbean scholars have borrowed from critical pedagogy to target inequitable schooling practices, critical theories of race have been virtually ignored within the 'generalized theorization of the development and future of critical pedagogy' (Wright, 2002, p. 6).

Given this absence of a theoretical discussion of race within critical pedagogy, we hope this paper performs three initial functions. Since Marvin Lynn has provided an overview of CRT by connecting it to other existing recent work on race, racialism and racism in this issue, we want to connect the tenets of CRT to the current color-blind ideology and discourse in education regarding race studies. Our purpose here is to highlight some of the limitations of critical pedagogy regarding the permanence of racism, and how CRT perspectives have been utilized to analyze the racism, coupled with social class bias, sexism, etc., that still exists in education. Second, we want to present an argument for why there is a need for CRT and critical race studies (more broadly) to connect with critical pedagogy. Finally, we will speculate about what lies ahead regarding possible points of agreement and conflicts between CRT and critical pedagogy.

White Supremacy, Color-blind Ideology, and Problems With Critical Pedagogy In Education

One of the main problems in critical theory is dealing with the centrality of racism in education and its strong philosophical roots and connections to the political economy. Race has played a major part in shaping the modern and postmodern world (McCarthy & Crichlow, 1993). Even though race is a mythology that has been socially constructed for purposes of control, power and economic exploitation, racialism (e.g., attitudes, actions of stereotyping, discriminatory policies, unequal distribution of resources) is fundamental to everyday life, the shaping of moral character, the formation and implementation of law, policy, and the study of social context in education and other social science fields (Stanfield, 1999). Critical race theory (and its connecting parts, e.g., LatCrit, Asian American poststructural critical legal positions, critical race feminism) argues that race is central in the making of our world. Race has played a fundamental role in: (1) the making of nation—empire that evolves into a system of conquest and enslavement; (2) the creation of capital; and (3) the shaping of culture and identity, especially in the creation of subordinate racialized groups (Winant, 2002). Modern white racism evolved ideologically and philosophically in Europe and North America as a system of human classification based on physical characteristics that were considered fixed (Smedley, 1999; Feagin, 2000). Goldberg (1993) argued that in order to understand modernity and its evolution, one has to understand the ontology of race, racialism, and how each played a fundamental role in shaping major philosophical, political, and scientific thought. Smedley (1999) traced the origins of racial ideology in North America, to British conflicts with other national groups such as the Irish, in order to fully examine how those conflicts over national origin, land, and religion seeded the ideology of British racism and justification of colonialist expansion and domination. As an ideology, white supremacy was imposed in North America, as it was used hierarchically to rank races and justified horrific acts in the form of slavery, colonialist domination of land and populations, and forced assimilation.

The current racialized discourse in the U.S. has taken on a different form through the ideology of color-blind interpretations of law and political, social, and economic relations (Lipsitz, 1998). The core of these racialized arguments posits that there are no fundamental differences between the races based on inequality (Bonilla-Silva, 2001). Overt discriminatory laws have been repealed and there is more popular acceptance of different racial groups within the current conservative multicultural discourse that accepts symbolic individuals such as Colin Powell or Condoleezza Rice, the mainstreaming of Latino popular culture, and Asian Americans' children as 'model minority' students, as evidence of racial and ethnic acceptance in the current conservative U.S. political climate (Dillard, 2001). This ideology of color-blindness and 'racial progress' has also been reflective of an overarching trend in K-12 education for teachers and administrators to ignore race and racism in their schools, by assuming that if attention is not paid to racial implications of problems related to low minority student achievement, school restructuring, or African American teacher disengagement with white staff, then these issues will simply disappear (Lewis, 2001; Lipman, 1997; Madsen & Mabokela, 2000). Another part of this conservative ideology in schools is the open racism that teachers and administrators have toward African Americans, Latinos, Navajos, and other racial groups. This has been illustrated through the case study research on small Midwestern 'liberal' university towns, where the image has belied the reality of white teacher hostility toward African American students and parents (Kailin, 1999). Deyhle (1995) presented evidence of racial warfare in the schools between the Navajo and Anglo population in southern Utah. Her research has been used to demonstrate the illegality of racial tracking practices by the district as well as other inequitable resource distribution issues. Deyhle argued that the role of race and racism has been central in creating 'racial warfare' between Anglos and Navajos (p. 409). Larson (1997) uncovered another aspect of racism that relied on administrative use of rigid policy processes and bureaucratic procedures in attempts to quell racial disturbances and tensions in a Midwestern high school, as African American students, parents, church leaders pressed for increased Black curriculum and representation in the school setting. As the Black student and community protests increased, the administrative staff in the district held on to tighter interpretations of discipline policies to achieve order for whites in the district. Larson found that, in hindsight, some of the administrators saw that they should have relied less on the bureaucratic rules, and more on honest communication and dialogue with the Black community. In the United Kingdom, Sewell (1997) documented a different example of racism regarding white teachers' relationships with Black male youth. On the one hand, there is an acceptance of Black popular culture through music and style. However, Sewell showed how white teachers felt threatened by Black males when they used popular culture behavior to act against unfair treatment in the schools by white authorities.

Given the phenomenon of white backlash toward students of color in predominantly white schools and colleges, critical pedagogy has to address not only the conditions of global capitalist exploitation, but also anti-racist pedagogy, and other commitments to social justice (see special issue of *Educational Theory*, fall 1998). We would argue that one of the main challenges for critical pedagogy has been the intractability of white supremacy in education institutions. This racism ranges from 'microaggressions' toward Latino students on predominantly white college campuses (Villalpando, 2000; Solórzano & Yosso, 2001), to race and social class disparities in financial aid, with college access reserved increasingly for upper-middle-class students (Orfield, 1992), and admission to elite colleges and universities being viewed as an educational 'property right' reserved for whites opposed to affirmative action (Harris, 1993). To be sure, we are in solidarity with one of the main radical purposes of critical pedagogy, which involves a politics of economic and resource distribution as well as a politics of recognition, affirmation, and difference (McLaren, 1998, p. 458). But one of the immediate problems of praxis that also needs to be confronted is the changing shape of racism reflected in the national trends that reveal this white backlash towards African Americans, Latinos–Latinas, Asian American/Pacific Islanders, and Tribal Nation students and communities in many schools. This backlash represents itself through an overwhelmingly white teaching and administrative force having control of, and conflict with, children and parents of color in urban, suburban, and rural communities, an example of which was illustrated in the opening narrative.[2]

The second challenge that race and racism has posed for critical pedagogy has been one of relevance and inclusion in the debate and discussion as to its theoretical underpinnings and practical utility for various racial groups. Appiah (1992), Outlaw (1996) and Mills (1998) have all called for the study and inclusion of African American/Black philosophy as a legitimate contributor to ontological and epistemological debates in the academy. This type of philosophy 'develops out of the resistance to oppression, it is a practical and politically oriented philosophy that, long before Marx was born, sought to interpret the world correctly so as to better change it'

(Mills, 1998, p. 17). An African American/Black philosophy counters the 'dehumanization to which people and the ideas of African descent have been subjected through the history of colonialism and of European racism' (Hord & Lee, 1995, p. 5). Yet, Wright (2002) posits that critical pedagogy has not been interested in how these race-based philosophic perspectives can inform the general theoretical discourse in the field. The debates between feminist and male respondents, or post-structuralists and post-Marxists, etc., have been 'discussions among white people from which people of color have for the most part been excluded' (p. 6). Wright points out that from its inception at the Frankfurt School, to its principal male theorists, to its mostly feminist critics, the figures involved in theorizing the discourse have been white. Wright raises the issue of representation in critical pedagogy as 'unremarked whiteness' (p. 6), yet sees an ambivalence or caution toward approaching critical pedagogy in terms of questioning the utility of entering the theoretical debate. Grande (2000) voiced skepticism about critical pedagogy, as she noted how its pedagogy of oppression failed to consider the ways that American Indians, as a sovereign tribal people within North America, experience a fundamentally different type of oppression that is incomparable to other minority groups. For example, she noted that the tenet of critical democracy as central in the struggle for liberation for critical pedagogy, fails to recognize tribal nations' struggles against inclusion into the democratic mainstream. Furthermore, the concept of democracy in critical pedagogy has not been seriously questioned regarding how it has been enacted as a lethal colonizing force against tribal nations (p. 468).

Third, critical pedagogy, with its roots centered in social class analysis and critique, can be faulted for not paying enough attention to when class matters, when race matters, and when both areas (along with gender, or areas such as sexual orientation which sometimes conflict) determine the life chances of families in the US. Conley (1999) opened his analysis of this issue by pointing out that, for example, in 1994 the median white family held assets worth more than seven times those of the median family of color. Going a step further, when one compares white and racial minority families of similar income levels, whites have more advantages in terms of total wealth and assets:

> For instance, at the lower end of the income spectrum (less than $15,000 per year), the median African American family has no assets, while the equivalent white family holds $10,000 worth of equity. At upper income levels (greater than $75,000 per year), white families have a median net worth of $308,000, almost three times the figure for upper-income African American families ($114,600).[3]

Conley posited that due to past discrimination against African Americans, especially in terms of home ownership, they were not able (until fairly recently) to acquire other wealth assets that they could pass on to their children. This, in turn, compounded the race and social class disparities between themselves and white Americans in areas such as education. Furthermore, whites benefited from racial segregation in terms of wealth accumulation when compared to African Americans. We are in agreement with the criticism of global commercialized capitalism and its influence on education. This is a sharp criticism that needs to be directed toward the current pro-business model that is used to create a community of consumers connected to education, primarily for the purpose of training the majority of low SES (socio-economic status) and racial minority students to become future depoliticized but literate high-tech assembly-line and service-sector workers (Anderson, 2001). However, in connecting this point to critical pedagogy, our concern is that an extreme turn back to rigid class analysis as the fundamental explainer of social position, and potential for democratic emancipation in the political economy primarily through class struggle, once again ignores the fundamental role that race and white supremacy have played in shaping the life chances of other racial groups to pursue educational opportunities and obtain equitable results.[4]

Critical Race Theory and Its Links/Conflicts With Critical Pedagogy

Critical race theory emerged from the legal arena as a challenge to the aforementioned ideology of color-blindness, and the accompanying political discourse, viewing it as a pretext for racial discrimination. African Americans, Latinos–Latinas, Asian-American/Pacific Islanders, and various Tribal Nation groups made significant strides in using the law and federal courts to dismantle symbolic racism during the civil rights era of the 1960s and early 1970s. However, critical race theory uses counter-stories or narratives, as well as historical triangulation of facts that have an impact on present-day discrimination, to argue that a color-blind view of race upholds white supremacy in terms of sweeping away racial classifications, but leaves political majorities intact, which in turn uses the power of racism to undermine minority interest (Delgado, 1989; Williams, 1991; Bell, 1992; Crenshaw et al., 1995). At present this is done not so much through legalized measures of overt discrimination; rather, it is through more general everyday racism, where racism and prejudice are embedded in the simple psychological decision-making rules that we use to make inferences and draw conclusions about groups (Essed, 1991; McMorris, 1996). Critical race theory offers a framework that would attack seemingly neutral forms of racial subordination, while counteracting the devaluation of minority cultural and racial institutions in a color-blind society (Gotanda, 1991). Essentially, the color-blind perspective on race calls for assimilation, while critical race theory calls for the full awareness and critique of the ideology of race as a determining factor in how the law has been used against racialized minority groups and how the law and social action can be used to bring groups together for common interests of racial and class struggle (Yamamoto, 1997).

Our interactions in educational sites of struggles over race (in schools and the academy) have led us to argue for the importance of connecting critical race theory to critical pedagogy. We also acknowledge the limits and possibilities of both at specific points of analysis and action. Critical race theory can move into critical race praxis and pedagogy through the use of critical race theory studies in education, and changes in teacher education through an emphasis on race, racism, and dealing with white supremacy. We posit that there are some salient positions which undergird critical race theory in education (particularly in terms of research and teaching) that in turn have implications for critical pedagogy; they are: (1) the experiences of racial groups merit intellectual pursuit because of the uniqueness of the cultural, historical, and contemporary experiences of persons of color; (2) the historical and contemporary experiences of people of color can prove instructive about human interactions; and (3) one of the most significant tasks of a teacher or scholar who plans to utilize CRT (or LatCrit, etc.) is to develop tools that help generate knowledge designed to describe, analyze and empower people of color and to help change negative social forces into positive social forces as they impact on everyday life. Subsequently, it would be essential for researchers, teachers, or educational administrators steeped in critical pedagogical theory, to know not only the history of race and race relations, but also the connection of race to a community of interest with regard to the group's struggle for power and self-determination.

One of the ways that critical race theory can serve this end is to generate informed perspectives designed to describe, analyze and challenge racist policy and practice in educational institutions. The connection between critical race theory and education would entail linking teaching and research to general practical knowledge about institutional forces that have a disparate impact on racial minority communities. For example, the emphasis on narrative life and perspectives among African American graduate students in the class (mentioned in the opening narrative), would highlight an important aspect of critical race theory's power to illuminate and connect the African American experience of institutional racism as initially documented through the high discipline rates and low achievement of the African American students in these school districts. The narrative or storytelling would not only let the informants speak for themselves, but also deliberately challenge racist assumptions and design the research to be part of the solution and not part of the problem. It is here that CRT differs somewhat from critical pedagogy. Critical theory has been used to provide a lens for seeing and acting upon racial change in order to deal with inequality related to the hidden curriculum and overt schooling practice. Critical theory in education is currently concerned with various forms of critical multiculturalism or anti-racist education, particularly among white European Americans (Derman-Sparks, 1989; Giroux, 1983; Lewis, 2001). CRT work, presented in the opening narrative, seeks to disrupt the portrayal of the 'problems' with African American education as residing with African American students or parents. Rather, critical race theory in education connects with the experiences, ways of thinking, believing, and knowing the racial communities in their struggle for self-determination and equity in the schools. This is not to completely discount the efforts by critical pedagogy to deal with race. However, from a CRT perspective, racism, its historical dimensions, social construction, and political/social ramifications become much more central to the debate surrounding power relationships in school policy and practice. So it is also important to make various testimonies of discrimination a part of the legal, social and public record through discourse and demonstration. For example, the actions of the students mentioned at the start of this paper led to them pulling their individual efforts together in the schools and the African American community to document various aspects of the problem of underachievement of African American students in the east-central Illinois public schools (Bartee *et al.*, 2000). In turn, the information has been used in connection with other individual efforts to work with students in the schools, and Black community leaders and parents, to support their efforts to press the districts for equitable remedies.

The current work in critical race theory and education seeks to foster an engagement with praxis and movement toward racial justice in the schools and higher education institutions (Solórzano, 1998; Solórzano & Yosso, 2001). Much of the literature in education related to CRT addresses its origins and links to specific educational issues and policies. Ladson-Billings and Tate (1995) pushed for using CRT in education to deconstruct fundamental assumptions behind seemingly race-neutral policies and ideology about the education of African American children and other students of color. Tate (1997) traced the origins of CRT and elaborated on the positions of founders on the formation of the CRT movement. He also suggested ways in which CRT could be linked to educational research by calling for specificity in using CRT and pinpointing it as the tool used to unmask the effects of racism and how it has been operationalized in educational institutions. Solórzano (1997, 1998) and Solórzano and Yosso (2001) looked at using CRT in higher education settings, first as a theoretical framework to examine teacher education racial discourse about the abilities of children of color, and then to look at its cumulative impact on Chicano–Chicana fellowship students in graduate school settings. Solórzano and Yosso used CRT and LatCrit to analyze the seemingly race-neutral policy language of equal educational opportunity in providing high status education for meritorious minority graduate students. However, the student counternarratives illustrated how they endured the everyday racism of graduate school, as White European American professors and students made these Chicano–Chicana students feel as if they did not deserve to be at elite institutions of graduate study. Building on this theme, Villalpando (2000) used CRT and LatCrit and case study research methods to identify institutional climates related to race in higher education settings and found that some of the campus environments were inhospitable to Chicano–Chicana students. He also used CRT, LatCrit, and critical race praxis to analyze how these students forged racial–ethnic support networks to combat the racism on campus, and take advantage of educational opportunities and serve the local Chicano community. Delgado Bernal (2002), González (1998), Pizarro (1998), and Hidalgo (1998), all discussed how CRT and LatCrit could be linked to Chicano/Latino epistemology, particularly Chicana feminist epistemology and the validation of the experiences of Chicana/Chicano students and Puerto Rican families. Ladson-Billings (1998) discussed CRT's use in analyzing the impact of racism in school policy actions related to curriculum, instruction, and school funding. Lynn (1999) added to this perspective by researching African American teachers who utilized a critical race pedagogical framework when informing African American students as to the importance of their race/culture as a bridge to learning and success. In sum, connections between CRT and critical pedagogy can be forged by using both to examine the origins, development, implementation, and evaluation of educational practices, and both should be useful to help guide this inquiry.

CRT and the Implications for Teacher Education, Educational Leadership, and Critical Pedagogy

We also believe CRT in teacher education and educational leadership could potentially serve as a useful framework with which to explore possibilities of change in both areas. For example, Ladson-Billings (1999) made reference to exemplar programs led by key leaders in the field of teacher education (e.g., Jacqueline Jordan Irvine, Marilyn Cochran-Smith, Joyce King, Martin Haberman), which have all strived to challenge preconceived notions of race and guide new, more critical thinking about race among the teacher education candidates. Some of these programs make an appeal to professionalism regarding the teaching of diverse urban K-12 students. Others stress the generation and development of different thinking about race based on critical reflections and narratives in schools and communities of color. These programs stood out as ones which deliberately prepared new teachers to think and act critically about race and racism in the schools and larger society. Michelle Young, the late Julie Laible, Jim Scheurich, Linda Skrala and others are also seeking to challenge educational leadership in the area of white racism through teaching courses that explore building new foundations of administration knowledge based on more critical perspectives related to race, gender and social justice for children and minority communities of color (Young & Laible, 2000). The work of Annette Henry (1992) and Michelle Foster (1997), which documents the importance of Black teachers' use of critical teaching instruction and role modeling for African American and African Canadian youth in the interest of the Black community, is also important for critical pedagogy to consider with respect to specific critical race perspectives related to Blacks. Similarly, critical pedagogy should take into account various other important aspects of race and critical teaching in the centrality of the theoretical and practice-based discussions about teaching. These range from the review of the literature on the role that minority teachers play in African American and Latino/a student achievement (Quiocho & Rios, 2000), to the importance of African-centered epistemology and culturally appropriate pedagogy for curriculum and instruction with African American students (Hale, 2001; Henry, 2001; Ladson-Billings, 2001; Lee, 2001). The future challenge for CRT in teacher education and educational leadership will also be to link it to anti-racist efforts in teacher education in order to incorporate critical challenges to 'whiteness' in teacher education.[5]

Critical pedagogy should look to specific areas of race-based pedagogy, and examples of successful schools that are comprised of low SES students of color, for ways in which race can be central to achievement in education. Nevelle and

Cha-Jua (1998) outline a model of critical pedagogy for Black studies that incorporates many of its fundamental facets but includes race/nationality as a category of analysis in the curriculum and instruction process. Their model for critical pedagogy in Black studies is influenced by Marxist and Black feminist perspectives, and grounded in the accurate documentation of the sociohistorical and cultural realities of African descended people, and a scholarship that advocates the core values of resistance, freedom, self-determination and education (pp. 450–454). Nevelle and Cha-Jua have discussed incorporating knowledge of a variety of learning styles characteristic of the diversity of African American students, and pedagogical choices that provide structure for learners; linking subject matter to students' experiences; and drawing upon cultural roots (pp. 456–459).

The lived experience of success in low SES schools with majority students of color was the focus of Scheurich's (1998) research. The HiPass elementary schools he and his research team evaluated engaged in learning not only met the base-level state standards of achievement. They also encompassed a set of core beliefs and cultural characteristics that emphasized the success of all students with no exceptions, allowed child-centered schooling, children and adults being treated with love and respect, valuing the first language of students and their families, and openness to innovative and experimental ideas. At the center of these schools is a commitment to children and families by the entire staff and community. The schools profiled in Scheurich's study serve to show ways we can look at how race and socioeconomic status do not have to serve as barriers and how high levels of success can be achieved not only on the standardized tests, but also in guiding low SES youth of color towards a different future than what has been stereotyped and scripted for them.

Conclusion

What is the role of race in educational research, teaching and praxis? Critical race theory can hopefully provide some help as we grapple with this question. This paper has introduced the concept of critical race theory and its problematic and potential ways of providing us with openings to theorize and take action in the area of race and education. Furthermore, it holds possibilities for intersection and conjunction with other areas of difference in educational struggles. To be sure, the legal debate surrounding the legitimacy of the theory in relation to the color-blind approach to the law will become even more prominent in education and the social science research circles as well. Yet, we feel that the future of critical race theory is part of a larger on-going power struggle pertaining to the dominant ideological racial context. It is one that concerned researchers, teachers, and activists will discuss and be engaged with in the academy, the schools and the larger community. It is one that will separate camps of concerned scholars by age, class and position. By engaging this new space, the project becomes a contested space with social justice at its center. As we continue to redevelop older positions and bring new perspectives to the table, the responsibility becomes to historicize CRT and embrace its marriage to issues of gender, class and sexuality in education. CRT is not mutually exclusive. Instead, it is the attempt to provide a space for excluded voices in education and the responsibility to produce praxis geared to address the human condition of victimized groups struggling for respect and self-determination through the expansion of their contexts of choice (Moses, 2001).

Culture-centric schools was how Scheurich (1998) described them in his research findings as to how schools in low SES areas, with majority students of color, have been successful in valuing the racial culture and the first language of the child; treating children of color with love, appreciation, care, and respect; believing and proving that all children of color can achieve at the highest academic levels; and focusing on community more than competitive individualism. Community members who work within the school structure as non-teaching and non-administrative professionals embrace these themes with teachers and administrators who share the same sentiment. The work at this level points toward one example of the direction that critical race theory and critical pedagogy could indeed move toward working in various ways to create successful schools that embody the aforementioned values and core beliefs, and cultural characteristics. Unfortunately, the former is not easily achieved. As CRT and critical pedagogy converge on this space, it is crucial that proponents of both projects do not envision an adversarial relationship. If we are honest with ourselves about the end of oppression, we must be willing to consider all approaches that do not contribute to the further oppression and marginalization of children of color. The space is not always a safe one, but it is necessary if we profess a commitment to the development of safe spaces for young people to recognize their importance to themselves and the world.

Notes

1 Part of this paper was presented as a symposium session for the *International Journal of Qualitative Studies in Education* at the British Educational Research Association annual conference, University of Leeds, September 13–15, 2001.
2 The problem of white predominance in the teaching force has become more acute over the last few years. For example, Wilder (2000) noted that, over the past thirty years, white teachers comprised approximately 87% of the national teaching force. African Americans only comprised 8%, while the African American student population was at approximately 16% of the total national enrollment. The situation is even worse for Latinos–Latinas, as they only make up 3% to 4% of the national teaching force despite the large increases in Latino–Latina students nationwide.
3 D. Conley (1999, p. 1).
4 We are not dismissing the crucial role that social class and post-Marxist analysis plays in explaining the disparate treatment of groups in the U.S. and the importance of global capitalist forces in creating these growing inequalities and unequal distribution of power that need to be challenged on multiple fronts. More discussion of this and social action needs to take place in the U.S. and elsewhere to address social class inequality and power, to be sure (McLaren, 1998). However, race does matter in the post-civil rights era and there are times when critical pedagogical theorists need to

acknowledge this and specifically tease out when it does matter and when race does indeed act as a stand-in for class analysis (Conley, 1999, p. 1).

5 See Thompson (1999), Cochran-Smith (2000), and Schick (2000) for more discussion on this point, as well as the work by scholars in the UK such as Cecile Wright (1995) and the late Barry Troyna (1995), and various works on anti-racist teaching, policy and research on white teachers and Afro-Caribbean and Pakistani student interactions.

References

Anderson, G. L. (2001) Promoting Educational Equity in a Period of Growing Social Inequity: The silent contradictions of Texas reform discourse, *Education and Urban Society*, 33, pp. 320–332.

Appiah, K. A. (1992) *In My Father's House: Africa in the Philosophy of Culture* (New York, Oxford University Press).

Banks, J. A. & McGee Banks, C. A. (eds) (1997) *Multicultural Education: Issues and perspectives*, 3rd edn (Boston, Allyn & Bacon).

Bartee, R., Beckham, J., Gill, C., Graves, C., Jackson, K., Land, R., Williams, D. & Parker, L. (2000) Race, Discipline, and Educational Leadership: African American Student Perspectives on the Decatur, IL Incident, *Journal of Special Education Leadership*, 13, pp. 19–29.

Bell, D. (1992) *Faces at the Bottom of the Well: The Permanence of Racism* (New York, Basic Books).

Bernal, D. D. (2002) Critical Race Theory, Latino Critical Theory, and Critical Raced-gendered Epistemologies: Recognizing Students of Color as Holders and Creators of Knowledge, *Qualitative Inquiry*, 8, pp. 105–125.

Bonilla-Silva, E. (2001) *White Supremacy and Racism in the Post-Civil Rights Era* (Boulder, CO, Lynne Reiner).

Cochran-Smith, M. (2000) Blind Vision: Unlearning Racism in Teacher Education, *Harvard Educational Review*, 70, pp. 157–190.

Conley, D. (1999) *Being Black, Living in the Red: Race, Wealth, and Social Policy in America* (Berkeley, CA, University of California Press).

Crenshaw, K., Gotanda, N., Peller, G. & Thomas, K. (eds) (1995) *Critical Race Theory: Key Writings that Formed the Movement* (New York, New Press).

Darder, A. & Torres, R. (2002) Critical Race Theory or a Critical Theory of Race? Symposium Conducted at the Annual Meeting of the American Educational Research Association, New Orleans, LA.

Delgado, R. (1989) Storytelling for Oppositionist and Others: A Plea for Narrative, *Michigan Law Review*, 87, pp. 2411–2441.

Derman-Sparks, L. & ABC Task Force (1989) *Anti-Bias Curriculum: Tools for Empowering Young Children* (Washington, DC, NAEYC).

Deyhle, D. (1995) Navajo Youth and Anglo Racism: Cultural Integrity and Resistance, *Harvard Educational Review*, 65, pp. 23–67.

Dillard, A. D. (2001) *Guess Who's Coming to Dinner Now? Multicultural Conservatism in America* (New York, New York University Press).

Essed, P. (1991) *Understanding Everyday Racism: An Interdisciplinary Theory* (Thousand Oaks, CA, SAGE).

Feagin, J. (2000) *Racist America* (New York, Routledge).

Foster, M. (1997) *Black Teachers on Teaching* (New York, New Press).

Giroux, H. (1983) *Theory and Resistance in Education: A Pedagogy for the Opposition* (South Hadley, MA, Bergin & Garvey).

Goldberg, D. T. (1993) *Racist Culture: Philosophy and the Politics of Meaning* (Oxford, Blackwell Press).

Gonzalez, F. E. (1998) Formations of Mexicanness: Trenzas de Identidades Multiples/Growing up Mexicana: Braid of Multiple Identities, *International Journal of Qualitative Studies in Education*, 11, pp. 81–102.

Gotanda, N. (1991) A Critique of 'Our Constitution Is Color-Blind', *Stanford Law Review*, 44:1, pp. 1–68.

Grande, S. M. A. (2000) American Indian Geographies of Identity and Power: At the Crossroads of Indigena and Mestizaje, *Harvard Educational Review*, 70, pp. 467–498.

Hale, J. E. (2001) Culturally Appropriate Pedagogy, in: W. H. Watkins, J. H. Lewis & V. Chou (eds), *Race and Education: The Roles of History and Society in Educating African American Students* (Boston, Allyn & Bacon).

Harris, C. I. (1993) Whiteness as Property, *Harvard Law Review*, 106, pp. 1701–1791.

Henry, A. (1992) African Canadian Women Teachers' Activism: Recreating Communities of Caring and Resistance, *Journal of Negro Education*, 61, pp. 392–404.

Henry, A. (2001) Comment: Researching Curriculum and Race, in: W. H. Watkins, J. H. Lewis & V. Chou (eds), *Race and Education: The Roles of History and Society in Educating African American Students* (Boston, Allyn & Bacon).

Hidalgo, N. M. (1998) Toward a Definition of a Latino Family Research Paradigm, *International Journal of Qualitative Studies in Education*, 11, pp. 103–120.

Hord, F. L. & Lee, J. (eds) (1995) *I Am Because We Are: Readings in Black Philosophy* (Amherst, MA, University of Massachusetts Press).

Igleias, E. M. & Valdes, F. (1998) Religion, Gender, Sexuality, Race and Class in Coalitional Theory: A critical and Self-Critical Analysis of LatCrit Social Justice Agendas, *Chicano-Latino Law Review*, 19, pp. 504–588.

Kailin, J. (1999) How White Teachers Perceive the Problem of Racism in their Schools: A Case Study in 'liberal' Lakeview, *Teachers College Record*, 100, pp. 724–750.

Ladson-Billings, G. (1998) Just What Is Critical Race Theory and What's It Doing in a Nice Field Like Education?, *International Journal of Qualitative Studies in Education*, 11, pp. 7–24.

Ladson-Billings, G. (1999) Preparing Teachers for Diverse Student Populations: A critical Race Theory Perspective, in: A. Iran-Nejad & P. D. Pearson (eds), *Review of Research in Education* (Washington, DC, American Educational Research Association).

Ladson-Billings, G. (2001) The Power of Pedagogy: Does Teaching Matter?, in: W. H. Watkins, J. H. Lewis & V. Chou (eds), *Race and Education: The Roles of History and Society in Educating African American students* (Boston, Allyn & Bacon).

Ladson-Billings, G. & Tate, W. F. (1995) Toward a Critical Race Theory of Education, *Teachers College Record*, 97, pp. 47–63.

Larson, C. L. (1997) Is the Land of Oz an Alien Nation?: A Sociopolitical Study of School Community Conflict, *Educational Administration Quarterly*, 33, pp. 312–350.

Lee, C. D. (2001) Comment: Unpacking Culture, Teaching, and Learning: A Response to the 'Power of Pedagogy', in: W. H. Watkins, J. H. Lewis & V. Chou (eds), *Race and Education: The Roles of History and Society in Educating African American Students* (Boston, Allyn & Bacon).

Lewis, A. E. (2001) There Is No 'Race' in the School Yard: Color-Blind Ideology in an (Almost) All-White school, *American Educational Research Journal*, 38, pp. 781–811.

Lipman, P. (1997) Restructuring in Context: A Case Study of Teacher Participation and the Dynamics of Ideology, Race, and Power, *American Educational Research Journal*, 34, pp. 3–38.

Lipsitz, G. (1998) *The Possessive Investment in Whiteness: How white People Profit from Identity Politics* (Philadelphia, Temple University Press).

Lynn, M. (1999) Toward a Critical Race Pedagogy: A Research Note, *Urban Education*, 33, pp. 606–626.

Madsen, J. A. & Mabokela, R. O. (2000) Organizational Culture and Its Impact on African American Teachers, *American Educational Research Journal*, 37, pp. 849–876.

McCarthy, C. & Crichlow (eds) (1993) *Race, Identity and Representation in Education* (New York, Routledge).

McLaren, P. (1998) Revolutionary Pedagogy in Post-Revolutionary Times: Rethinking the Political Economy of Critical Education, *Educational Theory*, 48, pp. 431–462.

McMorris, G. (1996) Critical Race Theory, Cognitive Psychology, and the Social Meaning of Race: Why Individualism Will Not Solve Racism, *University of Missouri-Kansas City Law Review*, 67, pp. 695–729.

Mills, C. (1998) *Blackness Visible: Essays on Philosophy and Race* (Ithaca, NY, Cornell University Press).

Moses, M. S. (2001) Affirmative Action and the Creation of More Favorable Contexts of Choice, *American Educational Research Journal*, 38, pp. 3–36.

Nevelle, H. A. & Cha-Jua, K. S. (1998) Kufundisha: Toward a Pedagogy for Black Studies, *Journal of Black Studies*, 28, pp. 447–470.

Orfield, G. (1992) Money, Equity, and College Access, *Harvard Educational Review*, 62, pp. 337–351.

Outlaw Jr, L. T. (1996) *On Race and Philosophy* (New York, Routledge).

Parker, L. (1998) Race Is . . . Race Ain't: An Exploration of the Utility of Critical Race Theory in Qualitative Research in Education, *International Journal of Qualitative Studies in Education*, 11, pp. 43–57.

Pizarro, M. (1998) Dialogical Praxis-Oriented Research: A Response to Contemporary Educational Methodological Discourse, *International Journal of Qualitative Studies in Education*, 11, pp. 57–80.

Puch, D. (2000) Decatur Ruling Relief for Other School Officials, *Champaign-Urbana News Gazette*, 16 January, pp. A1, A8.

Quiocho, A. & Rios, F. (2000) The Power of Their Presence: Minority Group Teachers and Schooling, *Review of Educational Research*, 70, pp. 485–528.

Scheurich, J. H. (1998) Highly Successful and Loving, Public Elementary Schools Populated Mainly by Low-SES Children of Color: Core Beliefs and Cultural Characteristics, *Urban Education*, 33, pp. 451–491.

Schick, C. (2000) 'By Virtue of Being White': Resistance in Anti-Racist Pedagogy, *Race Ethnicity & Education*, 3, pp. 83–102.

Sewell, T. (1997) *Black Masculinities and Schooling: How Black Boys Survive Modern Schooling* (Staffordshire, UK, Tentham Books).

Smedley, A. (1999) *Race in North America: Origin and Evolution of a World View*, 2nd edn (Boulder, CO, Westview).

Solórzano, D. (1997) Images and Words that Wound: Critical Race Theory, Racial Stereotyping and Teacher Education, *Teacher Education Quarterly*, 24, pp. 5–19.

Solórzano, D. (1998) Critical Race Theory, Race and Gender Microaggressions, and the Experience of Chicana and Chicano Scholars, *International Journal of Qualitative Studies in Education*, 11, pp. 121–136.

Solórzano, D. G. & Yosso, T. J. (2001) Critical Race and LatCrit Theory and Method: Counter- Storytelling, *International Journal of Qualitative Studies in Education*, 14, pp. 471–497.

Stanfield, J. H. (1999) Slipping Through the Front Door: Relevant Social Scientific Evaluation in the People of Color Century, *American Journal of Evaluation*, 20, pp. 415–431.

Tate, W. F. (1997) Critical Race Theory and Education: History, Theory and Implications, in: M. Apple (ed.), *Review of Research in Education* (Washington, DC, American Educational Research Association).

Thompson, A. (1999) Color Talk: Whiteness and Off White, *Educational Studies*, 30, pp. 141–160.

Troyna, B. (1995) Can You See the John?: A Historical Analysis of Multicultural and Antiracist Education Policies, in: D. Gill, B. Mayor & M. Blair (eds), *Racism in Education: Structures and Strategies* (London, Sage and Open University Press).

Valdez, F., Culp, J. & Harris, A. P. (eds) (2002) *Crossroads, Directions, and a New Critical Race Theory* (Philadelphia, Temple University Press).

Villalpando, O. (2000) Symposium: Critical Race Perspectives, Interdisciplinary Implications and Teaching Concerns, paper presented at the meeting of the American Educational Studies Association, Vancouver, CA.

Wilder, M. (2000) Increasing African American Teachers' Presence in American Schools: Voices of Students Who Care, *Urban Education*, 35, pp. 205–220.

Williams, P. J. (1991) *The Alchemy of Race and Rights* (Cambridge, MA, Harvard University Press).

Winant, H. (2002) *The World Is a Ghetto: Race and democracy Since World War II* (New York, Basic Books).

Wright, C. (1995) Early Education: Multiracial Primary School Classrooms, in: D. Gill, B. Mayor & M. Blair (eds), *Racism in Education: Structures and Strategies* (London, Sage & Open University Press).

Wright, H. (2002) Homes Don't Play Posties, Homies Don't Play Neos: Black Ambivalent Elaboration and the End(s) of Critical Pedagogy, Symposium presentation at the annual meeting of the American Educational Research Association, New Orleans, LA.

Yamamoto, E. K. (1997) Critical Race Praxis: Race theory and Political Lawyering Practice in Post-Civil Rights America, *Michigan Law Review*, 95, pp. 821–900.

Young, M. D. & Laible, J. (2000) White Racism, Antiracism, and School Leadership Preparation, *Journal of School Leadership*, 10, pp. 374–414.

Chapter 5

After the Glow

Race Ambivalence and Other Educational Prognoses

Zeus Leonardo

Editors' introduction

This 2011 essay by Zeus Leonardo explores the myriad meanings of race and ambivalence surrounding race in what has been called the 'post-race' era. As Leonardo notes, after the United States presidential election of Barack Obama in 2008, many questioned the concept of race and the continued value of race-based discourse. Those on the right criticized the usefulness of race as a social category in relation to the possible merits of color-blind, non-racialized discourse. Those on the left also conceded the limitations and incoherence of race as a concept, but continued to witness and emphasize the pernicious impact of racialization on racialized people's lives. One key issue here, Leonardo observes, is that racism has never been only about skin color, and it has not been conceptualized in a universal way across countries or over time. Furthermore, race as an essentialist notion is different from, and less useful than, other key social categories like culture and ethnicity, which (also) continue to have significance in education and social life. Thus, ambivalence about race marks the 'post-race' era, where race cannot be ignored, but any account of it must confront its inadequacy. What racism means to diverse racialized groups and white groups is also discussed in this essay, which concludes that racialized groups must remain hopeful about the possibility of a post-racial time, while white people seem 'optimistic' but less 'hopeful', regarding the history and ongoing saliency of race. This is a powerful essay that engages various debates about what race and racism have been, are, and may look like in the future.

On 4 November, 2008, the US entered a new era of race relations when the nation elected its first-ever black president, Barack Obama. Whether intellectuals want to brand the event as a new day of post-racial proportions or a new stage for a continuing race politics, or whether it ultimately signifies racial progress or a reconfiguration of white hegemony, *something significant happened*. For some, Obama's election confirmed a prediction that the US was over the racial hump from which it has been running away for centuries, like a dog escaping its own tail. That said, we also hear objections to the idea that Obama is a 'real' African American man, casting aspersions over his authenticity by virtue of the fact that he is mixed-race with white, part of the educated and political elite, among other things. Perhaps ironic and germane

DOI: 10.4324/9781003346104-6

to this discussion, doubt about Obama's blackness is also a blow to the one-drop rule that transforms any part-black person fully black in the US, which paradoxically signals a dismantling of the rule of hypodescent, a staple of US racialization. All that said, it is more likely that Obama is a mixed-race black man, and a brilliant politician at that. His mixed-race heritage is a topic he did not eschew during his campaign, embracing the fact that he has a Kenyan father while his mother is white and hails from Kansas. Much has been made of the idea that Obama represents the poster child of 'post-race' identity, indeed the symbol of a new race era.

What was unimaginable not long ago to many US citizens has now become a reality. The deceased rapper, Tupac Shakur, in a track titled 'Changes', once opined that the US was not likely to have a black president. To some, surely this moment is indicative of the US approaching a post-race condition. This would overstate the case in light of the fact that Obama's campaign against Senator Clinton was highly racialized, not to mention the lynch mob mentality of the protestors who stormed the Capitol ostensibly to display their dissatisfaction with Obama's health reform. The irony is not lost when one considers that his health reform would likely help the modest white American protestors. At stake here is precisely whites' long-term interests of racial supremacy even as they are willing to forego short-term benefits by adopting the new health plan. We are tempted to interpret the situation as an expression of white *ressentiment*. Acknowledging white retrenchment in the face of a black man in the White House, Obama's ascendancy also signals another trend in the form of ambivalence with otherwise entrenched notions of race, such as the rule of hypodescent. Whether or not a sea of change is about to happen, these are interesting times to the intellectual of race relations. The noted ambivalence may represent an opportunity for a discussion on the merits of a post-race analysis rather than the more usual suspicion that it is another limp attempt at color-blindness, a moment which progressive educators can utilize.

With the Obama moment setting the tone, this essay considers the insights of post-race writings within the general field of race theory. It is necessary, at least as it concerns the US, to begin with Obama who has sparked interests in the debates around post-race thinking. To some, it represents *the* signature example of post-race possibilities. First, I introduce the main contours of post-race thinking as a form of aspiration rather than a description of society as it exists. That is, whereas conservative thought uses post-raciality as a *fait accompli*, progressives have the opportunity to consider it as a future goal and in effect wrestles the concept away from its commonsense use. With Omi & Winant (1994), I define race as a contested formation comprised of material and cultural projects along the color line.[1] The task at hand is to ask questions about the possibility of a 'post-racial project'. Second, I analyze the theoretical space of race ambivalence as a source of possible insights when race theory becomes aware and reflective about its own conceptual apparatus. Here, I favor the concept of ambivalence over the usual and helpful construct of racial contradictions because the former allows educators to establish some distance from the naturalness of race, its seeming permanence, which is the first step at making its familiarity appear strange. It does not suggest reconciling contradictions if it means

leaving the domain of race unquestioned and conjuring up a non-racist racial formation, something Hirschman (2004) argues is an anachronism. Third, I present
post-race thinking as precisely the opportunity that affords educators the space to
move race pedagogy into a different direction. It is important to note that color-
blindness is the shell of post-race thinking, while its kernel fully endorses racial perpetuity through its denial of race's daily effects as a structuring principle of society.
This is hardly post-racial. Finally, I imagine the long-term implications for hope in a
post-race society that counters the short-term optimism of whiteness.

Introduction: From Racial to Post-racial Imaginary

Engaging post-race discourse is driven less by the need to pronounce that race is
walking out the door, that it is an interpellation that is getting increasingly harder
to hear, and more about the future status of race—or better yet, its future standing. Racial hailing still occurs and many of its subjects still turn around when their
subjectivity is called upon to answer (Leonardo, 2009a). Race, as Warmington
(2009) argues, is still a powerful mediating tool, and 'we live race as if it has meaning and we live within a society in which those raced meaning have innumerable
consequences. We live with race as a social fact' (p. 284). As Derrida (1985) notes,
although linguistic discrimination is not the only form of racism we can imagine
(e.g. labor and wealth disparities), racism *requires* language to do its daily work:
no language, no racism. Its meaning is deciphered through language and its enactment requires recruiting language into its logic. While guarding against linguistic
idealism or determinism, the racial critic recognizes that racist acts depend on language in order to signify self and other, therefore rationalizing the disparagement
of racialized minorities and valorization of whiteness. Although racism involves a
whole range of social processes, as I argue later, it never does not involve language,
which is always in play. It is not language *qua* language that concerns us, but language as a form of social practice. Subjects do not merely describe the world of
race, but actively perform and constitute it through discourse. This establishes the
fact that in order to know racism, we must know language intimately. Consistent
with this special issue's focus on language and domination, I want to establish the
centrality of language in the enactment of race. But I also have another curiosity
regarding racism: that is, whether or not the discourse of race, or race language in
practice, is itself intimately tied to racism and any hopes of ending racism may have
to pose the end of racial signification. Particularly in the US, racialized language is
still the dominant public discourse and represents the nation's anxiety with difference. I hope to make this argument clearer below.

The Stubborn Significance of Race and Racism

In terms of a material organization of US society, there is nothing to suggest
that race is on the wane when the racial wealth gap (Oliver & Shapiro, 1997) is
still a force, yet talks of reparations receive less attention than Paris Hilton's latest

exploits. The language of race is still part of everyday life in the US and Obama's case is not an example of transcending race altogether and rather highlights the ambivalent share of it. But suggesting that US society is still organized around the language of skin color says nothing about our preference that it discontinue in this vein. This is the third space of post-race discussion, which exists uncomfortably alongside the first space of race-in-perpetuity and second space of color-blindness. One might suggest that we live in an **era of race ambivalence**. It does not prevent most scholars from engaging the question and study of race; in fact, I argue we must. But it is becoming increasingly difficult to rely on its stability. Brett St. Louis (2002) explains this ambivalence,

> As the intellectual descendants of DuBois we inhabit, for the most part, a scholarly age wise to the scientific myths, spurious rationality and dubious facticity of 'race'. We have long been aware that 'race' has no sustainable biological foundation and, convinced of its socially constructed basis, we instead recognize the *racialization* of different 'groups' that are culturally, socially and historically constituted. We also largely agree that socially recognizable 'races' demonstrate significant degrees of *internal* as well as *external* differentiation. It is clear therefore at least for much of the academy, that the inviolable sanctity of race is under fire, it is under erasure. (pp. 652–653; italics in original)

Race scholars carry on as usual, but we do so with an increasing sense of doubt and doom about the very nature of our topic. It is possible that racial organization has always been under the threat of erasure or obliteration and the latest set of challenges speak to its continuing evolution. The intellectual's livelihood may also be under erasure but something more important than this remains: our search for racial emancipation. When Gilroy (1998) announces that 'race ends here', he points to the conceptual flimsiness of racial organization that may create as many problems as it purports to solve. It leads St. Louis (2002) to propose a nominalist or 'weak' form of race thinking that claims 'race is a contributory, not determining or principal, local existential element within human existence' (p. 670) in order to observe its social materiality without further reifying its fallacious ideality (see also Leonardo, 2005).

Race is not declining as a structuring principle of US society. Moreover, the US is not alone, as demonstrated with experiences from Canada and Australia (Graham, this issue; Ibrahim, this issue). There may be signs for the prognosis of race's decline, as Gilroy (2000) clearly provokes, but they are inconclusive at best and mistaken at worst. This fact notwithstanding, the current moment or 'crisis' presents an opportunity to ask new questions, to search for new understandings. It may be the case that two apparently contradictory trends of color-blindness and racial progress are occurring. Gilroy's argument does not depend primarily on its empirical veracity but its logical conclusions. That is, scholars cannot wish away race but we can recommend its impeachment. Contrary to the declining significance of race, we can make a good case that race relations pulsate as strongly as ever, perhaps even more significantly than previous eras. It is possible that both phenomena are happening simultaneously: race entrenchment and ambivalence. As Mills (1997) asserts, there is neither a transracial class nor gender solidarity and therefore race, at least for the moment, remains axiomatic.

Post-race Thought Versus Color-Blindness

A society does not reach a post-race situation by downplaying race and the reality of racial contestation, as in policies that turn a color-blind eye to race and education in a desperate attempt *to make the States united again* (if it ever was). Downplaying race struggle will ensure that it continues at the level of social practice as both race and racism have 'gone underground' (Chesler *et al.*, 2003, p. 219). Of course, racism may be overt and above ground, and receive insufficient attention as denial becomes the easier route. Suggesting that race does not matter does not necessarily make it so, as Gotanda (1995) clearly shows in his debunking of the apparent color-blindness of the US constitution. Haney Lopez's (2006) study of prerequisite case laws displays in full splendor the awkward way that the courts used both scientific and common sense arguments to legalize the construct of whiteness. In the Thind case, the highest court argued that despite the fact that he has legitimate claims to Caucasian identity by virtue of his geographical ancestry (compatible at the time with Blumenbach's 'scientific' typology of the races), by all commonsense understandings of whiteness, Thind fails to establish his identity as such. He may be Caucasian but he is certainly not white by commonsense law.

This essay's argument goes against the notion that the best way to rid society of racial discrimination is to stop making distinctions based on race, which is more of a slogan than a sign of a genuine engagement of racism (see Lewis, 2003). However, that race matters does not suggest that society should continue existing in a racial form, that race should keep mattering. That is, insofar as the US is racially structured, skin color stratified, and somatically signified does not automatically recommend their perpetuity. So the task is not only to promote anti-racism but also to consider the post-race position, which is to say, the *politics of being anti-race*, or the dispreference for the continuation of a racially organized society. To be clear, this is a race-conscious, as opposed to a race-neutral, proposition. It does not only require acknowledging the fact of race, but also necessitates entering the field of racial contestation in order to end, rather than to perpetuate, it.

The prognostication of race's future asks neither the question of race's current significance nor its real past but more important, its projected destiny. It takes from Nayak's (2006) assertion that 'post-race ideas offer an opportunity to experiment, to re-imagine and to think outside the category of race' (p. 427). To be more precise, post-race ruminations allow educators to recast race, even work against it, as Gilroy suggests, but this move cannot be accomplished with the pretense of thinking *outside* the category of race. As I argue elsewhere (2005; 2007, 2009a), in a racialized formation, *race has no outside*. As Graham and Slee (2008) note, following Deleuze, assuming an outside maintains an illusory interiority, thus reproducing the original problems associated with margins and centers (see also Lather, 2003). At this point, in many societies, like the US, there is no way to deal with race from a position outside of race relations. We are caught up in racemaking at every turn and presuming access to its outside comes with dangerous implications, usually complicit with color-blindness. Rather, it suggests the possibility of *undoing race from within rather than from without*, of coming to full disclosure about what race has made of us to which we no longer consent. If race has no outside, is it possible to talk of its *elsewhere*? If color-blindness does not work as policy, is it supportable as a utopic aspiration? Is there a foreseeable end to the language of race? In this sense, the unmaking of race interests the oppressed races more than the master race, the latter arguably more invested in its continuation (see also Ibrahim, this issue). Therefore the analysis does not proceed from the audacious pronouncement that this move is plausible but asks whether or not it is possible and more important, preferable.

Problematizing the Vague Uses of Race

Given the bogus beginnings of race, dismantling race from the inside seems warranted and within the realm of possibilities. The language of race and the racial dimensions of language are a source of much symbolic violence (Bourdieu & Passeron, 1990) the moment that human differences were reduced to skin differences. Although racialized minorities, as skin collectives, may mobilize around the concept of race and find strength (indeed a source of pride) in their survival from and resilience against white supremacy, skin ontologies are not sustainable ways to organize society, even after the demise of racism. What would it mean to dismantle racism but not disband social groups based on skin color? It is possible to discredit race at this level of analysis. However, given race's omnipresence, in US society in particular, the task seems impossible in the Derridean sense. Although race arguably has a five hundred year pedigree, ideologically it feels eternal, just like the unconscious (Leonardo, 2005; Althusser, 1971). That is the space this essay occupies, wedged as it is between the possible and the impossible, between the precept of and a preference for race. It not only requires a language of possibility (Giroux, 1988), but equally a language of impossibility (Biesta, 1998; Cho, 2006). Post-racial analysis is ethically justifiable despite the independent issue of and slim chances for success because whites show such low levels of investment in critical race work (McPhail, 2003). But as I argue later, alongside McPhail, the hope in ending racism trumps the despair in whiteness.

The concept of race and utility of race analysis have been staples of social theory and education for quite some time. One can hardly read or write about the challenges of education without confronting the 'problem of race'. In fact, the ubiquitous language of the 'achievement gap' is inherently a racial gap. That said, the future of the race concept has been left relatively untouched—e.g. in its leading discourses of multiculturalism, critical race theory, and anti-racism. *As a relation*, race is seldom deemed problematic. Questioning race becomes tantamount to interrogating the very existence of racial groups, risking the very self we have come to know. Or worse, sometimes race is elided and dangles as a proxy for the vague identity of 'social group', sometimes conflated with ethnicity, sometimes sliding into nationality. No doubt these concepts are interrelated but they are by no means equatable, at least not without some loss in clarity. For example, it is not uncommon to read treatises on race in education, which comfortably analogize it with ethnicity and leave the educator unsure how culture achieves a color in the process. Racism then becomes a descriptor of any institutional arrangement, as opposed to prejudice, where a group has suffered at the hands of another group because of race's currency in the US imagination. However, there are other sources of injury, such as zenophobia and ethnocentrism, which are related to race but not reducible to it. *In the US, a group's grievance is not recognized until it becomes racialized.* In a literal sense, oppression is not understood before it is expressed in a racial language, tied to racial terms, and does not enter popular cognition until it enters racial reasoning. To repeat Derrida's point, no language, no racism, therefore we must know language in order to know racism. This does not mean that recognition equates with resolution of the problem and nearing 150 years since the fall of slavery, the US is no closer to granting African Americans forty acres and a mule. The upshot is that until the point of insertion into race, a claim to historical reparations only meets with glancing interest.

In the US, race has become common sense and sometimes loses both its specificity and edge. Our attempts to intervene into racism come with difficulties when the language of intelligibility contained in race is not held up to be problematic. The language of race has saturated US society to the point that it loses its strangeness as a bogus social relation. Schools are part of how race is maintained through race's pedagogical dimensions. In other words, educators daily teach young people the naturalized status of race, its foreverness. Educators may question racism, but they rarely interrogate the status of race. The color-blind teacher is perhaps most guilty of this crime as s/he enacts race while denying its reality, but s/he is not the only one who takes race for granted. In general, racism has to end, as the saying goes, but race has a different destiny; it should stay. It acquires a privileged place in history and utopia, an explanation of where we have been but also an apparently inextricable part of our future. Here, I want to recognize that the possibility of race's disappearance does not mean that culture *in toto* goes with it.

The Permanence of Race

To the extent that black culture exists, it is possible that an African American ethnicity endures. A black or brown aesthetics may continue, but within the context of race, one cannot be sure that it is not, in some manner, a form of protection against white racism: aesthetics of color as a kind of weapon. Paul Taylor (2008) argues that within a racial formation, no theory of race is divorced from a theory of aesthetics and no notion of beauty is free from racialization. Such is the case with 'black is beautiful' during the 1960s–70s, when African Americans pushed back against the demeaning images of blackness in US society. As such, this establishes the fact that blackness or otherness may be a source of positivity when it fights against its dehumanization within race relations. The same cannot be said for a White American ethnicity insofar as this is the secret cousin of white raciality, which as Roediger (1994) and other abolitionists remind us is nothing but false and oppressive. Whiteness must go (Leonardo, 2002).[2] Dumas (2008) seems to agree when he admits that he has learned to love and trust certain whites, whereas whiteness is never to be trusted. Here we may notice that as a subfield of race theory, whiteness studies exhibits a tendency to recenter whiteness, even a sense of white fetishism. The Left's derogation of whiteness differs from its valorization from the Right but both recenter it. Whiteness studies disturbs the balance in its insistence on centering whiteness in order ultimately to dislodge it from its seeming permanence. In *A Black Theology of Liberation*, Cone (1990) goes further by arguing that whites can only destroy their whiteness by joining racially oppressed communities, whereby their white being passes into black being. This choice does not follow the usual election of blackness for whites who vicariously experience its benefits without its burdens. To be critical, it must be a simultaneous disidentification with whiteness and identification with otherness. In the end, they become neither white nor black but free.

Regarding racism and the status of race, even Bell's (1992) insurrectionary injunction of the 'permanence of racism' does not suggest that he *prefers* the continuation of racial inequality but in his deployment of racial realism, admits to its stubborn reality. Here he is right as there is more evidence to point to racism's perpetual status than to its eventual demise as white America has proven time and again its fundamental sheepishness toward racial equality. But with respect to race as a future organizing principle for society, Bell is more quiet and, one assumes, more accepting. Race appears permanent as well, and this time without the added irony given to the permanence of racism. What does it mean to clutch onto race but purge racism?

The permanence-of-race-as-skin-color thesis has received some criticism. Loic Wacquant (1997, 2002) interrogates not only the utility of this move, but also the questionable, folk-knowledge status of race that passes as scientific or analytical. Or worse, Wacquant fears that with the reality of US imperialism enacted at the level of theory, 'American' race analysis is exported as a general world analysis rather than a particular set of assumptions. Take the example of the Hutus and Tutsis, where an apparent race war is waged between the slender-constructed Tutsis against the Hutus (Freedman *et al.*, 2008). Although one recalls the traditional skin-based racialization introduced by the Belgian colonizers into Rwanda, this relation has mutated to a complex architecture of non-skin color driven racial distinction today. Slenderness is racialized and associated with Europeanness and therefore represents a higher aesthetics, but it is nominally associated with skin color since both Hutus and Tutsis are practically indistinguishable on this index.

On the Brazilian front, a well-known phenomenon goes by the phrase of 'money whitens'. That is, a higher class status affords (pun intended) people of color the power to purchase whiteness, which speaks to the intimate connection between race and capital. For now, I will not make more of these events more than necessary since alternative forms of racialization are outweighed by the more pervasive skin-based racism circulating globally, accelerating through the globalization of racialized beauty industries, such as cosmetic surgery and skin whitening creams (see Hunter, 2005).

With respect to the suggestion of a racial condition absent of racism, Hirschman (2004) observes that this anachronism belies the fact that race has always existed alongside racism. No race, no racism. To be clear on this point, racialization is not the mere recognition of skin color differences *qua* differences but an entire social system founded on a value system designed to elevate lightness (as a sign of godliness, among other things, see Dyer, 1997) and denigration of darkness as sign of an equally dark soul. When the Taíno people of Puerto Rico regarded as beautiful the Spaniards' armor, they were not expressing a preference for racial organization as much as they were enamored by a new form of difference; this event also challenges the otherwise naturalized assumption that human societies inherently fear and desire to control difference. The preference of lightness predates colonization of the Americas when we note that the Bible reminds us, 'there was light and it was good'. Race enters the room precisely when it becomes a justificatory discourse for an entire society. So it is less important to ask whether or not Jesus Christ is white (after all, whites did not exist then) but rather to ascertain the consequences of racializing Jesus and justice, of projecting race back into a raceless past because of a raced present, even to the point of distorting and whitening Christ's racial marking (arguably brown-toned) within current understanding.

As understood here with respect to race and racism, to continue the former while arguing to dismantle the latter is a bit like a Marxist imagining capitalism without exploitation. To the Marxist, no amount of restructuring capital rids it of labor exploitation. Likewise, no amount of resignification will rescue race (Gilroy, 2000). Decoupling race from racism to argue that racial hierarchy is the problem and not racial difference is a bit like suggesting that tracking practices that are hierarchical in schools can be reimagined *sans* the stratification. If that were to happen, it simply would not be called tracking anymore. By definition, tracking *is* hierarchical (see Oakes, 2005). Of course, we are tempted to imagine tracking as the lynchpin of racial oppression in schools but Oakes *et al.* (2004) remind educators of a more pervasive differential access to high status knowledge that, while exacerbated by tracking practices, recalls the near complete racial segregation of society, with the US as exemplar. Supported by Massey and Denton's (1993) *American Apartheid*, segregation studies explain the simple fact that in a racialized social system most blacks attend school with other black children, tracked with respect to one another rather than with whites.[3] In the same vein, race without racism simply would not be race as we know it. In all likelihood, it would be a society without race. With the arrival of post-race studies, new opportunities for analysis, insights, and recent ambivalences have made it possible to ask fundamental questions about the status of race.

On Race Ambivalence

Admittedly, a post-race analysis is not a simple task and is liable to make one an intellectual punching bag of critics from left to right. Currently, few spaces in the academy exist where a progressive discussion of a society beyond the color line can attract a sympathetic ear because it has been associated with color-blind pundits, like Dinesh D-Souza, reactionary politicians, like Ward Connerly, or conservative intellectuals, like Shelby Steele. Or, it attracts the wrong attention and becomes co-opted. In fact, one may be able to cite post-race tendencies in Martin Luther King, Jr.[4] or Frantz Fanon (see Gilroy, 2000; Nayak, 2006) but there is always the real and public fear that their message will be interpreted without its spirit, as Connerly once attempted when he appropriated King's platform in order to launch the 'Racial Privacy Act'.[5] Had it not been convincingly defeated in California, it would have outlawed any public institution's ability to gather racial data. It would have made it difficult—near impossible—to track racial discrimination in education, the health industry, and labor market. One treads on soft ground when it comes to engaging a post-race language.

But it is important to consider the implications of post-race in order to continually re-examine long-held beliefs about race and whether the ultimate existential choice of disappearing is warranted in order to reappear as something else we would rather prefer. But as Graham (in press) has noted elsewhere, in terms of identity this involves the risk of death in order to become a recognizable subject, of giving up certain identities to become something else. For subjects who have very little power to fall back on, it is understandable to desire holding onto current, but problematic identities in light of an unknown (and perhaps not better) option. Race sits strategically at a crossroad that demands scholarship that is attentive not only to its declining or rising significance but to its very future as a system of intelligibility.

Race Theory Becomes Aware of Itself:
The Case for Abolition

On one hand, race scholarship that forsakes a conceptual engagement of its own premises takes for granted the naturalized status of race. Questioning its solidity now seems unreal, caught up in unnecessary solipsistic arguments about the ostensible and unquestionable fact of race. After all, race groups exist and race history is indisputable. Race is real. End of story. There are several limitations to this approach. First, race was an invention and its matter-of-fact existence today should not be confused with its objective reality without the daily dose of reification. It is worthwhile intellectually to debate the conceptual status of race if racism significantly depends on the continuation of a *racialized mindset*. This is perhaps what James Baldwin was referring to, when he claimed that as long as white people think they are white, there is no hope for them (cited by Roediger, 1994, p. 13). After all, it is difficult to imagine white racism without the prior category of race that is responsible for white *perception* concerning which groups deserve a blessed or banished life. The challenge for whites is to unthink their whiteness because race trouble arrived at the scene precisely at the moment when white bodies began thinking they were white people. The birth of white people allows for the first premise of racism: put simply, that whites are better than people of color. This is a simplified reduction of a rather complex process but it captures the basic operation of racial superordination and subordination. If a group is simply better than another group, then the former in religious terms is saved, in epistemological terms represents the true knower, in aesthetic terms constitutes the beautiful, and in ontological terms plainly exists. This is not just the genesis of whiteness but of the very domain we know as race. Whiteness and race are the large and small arms of a clock that began over five hundred years ago. But if I (2002) am correct to announce the coming of *late whiteness*, their hours are numbered.

The abolitionist opposes encouraging an overt racial language and discourages greater awareness on the part of whites so common to racial pedagogy. Instead he asks them to forget their racial rootedness. The caveat is that it is a form of white privilege to even ponder 'giving up' one's racialization, a luxury that people of color simply do not possess. That established, it does not contradict the idea that this is the preferred collective path that abolitionists believe we should follow. The abolitionist assumption is that whites already know intimately their whiteness, which is different from suggesting that they understand their whiteness. Whiteness is the default position of the human and it is unnecessary to qualify one with the other. A white person need not describe his whiteness because it goes without saying. Toni Morrison (1993) says as much when she asserts that characters in novels are assumed to be white until the text explicitly writes them into the story as people of color. Writing 'white' into narratives can actually be jarring for whites whose self-identification with an unnamed whiteness exposes their racial investment. Increasing racial recognition is built on the faulty premise that whites are ignorant of their racial world, when in fact it does not take much of a threat to whiteness for whites to erect barriers around what Cheryl Harris (1995) calls 'whiteness as property'. In short, whites know they are white and do not need to be made aware of this first fact. More important, they know from whom they are set apart: people of color. Therefore, the common suggestion in education that teacher education programs ought to teach white pre-service teachers a heightened awareness of their whiteness misses the target. Becoming aware of one's whiteness is one thing but acknowledging how one's whiteness translates into political and social structures responsible for racial domination is quite another.

Or worse, education programs construct whites as passive observers of race, who must be taught to recognize their raciality. To the abolitionist, this move further embeds their whiteness. Everyday, US educators teach white children that they are white: from curriculum selection that prioritizes Western epistemology, to cultural classroom practices that bridge the home-to-school divide for whites and maintain the distance for students of color, to apparently race-neutral policies like No Child Left Behind, which make a casual, rather than causal, pass at race (Leonardo, 2007). Opposite racial awareness, whites must now forgo their whiteness, disowning it before they even own up to it. Although the abolition movement faces grim prospects about success, they are correct to challenge this oft-unquestioned premise of white ignorance. Said another way, post-race is intimate with post-white discourses. The abolition of whiteness is at the same time the abolition of white people, an invention that must now be forgotten. This move is not without ironies and waiting for whites to forgo their whiteness is like waiting for Godot (see also Ibrahim, this issue).

Second, conceptualizing race is intimately tied to performing it. Perceiving race as real is then tied to acting on it. The upshot is that taking up the race concept asks the primary question, 'What is race?' without which race analysis proceeds commonsensically rather than critically. For example, the question of which collectivities constitute a racial group is still unsettled in the US. Is race a black-white skin phenomenon that *implicates* other groups, like Asians and Latinos, which are quasi-races? If this is true, then it seems racial progress in the US will only result when the modern contradiction between whites and blacks is resolved.[6] One could call this model the modernist racial discourse of race-as-skin-color, a binary spectrum with whites and blacks at two poles and other races incorporated ambiguously along the continuum. Or are there multiple racial projects, each articulating itself in specific ways for different groups? For instance, in the US race has affected each group differently, such as the significant history of citizenship status for Asians, sovereignty and land rights for Native Americans, documented immigration for Latinos, and enslavement for African Americans. If this is true, then it necessitates a postmodern racial perspective (not always synonymous with a post-race philosophy) that decenters skin color from the focus of racial analysis and places it alongside other physical markers (as distinct from culture), such as Eastern eyes and Latino looks. In all, the obviousness of race is becoming increasingly strange.

Big Bang Race Theory Versus Steady State: Setting the Parameters

In both of these scenarios, racism maintains its distinction from cultural imperialism by emphasizing somatic relations as proxies for deciding human worth. Race is a relation of bodies and culture only enters the process when it is recruited, as in the case of 'new racism', which replaced the biological basis of racism with its cultural cognate (Barker, 1990). In this transformation, people of color are inferior to whites based on the former's cultural, rather than genetic, make up.

Moreover, in both of these offerings, the post-race imagination is mobilized as a mode of possibility after the glow of race relations. Although still surrounding us like the primordial warmth of the Big Bang, the heat of racialization will reach its end point and the possibility of a Big Squeeze ultimately develops, causing an eventual implosion. In contrast to a Steady State theory of race, which provides a portrait of racialization as changing but ultimately eternal as a social relation, a Big Bang theory posits a definite beginning and possible end of race as we know it. But this implosion, as in the field of physics, is not only catastrophic, but provides the elements necessary for life. Just as we are composites of the iron and other heavier atoms left over from supernovas, future generations will be comprised of debris gathered from the ashes of a racial involution. Like planets and stars, which result from gravity's ability to collapse material into a sphere, post-race society will represent the gradual accretion of race material from a time when race used to matter. Life does not start anew *per se* but a new history begins.

Without broaching these definitional debates and directional issues about the destiny of race, critical race analysis ceases to have a future because it cannot imagine a situation that makes it obsolete. For if, as an intervention into racist formations, race analysis is to realize its goal, it may eventually have to disappear as a condition of its own success. Marx predicted as much when it came to class and capitalism, which sowed their own seeds of destruction. This is different from the desire to organize around skin politics in order to end it altogether. A post-race perspective is not the attempt to elide and evade race in order to imagine its disappearance. Quite the opposite. Post-race discourse makes race visible, maps its operations, and enters its interpellations. It is not ambivalent about these commitments but on the issue that racial distinctions should be an endless ride without a destination. *If all good things come to an end, surely bad ones ought to.* One may be tempted to brand the inability to deal critically with the future of race as evidence of a certain anti-intellectual tendency. But that would be inflammatory and in the end does more harm than good. For a post-race project is not only an intellectual project but equally political, conceptual on one hand but actional on the other (see Fanon, 1967).

Reducing the problem of racism to the conceptual status of race comes with its own difficulties, as if racism were caused by a concept rather than racially motivated actions, such as educational segregation and labor discrimination. For Guillaume (1995), nothing short of dismantling the race concept can rescue us from racism. A concept not white supremacist institutions, like slavery. Not the attempt to exterminate Native Americans, to limit of Asian American mobility by curtailing their citizenship rights, or the constant attacks on Latino autonomy in the US. Not the forced removal of 'half caste' Aboriginal children from their family and communities to 'breed out' the indigenous peoples of Australia. Not the social engineering called 'whitening' in Brazil through selective immigration from Europe in the early decades of the 1900s. Not the South African social incarceration of Blacks. We could go on but it seems apparent that racism is not ultimately the problem of people who think there are races 'out there' but the materially coordinated set of institutions that result from people's actions. Certainly these actions have their root in the concept of race but a whip in the hand seems as responsible for racism as an idea in the head.

Creating a Racialized Society

These arrangements do not continue merely by virtue of our investments in a concept but through historical contestations over power within a racialized field of understanding. We may go a long way with Marxists' distinction between ideas and substance but this makes it all the more ironic that for all their materialist analyses, they would rather emphasize race as an idea rather than a set of material practices (see Bonilla-Silva, 2005). It is not just that people *think* they are white, but that they *act* on it. Like language, white is not reducible to a concept or idea but a social practice. As Appiah (1990) notes, counter-nationalisms may be a form of *intrinsic racism* insofar as they assume a family resemblance among people of color but *extrinsic racism* differs in the way that it enforces a group's assumed superiority on an(other). Just as we do things with words (Austin, 1962), we do things with whiteness, which is a performative, rather than an inert, identity (Youdell, 2004; Giroux, 1997). It is constituted through acts of whiteness, whose articulations are found in segregation in the housing and social spheres, and policies that reinforce black deviance through harsher expulsion and disciplinary actions against them (Gillborn, 2005) as well as blacks' over-representation in special education in the school sphere (Artiles, 2008). Deserving to be quoted at length, Gillborn (2005) writes,

> [T]he English education system appears to be a clear case where the routine assumptions that structure the system encode a deep privileging of white students and, in particular, the legitimization, defence and extension of Black inequity. In terms of policy priorities race equity has been at best a marginal concern, at worst non-existent. In relation to beneficiaries the picture is more complex than usually recognized (some minoritized groups do relatively well), but the most consistent beneficiaries are white students and, in key respects, Black students' position is no better than it was when the whole reform movement began in the late 1980s. Finally, an examination of outcomes clearly shows that central reform strategies (such as the use of selection and hierarchical teaching groups) are known to work against race equity but are nevertheless promoted as 'best practice' for all. These reforms are known to discriminate in practice (regardless of intent) and are, therefore, racist in their consequences. These [examples] establish the education system's active involvement in the defence and extension of the present regime of white supremacy in the contemporary British state. (pp. 4496–497)

Gillborn's study of the British educational system finds that whiteness is constituted through both informal, naturalized assumptions of white superiority as well as formal policies that solidify white advantage. Whiteness is not so much an identity, if by this we mean something of an essence that whites are born into, but the constellation of acts (beyond their intentions) that constitute whites as always an identity in the making.

Race does not disappear because we alter conceptualizing each other as post- or non-racial *if we act on the world in a racial way and with racial consequences*. Brazil is a case in point, where the concept of a post-racial democracy is compromised by the stubborn reality of racial stratification (see Caldwell, 2007; Telles, 2006; Warren & Twine, 2002). Whether or not we conceptualize Brazilian power relations as racial in the US sense of it, there is a clear color line among those who lead the country and those who follow. Brazilians may think through class, but they appear to act through race. This is not to argue that people of color in Brazil are worse off than those in the US, which is a legitimate argument. This is an empirical assertion with much veracity but is besides my point. The problem of racism cannot be reduced to the concept of race as much as religious warfare fails to be explained by divergent interpretations of sacred texts. Rather, racial contestation is decided by internal concepts (reified as they may be) externalized through social behavior and institutional arrangements. To racial realists, placing the word-race in scare quotes (i.e. 'race') appears as unduly intellectualist, particularly when other social relations that are socially constructed are not put under a similar, bracketed scrutiny (Warmington, 2009). It appears they have an axe to grind against racial analysis. To racial realists, for all the realness that Marxists claim, in the end they ultimately fail to 'get real' about race. Be that as it may, what does race relations look like after the innovation of a race ambivalent analysis?

As we have seen, in Marxist theory race retains its ideological status and a racial cosmology inevitably subverts a clearer understanding of social relations and the basis of an educational apparatus where race is reified through social practice. For example, in education people of color are dogged by racialized notions of intelligence, the most obvious and cruel forms of which were witnessed in the eugenics movement but whose legacy continues today in the knowledge apartheid that derogates minority students and scholars' experiences (Bernal & Villalpando, 2005: see also Stanley, 2006). Its everyday and almost universally accepted practice is tracking, where students are divided by curricular and instructional levels within subjects areas, particularly in high school (Oakes, 2005). Absent some critical race awareness, these intellectual currents and tracking assignments reify race as real, spurring on countless school reforms to 'fix the intelligence gap'. This does not mean that Marxism outright rejects race struggle but questions its scientific status and praxiological implications for change. They help us differentiate between the real and real-like. In sociology, Robert Miles' (2000) work proves instructive; in history, Barbara Fields (1990) assumes prominence; and in education, Darder and Torres (2004), and McLaren and Torres (1999) have taken the lead. Here, post-race is taken literally to mean *after* the usefulness of race analysis, something that may have had utility in 18th century US as a justification of plantation forms of capitalism used to convince whites of all class positions.

Post-race as an Opportunity

Instigated by cultural studies, post-race discourses distinct from Marxist ortho-doxy provide an opportunity to ask new questions about race through studies in the politics of representation, language being one of its privileged mechanisms. According to Gilroy (2000), post-race discussions signal an opportunity rather than something to be feared insofar as race understanding may be advanced in order that race may not remain standing. Like Marxism in the current conjunc-ture, post-race analysis is a politics that proceeds without guarantees, with race under possible erasure (see Hall, 1996, on Marxism). It is, as Gilroy (2000) punctuates, a politics of race abolition. It is a 'crisis of raciology', enabled by 'the idea that "race" has lost much of its common-sense credibility because the elaborate cultural and ideological work that goes into producing and reproduc-ing it' takes more than it gives, that race 'has been stripped of its moral and intellectual integrity', that 'there is a chance to prevent its rehabilitation', and that race 'has become vulnerable to the claims of a much more elaborate, less deter-ministic biology' (pp. 28–29). Earlier, Gilroy (1993) argued for a Black Atlantic perspective that would link historical continuities among the four continents of Africa, Europe, and South and North America to counter the bombastic claims of European enlightenment. Since then, it appears that Gilroy's ambivalence toward race thinking, or raciology, has increased, leading him to pronounce his position 'against race'. Gilroy finds that the amount of race work that goes into anti-racism fails ultimately to provide a positive alternative beyond the negation of racism. At the end of the day, absent the fight against racism, race becomes an empty vessel. In effect, Gilroy transitions from a trans-Atlantic racial argument to a trans-racial Atlantic argument.

Signifying the 'Post' in Post-Race Theory

As Paul Taylor (2008) has suggested, the innovation of post-race analysis does not signal the end of race as we know it. Rather, like the 'post' in post-analytic philosophy, the same 'post' in post-race analysis signals an opening made possible by a conceptual ambivalence, not the closing of race scholarship. It allows new questions, as products of intellectual and material development, to surface. Like the 'post' in many schools of thought among extant theories, post-race is the ability of race theory to become self-aware and critically conscious of its own pre-cepts. It signals the beginning of the end of race theory proper, which becomes near impossible to continue in the same vein. A race theory that becomes self-aware of its own constitutive activity enters the next stage of development in a dialectical movement of the thought process. Race theory becomes post-race pre-cisely for the same reasons that modern thought is compromised by post-modern theory. Modern theory still exists but only after it reckons with the postmodern (Lyotard, 1984). Likewise, race theory emerges as something different, if not new, through the filter of post-race. It alters the politics of race scholarship.

I believe Taylor is right to frame the discussion in this manner. It avoids the otherwise vulgar suggestion that we are 'beyond race' or have 'transcended race' for usually unsubstantiated reasons. It acknowledges the debt owed to race analysis proper but propels it forward without jettisoning it. What do we make of society as we remake race in a daily way? Like one might ask about modern theories after the postmodern moment, what does race analysis look like after the arrival of post-race thought? For all of Baudrillard's ranting against modern teleologies and determinisms, he did not succeed in making them irrelevant before his death (see Leonardo, 2003). However, he forced a response from modernist thinkers. As a carbuncle on their theories, Baudrillard and other postmodernists pushed social theory and their intellectual adversaries into different directions, if not forward. Post-race analysis accomplishes a similar move, forcing a hard and sometimes difficult look at race theory.

Race understanding stands at the uncomfortable street corner where our bodies meet their socially constructed racial identity and where we leave the same intersection unsure of what we have just become as a result of race. Gilroy (2000) writes, '[W]e always agree that "race" is invented but are then required to defer to its embeddedness in the world' (p. 52). Nayak (2006) laments, 'The problem that race writers encounter, then, is how do we discuss race in a way that does not reify the very categories we are seeking to abolish?' (p. 415). If race was a figment of the Occidental imagination, it is one of life's deepest ironies that people of color hang on dearly to a concept created in order to oppress them. Many centuries later, US minorities find it hard to imagine a post-race society, either because they suspect that color-blind whiteness is up to its old tricks again or they are invested in a hard-fought sense of an oppositional identity, the giving up of which means a fundamental loss of meaning. Of course, it goes without saying that many whites cannot imagine a post-race society either. As Nayak (2006) observes, '[F]or minority ethnic groups the erasure of race may equate with the obliteration of an identity and shared way of life . . . the concept of race, however tarnished it may appear, has provided an important meeting place for political mobilization, inclusion and social change' (p. 422). Although Nayak commits the usual slide between ethnicity and raciality, something he misrecognizes when he asserts that 'whiteness is not homogeneous but fractured by the myriad ethnic practices', (p. 417), he is correct to note that race (not only racism) is a source of problem as well as a resource of meaning for racially despised groups. Yet he misses an opportunity. Whiteness is precisely homogenizing, wiping out ethnic differences in favor of racial solidarity. This is whiteness' *modus operandi* and emphasizing myriad (white) ethnic practices misrecognizes white raciality. This does not suggest that ethnic differences are not relevant for whites as the Irish-English, German-Jewish, or Turk-Greek Cypriot relations make plain (see Zembylas, 2008).This fact notwithstanding, in places as diverse as the US and Australia white ethnic differences play second fiddle to whiteness because white ethnicity is a demotion whereas white raciality becomes a promotion because the former makes whites concrete while the latter keeps them abstract. For people of color, race is a condition of their being and to dispute its centrality in their lives violates their perceived right to be, and usually without the profitable returns that white ethnics gain as they shed their identity to ascend to white raciality. As a result, race takes away from, more than it gives to, people of color. It certainly benefits whites more than non-whites, even as whites give up their ethnic language, custom, and identity (see Ignatiev, 1995).[7] The upshot is that these losses were well worth giving up for whiteness. In fact, hanging on to ethnicity, which makes whites visible and concrete, decreases whites' ability to guard the invisibility and abstraction called whiteness.

This does not mean that whites are eager to give up race but there is less of an ironic return for them. This point extends Nayak's (2006) claim that 'It is precisely because whiteness is seen as an unmarked racial category that the loss of race for white theoreticians can appear inconsequential' (p. 422). We might distinguish between whiteness' discursive sleight-of-hand to conjure up a post-race reality and whites' general unwillingness to relinquish race privilege. Giving up race is consequential for whites for it is responsible for the lightness of their being, a sense of existential lack of tethers. Their sense of freedom and mobility is a direct and negative correlation with the restrictions people of color face. Their post-race attitude is belied by their racial behavior. A post-race situation is a threat to whites' very existence and can only come at a great loss for them, which may be greater than the loss of meaning for racial minorities. Racial recollections for minorities do not vanish with a post-race reorganizing, such as the South African case, but white domination and privilege may be eradicated structurally, which does not suggest that whiteness does not continue in the form of ideology. Arguably, race memory serves as the constant reminder against the return of white supremacy just as Jewish remembering of the Holocaust guards against its repeat. Race comes with advantages for whites and it is precisely the lack of guarantees that accompanies post-race analysis that threatens white privilege for it unsettles expectations on which many whites have counted. To the white race abolitionist, the antidote includes acting against whiteness as if it were an affront to one's humanity (see Ignatiev & Garvey, 1996). To be sure, people of color have relied on race as a stable system of meaning on which to base their self-understandings but this process occurs as a response to the first fact of white domination. Without white domination, there is little need to assert black, brown, red, or yellow self-love, whose history is a defense against the imposition of white power. Race ambivalence is intended to challenge white supremacy before it is designed to threaten its victims. Although post-race scholars do not underestimate this loss of meaning, they consider it worth the risk for it is a system of meaning that creates more problems than promises. This loss, as Nayak suggests, can be turned into a gain.

Making Sense of the Crisis in Raciology

To dispel further any notions that this model mystifies the innerworkings of race, education under post-race assumptions makes it clear that it is made possible precisely by testifying to the inhuman tendencies of a racialized humanism.

Gilroy (2000) contends that his '[planetary] humanism is conceived explicitly as a response to the sufferings that raciology has wrought' (p. 18), not its obfuscation. To Gilroy, the crisis in raciology represents less a crisis of identity and more the uncertain status and preferable (rather than inevitable) demise of race, not only at the level of signification but also at the level of social organization. Sweeping global changes in the economy and diasporic movement complicate and compromise racial worldmaking, stripping it of previous guarantees and predictive value as an autonomous relation. New events in history disturb our race-as-skin-color expectations, such as the apparent racial contest undetermined by skin color but mediated by somatic politics between Hutus and Tutsis in Rwanda. In Australia, one may look white but identify as indigenous, or whites with black features are not accepted as authentically indigenous. Of course, in the US there is a long tradition within communities of color regarding the colorism that affects their lives (Hunter, 2005). Although the Rwandan case should not be overinterpreted as proof of the waning effect of skin color difference, for which we have more worldwide evidence, the Rwandan situation brings new insights to race analysis by introducing the reinterpretation of bodily differentiation through primary markers besides skin color. Even the multiracialization of beauty images, which includes increasingly more black and brown faces, signals new anxieties about race, but this time by disturbing clear lines of racial demarcation rather than their enforcement. Whereas race thought was revolutionary in its own right, this new stage of development represents a revolution of the revolution, or the dynamic continuation of that transformation. To the extent that raciology introduced white subversion of the humanity inhered in people of color, post-race represents the attempt to subvert the subversion, to negate the negation. Race changed some subjects into people of color; it may be time to change again. This does not suggest that racism or racialization fails to exert its dominant imprint on social processes, subject formation, and State-sponsored policies. However, it means that both race struggle and raciology may begin the day but in no way end it, giving way to the era of race ambivalence.

I have no desire to overstate the case. Made clear by the stubborn standard of whiteness—from Tyra Banks, Halle Berry to Beyoncé Knowles, to Jennifer Lopez and Selma Hayek—light skin still, according to Hunter (2005), approximates white beauty standards. But as colonized peoples challenge white supremacy across the globe and gain access to networks of power monopolized by whites, counting on race stratification becomes ironically ambiguous and upsets racial expectations. This is a condition not to be deplored ultimately as a sense of loss, at least not in the manner that one grieves the passing of a seemingly endless war that has given this life much meaning. Putting race to peace may open up possibilities for other ways of being, other ways of knowing that have been heretofore limited or closed, particularly for people of color. The loss should not be minimized but countered by a sense of clarity concerning the neuroses of race about which Fanon (1967) spoke so forcefully and which Gilroy calls the 'rational absurdity of "race"' (p. 14). But like the absurdity of life as we know it, which existentialists and phenomenologists alike argued, we can avoid racial dread by fully committing to our choices. Gilroy taps a certain post-racial tendency in Fanon whose attempts to restore blacks in their proper human place represent black analytics, or negritude, in order then for blackness to vanish under its own weight (see also Nayak, 2006). Just how the problems of humanism fold into the refashioning of the human in a post-race condition remains contested, opening the door for Gilroy's pragmatic, planetary and postanthropological humanism. Blackness, for example, may remain a culture and disappear as a racial category. Gilroy clarifies, 'There will be individual variation, but that is not "race"' (p. 42). Gilroy is quite clear that race does not equate with 'group' and his goal is not to deride human difference. This last point is worth elaborating.

Human differences continue but whether or not skin color variation should form the basis for social organization is the question. As a modern principle, race is a particular grouping of individuals into social groups. As embodied collectivities, these social groups could very well continue intact as we enter a post-race society, but they will no longer be considered skin groups once the race principle has been discredited. The bodies remain but they will be conceptualized differently as post-racial subjects. African Americans may continue as an ethnic group so blackness as a form of cultural practice may thrive in the absence of race where 'skin, bone, and even blood are no longer the primary referents of racial discourse' (Gilroy, 2000, p. 48). African Americans will neither sever completely their relation with blackness as a racial experience, which is historical, nor be reduced to it. Racial solidarity will be liberated from the 'cheapest pseudo-solidarities: forms of connection that are imagined to arise effortlessly from shared phenotypes, cultures, and bio-nationalities' (Gilroy, 2000, p. 41). Of course Gilroy is speaking of both non-whites and whites who desperately cling to identity as a visual confirmation of one's politics.

On one hand, it is whites who, in their fetish of color, clearly profit from racial politics as a form of interest consolidation than people of color who mobilize identity movements as a form of defense against white supremacy (see Lipsitz, 1998). On the other hand, although clearly necessary at this juncture, race-based identity politics brings with it essentialized forms of belonging that may be secondary concerns to the problem of white supremacy but smacks of what Appiah earlier called intrinsic racism. As much as race politics may bring people of color together in a common struggle against white supremacy, it also becomes a source of division when it comes to that elusive grail of authenticity in one instance and the assumption of sameness that denies people of color their uniqueness in the other. They are literally thrown into some situations where the only possible commonality they have with others is the fact that they are people of color. These cheap forms of 'pseudo-solidarities' among minorities of which Gilroy speaks, are tyrannies that remain even after we write the obituary of racism, where race continues to encourage 'ready-to-wear racial identities' (St. Louis, 2002) or what Pollock (2004) calls 'lump sum' identities. It is hardly conducive to progressive politics. In the end, race creates emotional investments that lead to what Cheng (2001) calls 'melancholy', a sense of loss, for both whites and people of color.

Towards a New Day

As race relations enters its late phase of development, its contradictions become more ripe and obvious. Its logics hang desperately onto a worldview that becomes more anachronistic. This does not mean that race struggle becomes obsolete. On the contrary, post-race condition is reached precisely by exposing the myths held up for so long by a pigmentocracy that is whiteness, which people of color both love and hate because they have been taught for so long to admire the white and hate the black. Self-love in this instance is always uncertain for it is bound up with self-doubt. The possibility of ending race is the task of bringing back clarity to a situation that for so long has been clouded with the miseducation of racialized humans. This is the challenge of post-race thinking.

We live in a time when race is under intense questioning. Color-blind race discourse challenges the invocation of race analysis even in its most mainstream versions. However, progressive scholarship has taken this situation and reversed people's normal expectations. Like Judo, post-race analysis takes the otherwise reactionary implications of color-blindness and uses its momentum against itself. For color-blindness is often the performance of feigning indifference to race while enforcing its practice. In a complicated dance with hegemony, post-race scholars strike a compromise that upsets the head-to-head confrontation that usually results in racial antagonism. There is something subversive in this move. Arguing for the moribund status of race, post-race proponents do not rehabilitate race but argue against it. Where they differ from color-blind pretenders is their ability to go *through* race instead of *around* it. They are able to speak to race rather than about it.

Hope in Post-Race Versus Optimism of Whiteness

Ultimately, a post-race perspective enables educators to distinguish between hope and optimism. Whereas color-blindness is usually associated with a white mind-set or lived experience, post-race is a theory of color, which does not mean that scholars of color are always its author. A bright student of mine once suggested that 'hope is white'.[8] By this she meant that whites exhibit an abundance of hope concerning racial progress when compared to a rather pessimistic black progno-sis of the same problem. I took it to mean that even hope is racial and subject to its rationality. It struck me as insightful and I would like to end this essay with a commentary on hope and optimism. I would refine the insight this way: while whites are optimistic about race they are not hopeful, whereas people of color are precisely the opposite, hopeful but pessimistic. When it comes to race progress, whites show much optimism because small increments of improvement are taken as signs of white tolerance. It produces the psychological advantage of focusing on 'how far we have come' instead of the more loaded 'how far we still have to go'. For if whites compare present inequalities with past cruelties, not only do black lives look that much better but white tolerance looks that much greater. Whereas Gramsci (1971) once distinguished between the 'pessimism of the intellect and the optimism of the will', *whites show an optimism of the intellect and pessimism of the will*. In short, we cannot equate white optimism with real hope, which takes a certain will that whites have shown themselves to lack. They are prone to exaggerate racial progress because focusing on the continuing significance of racism indicts their collective inability to end the problem once and for all. They feel good without necessarily having to make good. For all the optimism they express toward racial progress, they lack hope in its actional sense. For whites, hope is abstract. This is hardly post-racial.

In contrast, if people of color have represented anything in the history of race relations, it is hope. It is one of the few 'advantages' that people of color have over whites. Hope is built into the experience of people of color as an ontological part of their being (see Freire, 1993). How else does one explain their ability to withstand centuries of racial oppression? It is premised on the hope that it will one day end despite the fact that they are disappointed by whites' ability to converge racial progress with their own interests (Bell, 1992). Time and time again, people of color cling on to hope as the force that prevents them from despair and resignation. It is historical and allows them to see setbacks as opportunities for defiance. In fact, they project hope onto whites more than they sometimes deserve, a surplus hopefulness that whites underappreciate because they would rather emphasize people of color's animosity over their grace.

We have seen Barack Obama's campaign was built on the audacity of hope and Reverend Jesse Jackson's battlecry was 'keep hope alive'. Even Derrick Bell's apparent bleakness is contradicted by his early endorsement of Obama for president, as evidenced by his public support of him many months preceding Obama's victory over his then favored opponent, Senator Clinton.[9] Hope is what propelled Bell to support change. As Obama accepts his Nobel Peace Prize, we recognize that it was made possible by his going to war with a unilateral decision-making process turned into a science by eight years under the Bush regime. As a concrete possibility, peace will be approached by people of color through a critical, honest appraisal of racialization. Their hope attenuates the otherwise realistic pessimism they feel about race relations, which may keep them bitter. A language of hope is concrete for people of color because it is not just a projected ideal but a way to exist in the present. It is a dream, not a fantasy. It is not an abstract feeling but a concrete emotion, or better yet, an emotional praxis (Chubbuck & Zembylas, 2008).

Post-race thought is ultimately hopeful. It may be a form of surplus hopefulness in light of the formidable presence of race and the fact of racism but people of color have always relied on a certain distortion of reality as someday better than itself, also called utopia. As part of emotional praxis, post-race perspectives allow racially oppressed minorities to recognize anger as part of history without it cementing into a form of indignation (Hattam & Zembylas, 2010). Like post-indignation, post-race analysis does not allow race to cement more than necessary. It recognizes race thinking as historical, and, like anger, is a natural consequence within a condition of racialization without graduating to the victimhood that can result from both indignation and raciology. In effect, post-race analysis is the sublimation of racial anger into a form of hope because 'investing in anger cannot form a particularly skillful political/pedagogical strategy for responding to colonization, racism or nationalism' (Hattam & Zembylas, 2010, p. 25). Post-race analysis is the recognition that the language of race has been necessary in order to understand what we have made of race and what it has made of us. But race is ultimately insufficient and shows its weakening grip over us. Post-race opens up our ambivalence in our search for a more humane and humanizing language.[10]

Notes

1 Below, I discuss the relationship among race, ethnicity, culture, and nation. These concepts are related but often used interchangeably in the literature. In this essay, my main concern is with the concept of race.
2 White abolition sees no redeeming aspects of whiteness, which articulates white bodies with the ideology of whiteness in order to create white people. The results of this partnering have been consistent and predictable: racial violence. In contrast, a pedagogy of white reconstruc- tion forges a new whiteness, a resignified subjectivity that is not hopelessly stuck in the quicksand of racist understandings. For an extended discussion regarding the merits and problems of both white abolition and reconstruction, see my (2009b) essay, 'Pale/ontology: The Status of Whiteness in Education'.
3 Massey and Denton's treatment of undeclared Apartheid in the US is very convincing and sound on many fronts. In terms especially of housing, the extreme isolation of blacks in US society explains their lack of access to 'good' (read: white) schools, neighborhoods, and social networks; this affects their ability to secure decent jobs and ability to acquire wealth (see Oliver & Shapiro, 1997). However, since Massey and Denton's argument rests on the value of integration as the antidote to the problems of segregation, their argument that the US was more integrated at the turn of the 20th century contradicts their basic premise since no one credible would argue that African Americans fared better in more or less racially integrated neighborhoods during early 1900s. Something else may explain the life chances of African Americans despite the fact that integration (in its true sense of an entire social system) is defensible. Moreover, Chapter Six of *American Apartheid* is positioned awkwardly within an otherwise rigorous sociological study of white supremacy. Revisiting the culture of poverty arguments extant from the 1960s on, Massey and Denton argue that ghetto culture, once a coping strategy for structural conditions, achieves *autonomy* and becomes an independent entity. Besides the fact that black culture from diverse class experiences is reduced to 'black street culture' (i.e. it would sound strange to evoke its counterpart in 'white street culture'), at *what point* it became autonomous is never explained. Furthermore, the authors rely on some questionable sources of evidence when they engage the song 'A Bitch iZ a Bitch' by NWA and its follow up by HWA of 'A Trick Is a Trick', as true expressions of black culture rather than what is more likely: embellishments through artifice like most songs.

4 We must recall here the observation that Martin Luther King Jr (and for that matter Malcolm X) was assassinated precisely at the moment when he broadened his mission to include the struggles of poor whites. In a white-oriented society, MLK Jr's nod to post-racial organizing represents a concrete threat against white supremacy *and* raciology.

5 In 2003, Ward Connerly of the University of California Regents drafted the 'Racial Privacy Act', which would remove data involving identity, including race, from official governmental documents in the state of California, USA. The initiative was voted down by the public, perhaps largely due to the mobilization of the medical and educational community, because it would make tracking of health disparities and school inequality based on race virtually impossible.

6 Admittedly, this is a US-centric point of view regarding race relations. Racial classifications differ across contexts, such as Brazil or Australia, where racial categories are more literal and reflect actual skin color and where miscegenation has created a larger group of mixed-race people in the former, and where Asians and Aboriginals occupy a higher percentage than Blacks among populations of color in the latter.

7 Alternatively, rather than loss, Arturo Cortez (personal communication) substitutes the concept of 'trade'. That is, whites did not lose ethnic practices as much as they traded them for white language, custom, and identity. This tack is preferable to the notion of 'white loss', which quickly degrades into a 'me tooism' (see Dyer, 1997).

8 Thanks goes to Rachel Lissy (personal communication) for provoking me to think critically about the distinctions between hope and optimism.

9 Professor Derrick Bell gave an address at the 2008 AERA in New York, USA, pronouncing his support for Obama.

10 I would like to take this opportunity to acknowledge and thank Linda Graham for putting together this excellent special issue, and for her gracious and critical commentary on my essay. In addition, much appreciation goes to the blind reviews of engaged and helpful colleagues. I have never seen such deep, sustained, and insightful critiques of my work. A simple thanks.

References

Althusser, L. (1971) *Lenin and Philosophy*. B. Brewster, trans. (New York, Monthly Review Press).

Appiah, K. (1990) Racisms, in: D. T. Goldberg (ed.), *Anatomy of Racism* (Minneapolis, MN, University of Minnesota Press), pp. 3–17.

Artiles, A. (2008) Special Education's Changing Identity: Paradoxes and Dilemmas in Views of Culture and Space, *Harvard Education Review*, 73,2, pp. 164–202.

Austin, J. L. (1962) *How to Do Things with Words* (Oxford, Oxford University Press).

Barker, M. (1990) Biology and the New Racism, in: D. T. Goldberg (ed.), *Anatomy of Racism* (Minneapolis, MN, University of Minnesota Press), pp. 18–37.

Bell, D. (1992) *Faces at the Bottom of the Well: The Permanence of Racism* (New York, Basic Books).

Bernal, D. D. & Villalpando, O. (2005) An Apartheid of Knowledge in Academia: The Struggle over the 'Legitimate' Knowledge of Faculty of Color, in: Z. Leonardo (ed.), *Critical Pedagogy and Race* (Malden, MA, Blackwell), pp. 185–204.

Biesta, G. (1998) Say You Want a Revolution . . . Suggestions for the Impossible Future of Critical Pedagogy, *Educational Theory*, 48,4, pp. 499–510.

Bonilla-Silva, E. (2005) Introduction—'Racism' and 'New Racism': The Contours of Racial Dynamics in Contemporary America, in: Z. Leonardo (ed.), *Critical Pedagogy and Race* (Malden, MA, Blackwell), pp. 1–36.

Bourdieu, P. & Passeron, J. (1990) *Reproduction in Education, Society, and Culture* (Thousand Oaks, CA, Sage).

Caldwell, K. (2007) *Negras in Brazil* (New Brunswick, NJ, Rutgers University Press).

Cheng, A. (2001) *The Melancholy of Race* (Oxford: Oxford University Press).

Chesler, M., Peet, M. & Sevig, T. (2003) Blinded by Whiteness: The Development of White college Students' Racial Awareness, in: A. Doane & E. Bonilla-Silva (eds), *White Out* (New York, Routledge), pp. 215–230.

Cho, S. (2006) On Language of Possibility: Revisiting Critical Pedagogy, in: C. Rosatto, R. L. Allen, and M. Pruyn (eds), *Reinventing Critical Pedagogy* (Lanham, MD, Rowman & Littlefield), pp. 125–141.

Chubbuck, S. & Zembylas, M. (2008) The Emotional Ambivalence of Socially Just Teaching: A Case Study of a Novice Urban School Teacher, *American Educational Research Journal*, 452, pp. 274–318.

Cone, J. (1990) *A Black Theology of Liberation* (MaryKnoll, NY, Orbis Books).

Darder, A. & Torres, R. (2004) *After Race* (New York, New York University Press).

Derrida, J. (1985) Racism's Last Word, *Critical Inquiry*, 12,1, pp. 290–299.

Dumas, M. (2008) Theorizing Redistribution and Recognition in Urban Education Research: 'How Do We Get Dictionaries at Clevelend?', in: J. Anyon (ed.), *Theory and Educational Research* (London, Routledge), pp. 81–108.

Dyer, R. (1997) *White* (London, Routledge).

Fanon, F. (1967) *Black Skin White Masks*, C. Markmann, trans. (New York, Grove Weidenfeld). Originally published in 1952.

Fields, B. (1990) Slavery, Race and Ideology in the United States of America, *New Left Review*, I, 181 (May-June), pp. 95–118.

Freedman, S. W., Weinstein, H., Murphy, K. & Longman, T. (2008) Teaching History after Identity-Based Conflicts: The Rwanda Experience, *Comparative Education Review*, 5,4, pp. 663–690.

Freire, P. (1993) *Pedagogy of the Oppressed* (New York, Continuum).

Gillborn, D. (2005) Education Policy as an Act of White Supremacy: Whiteness, critical Race Theory and Education Reform, *Journal of Education Policy*, 2:4, pp. 485–505.

Gilroy, P. (1993) *The Black Atlantic* (Cambridge, MA, Harvard University Press).

Gilroy, P. (1998) Race Ends Here, *Racial and Ethnic Studies*, 21:5, pp. 838–847.

Gilroy, P. (2000) *Against Race* (Cambridge, MA, Belknap Press of Harvard University).

Giroux, H. (1988) *Teachers as Intellectuals* (Westport, CT, Bergin & Garvey).

Giroux, H. (1997) Rewriting the Discourse of Racial Identity: Towards a Pedagogy and Politics of Whiteness, *Harvard Educational Review*, 67:2, pp. 285–320.

Gotanda, N. (1995) A Critique of 'Our Constitution is Color-Blind', in: K. Crenshaw, N. Gotanda, G. Peller & K. Thomas (eds), *Critical Race Theory* (New York, The New Press), pp. 257–275.

Graham, L. J. (in press) The Cost of Opportunity, in: J. Marshall & L. Stone (eds), *Handbook on Poststructuralism in Education* (Rotterdam, Sense Publishing).

Graham, L. J. and Slee, R. (2008) An Illusory Interiority: Interrogating the Discourse/s of Inclusion, *Educational Philosophy and Theory*, 40:2, pp. 277–293.

Gramsci, A. (1971) *Selections From Prison Notebooks*, Q. Hoare & G. Smith, ed. and trans. (New York, International Publishers).

Guillaumin, C. (1995) *Racism, Sexism, Power and Ideology* (London, Routledge).

Hall, S. (1996) The Problem of Ideology: Marxism without Guarantees, in: D. Morley and K. Chen (eds), *Stuart Hall* (London, Routledge), pp. 25–46.

Harris, C. (1995) Whiteness as Property, in: K. Crenshaw, N. Gotanda, G. Peller & K. Thomas (eds), *Critical Race Theory* (New York, The New Press), pp. 276–291.

Hattam, R. & Zembylas, M. (2010) What's Anger Got to Do with It? Towards a Post-Indignation Pedagogy for Communities in Conflict, *Social Identities*, 16,1, pp. 23–40.

Hirschman, C. (2004) The Origins and Demise of the Concept of Race, *Population and Development Review*, 30,3, pp. 385–415.

Hunter, M. (2005) *Race, Gender, and the Politics of Skin Tone* (New York, Routledge).

Ignatiev, N. (1995) *How the Irish Became White* (New York, Routledge).

Ignatiev, N. and Garvey, J. (1996) Abolish the White race: By Any Means Necessary, in: N. Ignatiev and J. Garvey (eds), *Race Traitor* (New York, Routledge), pp. 9–14.

Lather, P. (2003) Applied Derrida: (Mis)Reading the Work of Mourning in Educational Research, *Educational Philosophy and Theory*, 35,3, pp. 257–270.

Leonardo, Z. (2002) The Souls of White Folk: Critical Pedagogy, Whiteness Studies, and Globalization Discourse, *Race Ethnicity & Education*, 5,1, pp. 29–50.

Leonardo, Z. (2003) Resisting Capital: Simulationist and Socialist Strategies, *Critical Sociology*, 29,2, pp. 211–236.

Leonardo, Z. (2005) Through the Multicultural Glass: Althusser, Ideology, and Race Relations in Post-Civil Rights America, *Policy Futures in Education*, 3,4, pp. 400–412.

Leonardo, Z. (2007) The War on Schools: NCLB, Nation Creation, and the Educational Construction of Whiteness, *Race Ethnicity & Education*, 10,3, pp. 261–278.

Leonardo, Z. (2009a) *Race, Whiteness, and Education* (New York, Routledge).

Leonardo, Z. (2009b) Pale/ontology: The Status of Whiteness in Education, in: M. Apple, W. Au, and L. Gandin (eds), *Routledge International Handbook of Critical Education* (New York, Routledge), pp. 123–136.

Lewis, A. (2003) Some Are More Equal Than Others: Lessons on Whiteness from school, in: A. Doane & E. Bonilla-Silva (eds), *White Out* (New York, Routledge), pp. 159–172.

Lipsitz, G. (1998) *The Possessive Investment in Whiteness* (Philadelphia, PA, Temple University Press).

Lopez, I. H. (2006) *White by Law* (New York, New York University Press).

Lyotard, J. (1984) *The Postmodern Condition*, G. Bennington & B. Massumi, trans. (Minneapolis, MN, University of Minnesota Press).

Massey, D. & Denton, N. (1993) *American Apartheid* (Cambridge, MA, Harvard University Press).

McLaren, P. & Torres, R. (1999) Racism and Multicultural Education: Rethinking 'Race' and 'Whiteness' in Late Capitalism, in: S. May (ed.), *Critical Multiculturalism: Rethinking Multicultural and Antiracist Education* (Philadelphia, PA, Falmer Press), pp. 42–76.

McPhail, M. L. (2003) Race and the (Im)possibility of Dialogue, in: R. Anderson, L. Baxter & K. Cissna (eds), *Dialogue: Theorizing Difference in Communication Studies* (Thousand Oaks, CA, Sage), pp. 209–224.

Morrison, T. (1993) *Playing in the Dark: Whiteness in the Literary Imagination* (New York, Vintage Books).

Miles, R. (2000) Apropos the Idea of 'Race' . . . Again, in: L. Back and J. Solomos (eds), *Theories of Race and Racism* (New York, Routledge), pp. 125–143.

Mills, C. (1997) *The Racial Contract* (Ithaca, NY, Cornell University Press).

Nayak, A. (2006) After Race: Ethnography, Race and Post-Race Theory, *Ethnic and Racial Studies*, 29,3, pp. 411–430.

Oakes, J. (2005) *Keeping Track*, 2nd edn. (New Haven, CT, Yale University Press).

Oakes, J., Joseph, R. & Muir, K. (2004) Access and Achievement in Mathematics and Science: Inequalities that Endure and Change, in: J. Banks & C. Banks (eds), *Handbook of Research on Multicultural Education* (San Francisco, John Wiley & Sons), pp. 69–90.

Oliver, M. & Shapiro, T. (1997) *Black Wealth, White Wealth: A New Perspective on Racial Inequality* (New York, Routledge).

Omi, M. & Winant, H. (1994) *Racial Formation in the United States: From the 1960s to the 1990s*, 2nd edn. (New York, Routledge).

Pollock, M. (2004) *Colormute* (Princeton, NJ, Princeton University Press).

Roediger, D. (1994) *Toward the Abolition of Whiteness* (New York, Verso).

Stanley, C. (ed.) (2006) *Faculty of Color* (Bolton, MA, Anker Publishing).

St. Louis, B. (2002) Post-Race/Post-Politics? Activist-Intellectualism and the Reification of Race, *Ethnic and Racial Studies*, 25,4, pp. 652–675.

Taylor, P. (2008) The Racial Stance: Pragmatism and post-Analytic Race Theory. Paper delivered at the New Perspectives on Race Theory Conference, University of San Francisco, CA, April 26.

Telles, E. (2006) *Race in Another America: The significance of Skin Color in Brazil* (Princeton, NJ, Princeton University Press).

Wacquant, L. (1997) For an Analytic of Racial Domination, *Political Power and Social Theory*, 11, pp. 21–234.

Wacquant, L. (2002) From Slavery to Mass Incarceration: Rethinking the 'Race Question' in the United States, *New Left Review*, 13, pp. 41–60.

Warmington, P. (2009) Taking Race Out of Scare Quotes: Race-Conscious Social Analysis in an Ostensibly Post-Racial World, *Race Ethnicity & Education*, 12,3, pp. 281–296.

Warren, J. & Twine, F. W. (2002) Critical Race Studies in Latin America: Recent advances, recurrent weaknesses, in: D. T. Goldberg & J. Solomos (eds), *A Companion to Racial and Ethnic Studies* (Malden, MA, Blackwell), pp. 538–560.

Youdell, D. (2004) Identity Traps or How Black Students Fail: The Interactions between Biographical, Sub-Cultural, and Learner Identities, in: G. Ladson-Billings & D. Gillborn (eds) *The RoutledgeFalmer Reader in Multicultural Education* (New York, RoutledgeFalmer), pp. 84–102.

Zembylas, M. (2008) *The Politics of Trauma in Education* (New York, Palgrave MacMillan).

Chapter 6

Will They Ever Speak With Authority? Race, Post-coloniality and the Symbolic Violence of Language

Awad Ibrahim

Editors' introduction

In this 2011 essay, Awad Ibrahim explores personal experiences with racialization and racialized 'psychic violence' through ethnographic research with African Parisian French-speaking youth in a Canadian, Franco-Ontarian school. Theoretically, Ibrahim draws upon Jacques Derrida's discussion of language ownership to indicate how the students are racialized so as to be continually treated as deficient and effectively silenced as others by their white, Franco-Ontarian teachers. As Ibrahim notes, while Parisian French is normally a marker of high social capital in Ontario, the African Parisian French-speaking students are treated with incredulity and exaggerated astonishment by their teachers. Thus, the teachers' ignorance regarding Francophone Africa and their prejudiced treatment of the African youth are normalized, while the students' desires and interests, and their tools of expression and social power, are effectively muted. Here, Ibrahim notes that while teachers may have positive intentions, their minute, trivial day-to-day interactions with the students are 'hard-to-pin-down' as negative, yet 'psychically painful' for the students, as their testimonies demonstrate. Furthermore, the teachers harm the students educationally by tracking them into low-level classes and into physical education and sports activities despite the students' expressed interest in broader visions of academic success. This essay is exceptional for its intersecting issues of race, racialization, and language, as well as for its vivid writing which juxtaposes images of the African students' lived experiences in Ontario, Canada with theories on postcolonialism and the politics of language.

> [O]ne can *testify* only to the unbelievable. To what can, at any rate, only be believed; to what appeals only to belief and hence to the given word . . . [here] when we ask others to take our word for it, we are already in the order of what is merely believable. (Derrida, 1996, p. 20)

Indeed the hardest thing, especially in post-coloniality, is to testify to the unbelievable, that which is symbolic in nature and which is felt but hard to 'talk' or 'speak' about. We are always almost there, but it eludes language. As soon as we

DOI: 10.4324/9781003346104-7

'speak' it, as we are dealing with emotionality, it slips away. But we must speak it. When we do, however, we are constantly told: 'That's just unbelievable!'. We are left therefore wondering: is this an exclamation, a questioning or a reminder? Yet, this article dares to ask: Having fully mastered the colonial language, can post-colonial subjects ever speak with authority? Put otherwise, at what point do we own the language we speak? By way of an answer, the article tells the story of a group of French-speaking refugee and immigrant continental African youth who are attending an urban Franco-Ontarian high school in southwestern Ontario, Canada. They arrive at French-language schools with a highly valued variety of French, *le français Parisien* or Parisian French. As Monica Heller (2006) showed, the linguistic variety of French spoken in Ontario is both devalued and unauthorized in schools. However, Heller explains, most teachers in Franco-Ontarian schools speak this 'devalued' variety of French. Hence, I am arguing, we enter a 'linguistic war', where the struggle is no longer about language *per se*, but about power.[1] And in the context of this article, it is about race and language ownership. Because of race and legal status, I will show, this highly symbolic capital that African youth bring with them to Franco-Ontarian schools seems to become an unauthorized norm, a liability, a burden rather than an event to celebrate. Continental African students are treated, classified and streamed in either lower grades or in general levels, where their chances for advanced or university studies are limited. 'It was *unbelievable* how they spoke', one teacher exclaimed, expressing what Ben Rampton (1995), within the British context, calls *deceptive fluency*. For those who believe in this notion of deceptive fluency in Britain, Rampton explains, even though they may sound British and are born in Britain, South Asians cannot be native speakers of English. Therefore, the notion goes, their fluency or British accent is deceptive.[2] For Jacques Derrida (1996), this is an exemplary moment of 'performative contradiction,' an antinomy if you like, one where he would have declared: 'Yes, I only have one language, yet it is not mine' (p. 2).

Then, Who Owns Language?

Strongly worded, but Derrida (1996) is worth quoting at length here; after all he is my referent in intersecting authority-language-and-symbolic power. For Derrida, language is and has always been in the plural, and any claim especially by 'the master' to its possession can only be that: a claim.[3] In fact, 'the master himself' [sic], Derrida declares, is no longer:

> [C]ontrary to what one is often most tempted to believe, the master is nothing. Because the master does not possess exclusively, and naturally, what he calls his language, because, whatever he wants or does, he cannot maintain any relations of property or identity that are natural, national, congenital, or ontological, with it . . . [And] because language is not his natural possession, he can, thanks to that very fact, pretend historically, through the rape of a

cultural usurpation, which means always essentially colonial, to appropriate it in order to impose it as 'his own'.

(p. 13)

As we shall see, one has to be very careful in using the language of coloniality within the Franco-Ontarian context where I conducted my research. The discourse of coloniality does not lend itself easily here and the situation is tenuous if not confusing at best. Without entering the debate on the term's orthography or definition,[4] I will use interchangeably the two orthographies (postcolonial and post-colonial) more in the subaltern sense. When subalterns speak, said Spivak (1999), they are not heard. They are subaltern not because of total social immobility or for inherent reasons; they are subaltern because they are spoken for, they are authored and already talked about. Hence their silence is made possible if not expected. Spivak (1999) tells her own story as an Indian woman who is not heard (not even by other women) until recently: 'Here is a woman who tried to be decisive *in extremis*. She "spoke", but women did not, do not, "hear" her. Thus she can be defined as a "subaltern"—a person without lines of social mobility' (p. 28).

So picture this: It is Canada—an officially French-English bilingual country, and one of the most prominent countries worldwide in implementing bilingualism and multiculturalism. The study's population is French-language speakers in Ontario, an English-language speaking province that is situated next to Québec. Québec is the only French-language speaking province besides New Brunswick, which is the only bilingual province in Canada.[5] As we know, the so-called *français canadien* or Canadian French is older than Canada itself as a nation, goes back to 15th century France, and has unique lexical, morphological, syntactic and phonetic characteristics (Heller, 2006, 1994; Mougeon & Beniak, 1989). Ontario has the highest French-language speaking population outside Québec (StatCan.gc.ca, 2008). They are known as *Franco-ontariens* or Franco-Ontarians, comprising anywhere between 4.3-to-5% of Ontario's population, and concentrated primarily in Eastern Ontario, especially Ottawa (the national capital).

Franco-Ontarians are exceptionally savvy in using the apparatus of the State and in social and political mobilization. They pride themselves on this mobilization ability and refer to themselves as *francophones de souche* (old or 'original' French) to distinguish themselves from other francophones (e.g. Arabic speakers, Haitians or West Africans). Thanks to activism and the Canadian Charter of Rights and Freedom, which guarantees a prominent a place for the French language as it does English in Canada, Ontario has 12 French-language school boards (both public and Catholic), a number of community colleges and four universities that offer programs in French and the University of Ottawa as fully bilingual, attracting a sizeable number of Ontario's francophone population.

Francophone de souche is as much a linguistic, historical and cultural reference, as it is a racial one. It is a term commonly used for White Europeans who speak French and are part of the earlier settlers in Canada. They speak varieties of French that are similar to Québec French, but still quite distinct. Some of the distinct linguistic features of Franco-Ontarian French (FOF) include, among many others: 1) simplification (e.g. third-person plural that is cited as first-person singular: *ils veulent* [they want] turned into *ils veut* [they wants]); 2) the use of *sontaient*, a non-standard variant of *étaient* [were], the standard third person plural imperfect form of the verb *être* [to be]; 3) the common use of the possessive *à* in lieu of *de* (e.g. *la voiture à mon père* [my father's car]; the 'standard' use is: *la voiture de mon père*).[6] It is significantly important to note that these are mostly non-standard features which, as we shall see, create a very peculiar situation. On the one hand, internally, it creates a Franco-Ontarian linguistic community with its bond and intra-community recognition but, on the other, it becomes a simultaneous mechanism, a technology of exclusion.

To explain, those who speak standard French, oddly enough, would feel either excluded or highly valued. The 'lack,' as Édouard Glissant (1981) would have put it, is a better description for those who feel excluded. Postcolonial subjects, Glissant (1981) explains in *Le discours antillais*, are constantly identified and reminded by their lack of language possession. Here, language is locked in as a possession of a nation, a culture and a group of people. It *belongs* to 'them,' and identity (Franco-Ontarianness in this context) is no longer regarded as a being-of-the-entity [*l'être de l'étant*], a being-that-is-always-to-become (Derrida, 1996; Ibrahim, 2004, 2008), but as a *fait accompli*, an ontology whose essence and features are already known and non-changing. It may be a hyphen-identity in this context—Franco *and* Ontarian—but it is still purely 'French'.[7]

This is precisely why the real or imagined Frenchness is highly valued symbolic capital (Bourdieu, 1991). But for it to function as such, Frenchness has to have the 'right ingredients' in linguistic, cultural and racial terms. French, it seems, is a convoluted term referring mostly to White Europeans *belonging* to or *citizens* of France. The rest, as Derrida (1996) put it, is the 'Francophones *belonging*, as we strangely say, to several nations, cultures, and states' (p. 10; original emphasis). They are hyphened: Franco Maghrebian, Franco-Antillais, Franco-Senegalese, etc.[8] Because of this hyphen, or maybe thanks to it, they go through moments of mourning, where they speak a language—masterfully indeed—which they are told is not theirs. The source of that work of mourning (Todd, 2003) is in the psychic tension where, in many post-colonial moments, French is the only language they speak or they master it more than their mother tongues. Derrida (1996, p. 1) again:

—Picture this, imagine someone who would cultivate the French language. What is called the French language.
Someone whom the French language would cultivate.
And who [as post-colonial subject] would be, moreover, a subject of French culture, as we say.
Now suppose, for example, that one day this subject of French culture were to tell you in good French:
'I only have one language; it is not mine.'

Such 'exclusions,' Derrida continues, come to leave their marks on colonial, but as well on post-colonial subjects, and their identity formation. They create a 'disorder of identity', and are best captured in Paulo Freire's *Pedagogy of the Oppressed* (2000). Here, despite her/his presumed superiority, the so-called possessor of language, the oppressor in Freire's language, enters the work of mourning as much as the oppressed. That is, oppression and exclusion affect to a large extent the oppressed as they do the oppressor. Derrida pushes us further by, on the one hand, framing the work of mourning around language and, on the other, questioning the essence of language possession:

> But who exactly possesses it [language]? And whom does it possess? Is language in possession, ever a possessing or possessed possession? Possessed or possessing in exclusive possession, like a piece of personal property? What of this being-at-home [*être-chez-soi*] in language toward which we never cease returning?
>
> (Derrida, 1996, p. 17)

Season of Migration to Canada

In *Season of Migration to the North*, Tayyib Salih (1991) tells the story of Mustafa Sa'eed. Sa'eed is a post-colonial subject originally from the Sudan who finds himself in Britain. He goes through identity translation and re-configuration whereby he ends up in a Third-Space, a split-subject between two cultures, languages and ways of being (Ibrahim, 2008). This is the case with my research subjects. In 2007, I conducted a small-scale research study in an urban Franco-Ontarian high school in southwestern Ontario, Canada. This research was a follow-up to an earlier study conducted between January and June 1996 (Ibrahim, in press).

Both in 1996 and 2007, the research is a critical ethnography[9] and looks at the lives of a group of continental Francophone African youth and the formation of their social identity. Besides their gendered and racialized experience, their youth and refugee status was vital in their, what I termed elsewhere, *moments of identification* (Ibrahim, 2008): where and how they were interpolated in the mirror of their society (cf. Althusser, 1971; Bhabha, 1994). Put otherwise, once in North America, I showed, these youth were faced with a social imaginary in which they were already Blacks. This social imaginary was directly implicated in how and with whom they identified, which in turn influenced what they linguistically and culturally learned and how they learned it. What they learned, as I showed elsewhere (Ibrahim, 1999), is Black English as a Second Language (BESL), which they accessed in and through Black popular culture. They learned by taking up and repositing the Rap linguistic and musical genre and, in different ways, acquiring and rearticulating the Hip-Hop cultural identity (Ibrahim, 1999, 2004, 2009).

Here the research participants are a group of continental Francophone African youth who find themselves in a small French-language high school in southwestern Ontario, with a school population of approximately 400 students from various ethnic, racial, cultural, religious, and linguistic backgrounds, which I will refer to as Marie-Victorin or MV [all names in this article are pseudonyms]. Besides French, English, Arabic, Somali and Farsi were also spoken at the school. This group of continental Francophone African youth varied, first, in their length of stay in Canada (from 1–2 to 5–6 years); second, in their legal status (some were immigrants, but the majority were refugees) and, third, in their gender, class, age, linguistic and national background. They came from places as diverse as Democratic Republic of Congo (formerly Zaïre), Djibouti, Gabon, Senegal, Somalia, South Africa and Togo. With no exception, all of the African students in MV were at least trilingual, speaking French, English and an African language, a mother tongue. Given their postcolonial educational history, significantly, most African youths in fact come to Franco-Ontarian schools already possessing the highly valued symbolic capital: *le français parisien* (Parisian French, also known as *français standard* or *français international*).

Ethnography and Hospitality

[I]s there anything worse, said Nietzsche, than to find oneself facing a German when one was expecting a Greek?
(Deleuze & Guattari, 1994, p. 109)

As a critical ethnographic research project, I spent over six months in 1996 and three months in 2007 engaged in the research: I attended classes, talked to students, and observed curricular and extracurricular activities two or three times per week. I audio- and-videotaped classes and natural conversations, visited their houses, played basketball (a game dominated by African students) and became the basketball team coach, and was invited for picnics. In short, I literally lived with the students, and because of previous involvement before 1996 in another project in the same school for almost two years, at the time of this research I was well acquainted with MV and its population, especially its African students, with whom I was able to develop a good communicative relationship. What is more, my background as a continental African myself also helped me to decipher their narratives and experiences. Clearly, we shared a *safe space* of comfort that allowed us to open up, speak and engage freely.[10]

Of this growing continental francophone African population in Franco-Ontarian schools (Ibrahim, in press), I ended up choosing ten boys and six girls for extensive ethnographic observation inside and outside the classroom and inside and outside the school and interviewed all sixteen. Of the ten boys, six were Somali speakers (from Somalia and Djibouti), one was Ethiopian, two were Senegalese, and one was from Togo. Their ages ranged from sixteen to twenty years. The six girls were all Somali speakers (also from Somalia and Djibouti), aged from fourteen to eighteen years. Interviews were conducted either in French or English and French interviews were translated into English. Here, language was a crucial part of this comfort zone, this safe space.

This space was built against the backdrop of, first, total absence of diversity in the teaching, personnel or administration staff except for one teacher of Haitian descent and, second, the traumatic psychic experience of exclusion, discrimination and symbolic violence that students have experienced (see Ibrahim, 2009). Before the 1990s, MV had not experienced such a mass of diversity, especially the continental African presence. Teachers therefore had no experiential knowledge on how to interact with African youth in either comfortable or informed ways. Intentionally or not, students made it clear that there was a serious race-relation problem in the school.[11] This problem is manifested in three different ways:

1) *The host as hostage*: Here, one is hosted, but conditionally. In Jacques Derrida's (2000) language there are two forms or formulae of/for hospitality: conditional and unconditional (see Ibrahim, 2005 for full discussion). In the former, one is hosted, but under certain conditions, restrictions, choices and possibilities. Omer (M, 19, Ethiopia),[12] who came to Canada by himself when he was 15 years old, exemplifies this situation. Omer was living in a shelter at the time of the interview, yet enthusiastically he was longing and planning to go to Laurentian University. Following an Althusserian (1971) language, Omer conceives this conditional hospitality as interpellation: 'Hello there! You are Black you can't do anything. Muslims, you can do nothing. This is what astonishing to me. It is already seen [what Blacks and Muslims can or cannot do]' (individual interview, French). As Gayatri Spivak explained above, here the subalterns are already 'talked' about, authored and hence their silence is either made or expected.

2) *Undemocratic decisions*: This is when students *feel* they are not consulted on matters related to their lives. These decisions, then, are perceived as discriminatory, insensitive, if not plain racist. For instance, because all school teachers and personnel are White and Christian (except for one Jewish teacher), when the school decided that the midday Muslim prayer was no longer permissible, the decision was read in multiple ways, including as racism. Aziza (F, 18, Somalia) described it thus:

> So now there is this new rule. They met, the personnel of the school that is, they met. They agreed, like we were nothing at all. They said 'Oh, who cares!' you see. We have to just tell them not leave the class, because our class is more important than their pray . . . So, there wasn't, I am sure, there wasn't even one teacher who objected to that. They all agreed. (group interview, French)

Although students continued their protest, they found themselves submitting to the school decision after a few days. Their protest, they explained to me afterwards, was an expressed desire to participate in the democratic process of decision making. To soften the situation, the school brought in a Moroccan teacher from James High School, the other French-language high school in the city, who explained to students that midday prayer did not have a specific hour but an extended period of time from 12-noon to 3 p.m.

What is problematic here, however, besides the undemocratic decision taken by the school, is the way in which this Moroccan teacher was brought into the school. This outside teacher was brought in to reinterpret the students' experience of this decision for them in a way that reinforced the White and non-Muslim teachers assessment of this decision. This is akin to the common occurrence with a White person who tells a Black person: 'My Black friend told me that I am not racist, so [although they may have made a racist comment] what you are telling me [that I am racist] is wrong'. This is what George Dei *et al.* (2000) call 'everyday racism', which is hard to talk about and deal with (as we shall see below).

3) *The minute and the trivial:* This is the third and final way of racialization where *non-appartenance*, non-belonging or rejection is seen as an accumulative memory of small details, but when put together they tend to leave students with a clear message that they are not trusted, wanted or that they are deviant. Listen to Aziza again where she explains that even their names become a burden. The teacher's repetition of how African students' names should be pronounced has become a marker that sets them apart:

> I am going to give you an example. A female teacher always gives the absent sheet [*la feuille d'absence*], always to White students. Moreover, teachers are going to know the names when they know them, for a teacher always knows the names of all the students in class. He is going to know more the names of the White students than the names of African students. 'What's your name again? Bûralé? How do you want to me to pronounce that, Bûr-ralé, Boralé?' You see things like that. It's a bit, it gives, it gives you pain here [pointing to her chest]. This is like, these things are small small, but they can be big, which can also be something catastrophic you see. And you, you have to live with this every day, you see. (group interview, French)

Musa (M, 19, Djibouti) expands on Aziza's example. One day he was absent the first period. Because some African students live on their own, they confront adult life earlier: they pay their own bills, cook their own food, work odd jobs, etc. In many cases, in short, they need ears to listen to them or a helping hand. They aren't getting that at the school. Musa is worth quoting at length:

> The other day, I was absent the first period. I came to school in the second period. And that day, I didn't even see her [the principal]. I came the following day and I told her 'yesterday, I was absent.' 'All day? You were absent because you had problems.' I had problems with *Hydro*, [city name] *Hydro*. I told her that I was going there; if not, they were going to cut off electricity . . . She said 'no no, that doesn't concern me. That is your problem. If you have to solve that, you should do it during your holiday time.' But holiday times, they are closed. Saturday and Sunday, *Hydro* is not open. So, I have to go, I told her, I have to miss a class in order to go there and solve my problems. She didn't even listen, she said

'you were absent all day.' 'But Madame, how do you want me to [solve it?], and I was only absent the first period.' I didn't even finish, she said 'no no, you were absent all day for *Hydro*, to solve this *Hydro* problem.' I told her 'Madame, try to **listen**, try to **hear** me.' And I told her that I was only absent the first period. 'Ah,' she said, 'you were only absent the first period, I am sorry. Then, I give a paper to [the secretary] this time, but don't be late.' But that is me, I told her straight: 'That is your problem, you don't try to listen to the African students. You only scream. That is your problem, and you have to change this character.' I told her, straight up, I told her that. (group interview, French, emphasis added)

These examples are offered here as a demonstration for what Winant (2004) calls *racialization* or *racialized experiences*. They are insidious, convoluted, hard-to-pin-down, but psychically and painfully felt. As well, they are best captured as symbolic violence (Bourdieu, 1991).[13] The beauty (and I recognize the irony of the term) of symbolic violence in this case is that it works through slippage; that is, when the doers are confronted or called up to answer to their deeds, they can escape by saying: 'We didn't know; indeed we had the best intentions; we wanted to treat African students like any other students' (see also Graham & Slee, 2008 and their notion of 'benevolent humanitarianism'). *Intentions matter only in their final effect*, as we know. That is, in socio-psychic terms, how one makes people feel matters as much if not more than one's intentions. Intentional or not, African students in MV have built an experiential memory that is not so pleasant to remember, which is strongly expressed in language.

Race-in(g)-Language: Le *français parisien* Illegitimately Spoken

In MV, it is clear that race (read Blackness in this case) is experienced in at least three different ways, as we saw above, and with variable degrees of emotional intensity. My contention in this section is that language is central to this experience. Given their postcolonial education, by and large, African students arrive at school fluent in, and armed with, the highly valuable symbolic capital: *le français parisien*. Interestingly enough, as is noted many times by Heller *et al.* (1999), the role and the mandate of the French-language schools in Ontario is to introduce students to this variety of French as well as to the variety spoken by middle-class Franco-Ontarians. However, when African students come to school with this capital, there is an astonishment and disbelief on the part of teachers and school counselors. Their language, it seems, is *deceptively fluent*: they cannot be so fluent and speak the language with such mastery! This skepticism stems from the fact that, as Bourdieu (1991) would have said, the 'legitimate' language is spoken by an 'illegitimate' speaker: a refugee who is imagined to be, at least in the dominant media representations, a source of pity and not astonishment and envy. This mistrust of the linguistic capital that African students possess has led to a patronizing attitude that is easily open to a racialized, if not blunt racist reading. Without naming it as such, students were aware of both: the process of racialization and how it illegitimizes their speech. In my group interview with them, female students reflected on this situation thus:

Amani: The teacher could not stop thanking me every time I speak and tells me 'Here, your French, you can, it is different than the others. How that happens, where did you learn that? Are you sure that you are not in the wrong stream [this was a general level course]?'[14] You know, things like that. And then, she was really surprised you know. I told her 'No, I know what I have to know for my level, my my . . .' [interrupted]

Aziza: And then she was very impressed when we said that we learn our French in our country. And then things like that, and then she said, 'really, in your country, there is really this system?'

Samira: 'Are there professors who speak French like that? But my God you have *l'accent français!*' But of course we have *l'accent français*, there were teachers that taught us, no? And then this: 'you are coming from Somalia oh, we never heard that in Somalia people speak French with . . .' [interrupted]

Aziza: 'Really in Somalia you have this system?' You know, **they don't accept that** (group interview, French, bold added).

In my individual interview with Aziza, she expands on how teachers' disbelief is patronizing and grossly disturbing, especially given its racial connotation:

Aziza: The first day when I wrote my [evaluation] test, of my French level, he [the counselor] was really surprised because I spoke an excellent French. The good and rich French; you know when you live in Africa? He was really surprised, you see. 'You have an excellent French,' you see! Because that is new you see, **an African who speaks a good French, much better than they do**. It is a bit [too much? unbelievable?] you see. And also there is a teacher who said to me 'where did you learn your French? Your French is good.' And then I said that I learned there where I came from, in Africa. And then she said, she could not believe you see. You see; she said that all the time. (individual interview, French, bold added).

In spite of their 'good,' 'rich,' and 'excellent' French, continental African students are disproportionately streamed in the general, non-college-bound level. This disproportionate number is noted by the students themselves. Using his ethnographic gaze, Musa (M, 19, Djibouti) observed that, 'the majority of African students who are in Marie-Victorin take general level courses'. Although not all African students are in the general level, it is noteworthy that Musa introduced this observation to the discussion during my focus group interview with the boys without a question from me to this effect. Building on their memory of how schools functioned in Africa, African students were not fully aware of the difference between fundamental, general and advanced level courses. In Africa, reflected the boys during my group interview with them, all students go to the same class to perform the same academic task:

A male voice:	When you come, when you first arrive in the school, you don't know what general, advanced, fundamental courses mean. It is them [counselors and school administration] who give you your courses. You just want to go to school to study. They force you to take general courses [telephone rings]. You don't know what a general course means.
Musa:	With general courses you can't go too far. (group interview, French)

On the other hand, not surprising but exceptionally disturbing, most African students are pushed towards sports. In their studies, Dei *et al.* (2000), James & Shadd (2001), Mensah (2002), Nelson & Nelson (2004) and Yon (2000) have all observed the same phenomenon in Canada. Thinking about their counselor, the boys continue:

Mukhi:	But still, there is Monsieur Raymond [a counselor] who even if you took five physical education [courses], he is going to give a sixth.
A male voice:	*Yah, I don't know why.*
Mukhi:	I don't know why like, to make you waste time or something. (group interview, French)

The girls, on their part, seem to believe that it is the boys who are streamed more in the lower levels; but because of lack of statistical information, I can neither confirm nor overrule this observation. Nonetheless, I made the same ethnographic observation. Boys' presence in general level is substantially higher than the girls'; close to 90% boys as opposed to less than 10% girls. When asked why, the girls hypothesized that that has to do with the exclusivity the boys make between sports and academic performance. Always according to the girls, becoming a successful athlete for the boys is seen in opposition to doing well academically. When one is doing one's homework successfully, one is seen as a 'nerd', a term connected to what Ogbu & Fordham (1986) call 'acting white'. The girls have seen these boys 'back-home' where they were 'first class' students. Something has happened that caused them to see academics in opposition to athleticism.

Awad:	I have noticed that at the school, especially there is a very very strong majority [of the African students] who are present in the general level.

Asma:	That I know why. You know why?
Awad:	Why?
Asma:	The majority are the boys. The majority are the boys, they want *basket-ball. Dream Team*, I love the *basketball* [a girl talking], Yes, wait.
Ossi:	Yah, what does that mean?
Awad:	Yes, yes, what does that mean?
Asma:	They really want, they really could, I know these boys. They are really good. I remember in my country, they were really intelligent students.
Aziza:	First class.
Asma:	Yes, they know, they know. They know their academics, they know how to do this, how to do that. The problem is that if I start doing my homework, and I am a boy, this means I am a nerd. (group interview, French)

The gendered answer was exceptionally interesting here. When I asked the boys the same questions of why they dichotomize academics and athleticism, on the one hand, and why they are disproportionately in general, non-university-bound level courses, there was an unanimous response around their racialized experience, school counseling, or being refugees and living on their own as the reasons for their streaming and sense of alienation. Mukhi (M, 18. Djibouti) sums thus: 'Si tu allais faire un sondage, ça vient souvent de l'orientation ou des personnels' ['If you conduct a survey, the reason stems either from counseling or school personnel']. Taking the role of the African elder, Musa (M, 19, Djibouti) expressed the African students' agony concerning living on their own, working through the immigration papers and dealing with their social workers: 'The African students, they have a lot of problems. Here, the Canadians don't have problems, they have their parents, there is that. We, we have problems. You, you are late, she [the principal] sends you home. You go home for three or four days. We, we can't afford that because there is the immigration that calls us: "you have to come to see me today". You have to sign your check, things like that. There is back and forth. So, you have to go to the immigration, you have to go to, your, how do you call it, social worker?' (group interview, French)

Expanding on Mukhi's notion of school personnel and their role on student streaming in the general level, Musa continued his contention and elderly role: 'But the majority of the African students who are at Marie-Victorin, every time I see them, they take general level courses. I don't know why. "Why are you taking a general level course?" [explaining how he talks to other younger students] "It's Madame Robert [the principal] who gave it to me". "But, *gee* Madame Robert, [let her] go to hell, and take an advanced level course", I said' (group interview, French). In my field notes dated 5 February, 1996, I wrote, 'Musa came up to me requesting if I can offer an English-language tutoring course because he thinks that African students have problems with English'. What is significant in all of this is the fact that, first, unselfishly Musa is looking after other younger African students and, second, Musa's hopes are high that students can do much better. He knows they can do much better.

Consequently: Making Linkages and Conclusions

> Consequently, anyone should be able to declare under oath: I have only one language and it is not mine; my 'own' language is, for me, a language that cannot be assimilated. My language, the only one I hear myself speak and agree to speak, is the language of the other.
>
> (Derrida, 1996, p. 25)

At this point, I am sure my 'gentle reader' (as W. E. Du Bois would have called you), may be wondering if the connection was made between race, language, post-coloniality and authority of speaking. I certainly hope so. I have to admit though, tersely and speculatively, the paper is meant to be food for thought which some-times is more provocative than a French three-course meal. My intent was to show how, given students' racialized bodily experience, students' speech was illegiti-mized despite its highly symbolic value. This is what I am referring to as 'symbolic violence'. This is closer to Foucault's (1979) notion of punishment, where the flesh is replaced with psychic experience. That is to say, one is left questioning not only one's speech and language but even one's subjectivity (not to say humanity). Derrida (1996) again—talking about himself as an Algerian-Jew who has nothing else but French to 'speak': 'In what language does one write memoirs when there has been no authorized [language]? How does one utter a worthwhile "I recall" when it is necessary to invent both one's language and one's "I"?' (p. 31).

African students, it seems, are left with the same question: Can we ever speak with authority? They are to invent both their language and their subjectivity. Here students were conscious of what is involved in this (re)invention, this *linguistic return*, where one spells one's own name and names oneself. It involves:

1) A full mastery of the rules of the game, what Bourdieu (1991) would call the 'market of exchange'. In any market, Bourdieu explains, there are currencies or capitals that are needed, there are rules on how to exchange these capitals, and he emphasized that the players along with the rules determine the value of capital. Hassan (M, 17, Djibouti) was fully aware of his role in the school as a 'market of exchange' and the capitals he possesses:

> *Hassan:*   So, there are all these structures and differences that you have to play with [*jouer avec*]. Such include the fact that you have to have the competency of playing with others, you have to know how to play with others. (individual interview, French)

Clearly, we do not all enter the game the same way, nor with the same capi-tal. Nonetheless, 'gaming the system' or knowing how to play the game (i.e. system) is essential for Hassan.

2) Once aware of exclusion and discrimination, or knowing how the system works and how it excludes people, one is under the ethical responsibility to 'out' it, to talk about, and to turn it around to one's own benefit. To do so, however, one can work within the 'system,' from the inside. Hassan articulates it thus:

> *Hassan:* To begin with, there are all these stereotypes about Black people. There is discrimination and all that, OK! The only way to combat discrimination is outing [or publicizing] discrimination. Why do we have all this [discrimination]? We have to play their games to our own benefit. We don't have to do the impossible you know. (individual interview, French)

Since one is working with the system, the 'game' if you like, one does not look for alternative markets and identities—as did the boys when they chose basketball as opposed to volleyball and Hip-Hop as opposed to dominant identities. Instead, one chooses to affirm one's identity from within the particular *authorized, legitimized* and *dominant* market and identity. Yet, Hassan is mindful of the fact that, in the case of Blackness, there are no guarantees even when one possesses the market's required credentials and capitals. That is why, he adds in the same interview, 'if you come in [for an interview] with a tie, or with a suit, with your PhD, they are *probably* going to accept you more than before'. By 'they,' one may argue, Hassan is referring to the power bloc, those who have a larger control of the market, and who set themselves as the norm, the yardstick against which all is measured. Given their benefit from the dominant structure, 'they' have little incentive and lucrative investment in imagining others differently, especially Black people, and in decentering themselves. For to do so is to question one's own power and in some cases give all or some of it up.[15]

3) As educators, finally, and especially as anti-racism workers, we need to deconstruct the social structure of domination, discrimination and negation. Otherwise, some are damned to struggle all their lives and find themselves in the periphery of power with little or no resources and capitals. Thanks to these hegemonic structures, Black/African youth, by and large, find themselves putting in twice the effort to reach an average position (at least as defined by rules of the market). They carry the burden of 'proving' themselves, which means in some cases, they have to dichotomize, on the one hand, the school and the schooling process and, on the other, their personal desires, history, language and culture:

> *Hassan:* But, I can prove it, I can do whatever I want to, dress[16] however I want to, have whatever I want to, and be myself. You do what you have to do, you have 100% in your classes, and you are well-liked by everyone. It is really deceiving, it is really deceiving

that despite all of these, we have to prove what we have to everyone, or who we are, and the others don't. (individual interview,
French)

One way to do so, Hassan contends, is to 'flip the script' as Hip-Hoppers love to
say. That is, in place of failure one emphasizes pedagogies of hope, possibility and
success; and talks about the unsaid, the absent, and the silenced:

> *Hassan:* And the only way to do it [prove ourselves to others?] is not to
> conform or buy into stereotypical data like: 'Oh 50% of African
> youth had failed, they can't do it.' What has to happen is to show
> them that 50% had passed, not only to show them the 50% that
> failed. But they only see the part that failed, they don't look for the
> part that passed. We have to show them the part that passed, that's
> what we have to do; and this is one of my objectives: to do more
> in this regard, to leave a dream . . . (individual interview, French)

To materialize this dream Hassan is placing the onus squarely on himself. He is
not *Waiting for Godot*, as Samuel Beckett would have put it, to do something
about the social situation he sees around him. He is willing to 'sacrifice' and take
up that burden and he knows the price he has to pay. As the old African saying
goes: if the spirit is high, the body can only feel its height/weight. That is to say,
the body does not have too many choices when there is a will, since we are guided
by our will not our bodies.

> *Hassan:* I am sacrificing enormous amount of time. I have been in a chain of
> committees for example, so there are always prices to pay. He who
> wants something, he is going to pay prices. You want something, you
> have to pay for it. You may have to prove something, your strength or
> whatever. Personally, I know I sacrificed: I missed evenings and there
> is my mother, anxious [*debordée*]. 'You come really late at night. Why
> do you stay after school, occupied with so much work?' she says, you
> see! (individual interview, French)

Hassan's spirit of sacrifice, personal responsibility, and vision are vital in the struggle against exclusion and discrimination. However, the institutional and systematic nature of racialization, discrimination and exclusion motivate us to think
not only how discrimination takes place, but also, significantly, how it tends to
reproduce privilege, especially White privilege (Graham & Slee, 2008). As Peggy
McIntosh (1998) argues, for the longest time we tend to think about discrimination and racism and their effects on the victim. We need, she contends, to think
about discrimination and racism as technologies of power that end up reproducing privileges, ways of thinking, being and speaking. To conclude, Hassan's
mother is absolutely right in asking, 'Why do you personally, my son, sacrifice so

much?' What both Hassan and his mother need to ask as well is: 'Why do we as African and Black people have to prove who we are and what we have to anyone?' In an Obama-era, this latter question seems more than ever urgent since the silenced are yet to speak, and to speak with authority. They love but their love is yet to be heard as a creative margin for a radical pedagogy of hope, love and desire.

Notes

1 To clarify, there are two varieties of French that are talked about here: *français de France* and *français canadien*. I refer to the former as '*français parisien*' (Parisian French) and the latter as '*français de souche*' (original or old French; a term used both in Quebec and Ontario to refer to 'original' French settlers and their language). In the Franco-Ontarian context, the Parisian French is highly valued whereas *français de souche*, the variety spoken by most Franco-Ontarian schoolteachers, is both marginalized and discouraged. For further discussion, see the section in this article titled: 'Then, Who Owns Language?' For now, however, one may argue that we are dealing with 'racialized class conflict' where classism and racism are expressed through linguicism, that is, in the variety spoken and valued. Interestingly enough, Franco-Ontarian teachers speak *français de souche*, which they in turn devalued. This is a phenomenon of cognitive dissidence, if not a schizophrenic moment; one where one devalues what one speaks. However, when continental African youth arrived to the school with their *français international* (which I am provocatively calling *français parisien*), as we shall see, they are told: 'That's just unbelievable!'

2 Linda Graham & Roger Slee (2008) show a similar process taking place in Australia, where White Australians do not seem to fall under the umbrella of *deceptive fluency*, only the Other, it seems, are placed outside what they call 'ghostly center' (p. 284). In his book, *White by Law*, Ian Haney-Lopez (2006) addresses a similar notion which he calls 'rule of common knowledge'. Emerging in the 1930s–50s in the United States, the *rule of common knowledge* was used to preclude people of Asian descent from immigrating to the US, who were forced to argue in the courts that they were either 'White' or 'of African descent'. All the cases heard took the former tack, Haney-Lopez explains, partly because it was during Jim Crow segregation. In attempting to argue that Asians were White (a color, not a geographic or biological origin), those who called skilled anthropologists to testify on their behalf lost their bid to immigrate because the courts applied what was called the rule of common knowledge, in stating that, even if you are scientifically White, we all know that you are not what common knowledge tells us is White, so for that reason you cannot come into the country. Clearly, the so-called truth of Western science is subverted in the service of racist perception. To finish, I owe much of this text and the notion of the rule of common knowledge to one of the reviewers of this article.

3 In reality, 'language' is and has always been plural. For Derrida (1996), the French language, for example, always had (and still has) multiple speakers, accents and daily expressions. However, it was standardized as it was written, thus attempting to eliminate its multiplicity. This standardization, Derrida argues, is part of a colonial project, where even people within France who spoke a variety of French were brought into the project of the Republic, which is assumed to have one language, one accent and one voice.

4 See Mishra, 2005 for a comprehensive recent discussion of the term 'post-colonial'.

5 Quebec, as some might know, is a monolingual French-only province; and New Brunswick is the only bilingual French-English province. The rest of Canada is English-language speaking. This may be confusing to some since Canada is a bilingual country. Here, when Canada declares itself a bilingual country, this is usually in reference to the languages used by the federal government in its formal functioning. It does not mean that every province or every Canadian is bilingual. On its part, however, the federal government spends a substantial amount of money to make Canadians bilingual or at least functional in both official languages. For the purpose of this paper, two things are noteworthy: 1) more French speakers become bilingual (which puts them at a greater advantage when it comes to federal government jobs) and 2) for Franco-Ontarians, given the omnipresence of English in Ontario, this endangers the French language because by the second or third generation they become English-dominant speakers. That is, they tend to speak and be more functional in English than French and therefore their French-language schooling is marginalised if not put off in favor of the English language.

6 The detailed analysis and discussion of these features by Mougeon & Beniak (1991) has been my reference in this area.

7 For Franco-Ontarians, the French language (not to say France itself) is still their highly prized symbolic capital. Even though they may speak it little and in many cases, not at all, that identity (along with its language) is by and large *the* claimed identity. Put simply, though Franco-Ontarians are largely 'hyphened' and fluent in French and English, they will still claim French as their determining identity and language.

8 When it comes to Franco-Ontarians, notions of coloniality, postcoloniality and oppression are exceptionally complicated. Franco-Ontarians are a French-speaking minority in Ontario. They struggle as much as any minority does, and historically has been prevented from teaching their language or opening French-language schools (Heller, 2006). Yet, presently they have unearned privileges that others have to struggle either for or against: Whiteness, language, (institutionalized) power, school and social institutions, and above all the protection of the state. Because of these privileges, the population of my research (continental francophone Africans) finds itself a minority within a minority. Put simply, Franco-Ontarians do feel that their language variety is not as valued as *le français parisien* or *français de France*, but they ally themselves with this privileged symbolic capital by naming themselves: *Français de souche* [original or old French], hence creating complex situation where the oppressed or dispossessed can be an oppressor or a possessor, where the very notion of oppression and exclusion is no longer a unidimensional idea.

9 For Simon & Dippo (1986, p. 195), *critical ethnographic research* is a set of activities situated within a project that seeks and works its way toward social transformation. This project is political as well as pedagogical, and who the researcher is and what his or her racial, gender and class embodiments are necessarily govern the research questions and findings. The project, then, according to Simon and Dippo, is 'an activity determined both by real and present conditions, *and* certain conditions still to come which it is trying to bring into being' (p. 196). The assumption underpinning my project was based on the assertion that Canadian society is 'inequitably structured and dominated by a hegemonic culture that suppresses a consideration and understanding of why things are the way they are and what must be done for things to be otherwise' (p. 196).

10 Sandra Harding (1987) showed that the claim to objectivity in research has taxed both the research process as well as the research outcome. She thus called for a subjective notion of research, where the researcher and the questions she asks are always subjective; that is, they mean something to the researcher. We

end up reading the data we collect through a specific lens. This researcher therefore has always declared himself an organic part of his research. Though there was quite a considerable overlap between the mid-1990s and 2007 findings, for the sake of clarity, the focus for this paper will be on the 1990s findings.

11 To deal with issues of race and racism is to enter the chilling space of discomfort. Not to affect the student-teacher relationship, I decided not to speak with the teachers. But, elsewhere (Ibrahim, in press) I juxtaposed student narratives by talking to the only Black teacher at the school, who ended up leaving the school after a short time there. He expanded and confirmed student stories of racialization and exclusion. He had plenty of stories himself. It is worth noting here that, when I am referring to teachers' 'experiential knowledge' (or the lack thereof), I am invoking both the need for further multicultural sensitivity, especially within teacher education programs, and real life experience. Based on my teaching experience in French-language teacher education programs, I believe real life experience would be my choice in creating a higher level of multi/cultural/lingual awareness.

12 Each student pseudonym is followed by their gender, age and country of origin. I will also indicate whether the interview is individual or group or in French or English.

13 Violence is, by definition, violent, no matter the shape or form. In Bourdieu's (1991) language, however, 'symbolic violence' is no less violence or violent. It is 'symbolic' only in that it works at the psychic and intangible level. It is conceived in relation (not in opposition) to material and bodily violence. The two forms of violence, for Bourdieu, are complementary, go hand in hand, and can/do converge one into the other. (See also his notion of 'symbolic' and 'material' capital.)

14 In Ontario, there are two streams: general and academic. The former leads students either to vocation schools or community colleges, whereas the latter leads to university studies. Despite their language mastery, most African students find themselves in general level, as we shall see, which itself becomes part of their experience with the process of racialization.

15 Using Derrida's notion of 'play', Graham & Slee (2008) offer an interesting analysis on how the center/margin work. One of their main arguments is that, 'there *is no* centre but instead an *absence* of centre for which infinite substitutions are made, for there is no natural essence, origin or "invariable presence" . . . , supporting a legitimate claim to centre' (p. 284). We thus end up creating, what Graham and Slee call, discursive 'ghostly centers'; ones where there is a 'substitution of sign, substituting presence (i.e. singularity/normality/whiteness/ablebodiedness and so on) for absence (multiplicity/diversity)' (p. 284). Here, the authors add, 'privilege and position at centre is dependent upon the subjection and marginalisation of the Other,' and the 'maintenance of positions of power through discursive dividing practices as rhetorical strategies . . . that (re)secure domination and privilege results in the reinstatement of the politic of the powerful' (p. 284). I am also mindful that Hassan may have left a sense of the classic 'internalized racism', which goes something like this: If I can just be good enough, you will see I am like you, so embrace me! Hassan was too self-conscious and troubled this notion elsewhere (see Ibrahim, 2009).

16 Most of the time, Hassan had on elegant yet baggy clothes, bordering on Hip-Hop and dominant/ 'regular' clothes. Hassan was one of the most popular and elegant students at the school. He was the student Council President for two years and one of the most articulate students at the school. He was invited many times to school board meetings to address African youth concerns.

References

Althusser, L. (1971) *Lenin and Philosophy* (London, New Left Books).
Bhabha, H. (1994) *The Location of Culture* (London & New York, Routledge).
Bourdieu, P. (1991) *Language and Symbolic Power* (Cambridge, MA, Harvard University Press).
Dei, G., James, I., Karumanchery, L., James-Wilson, S. & Zine, J. (2000) *Removing the Margins: The Challenges and Possibilities of Inclusive Schooling* (Toronto, Canadian Scholars' Press).
Deleuze, G. & Guattari, F. (1994) *What Is Philosophy?* (London, Verso).
Derrida, J. (1996) *Monolingualism of the Other, or, The Prosthesis of Origin* (Stanford, CA, Stanford University Press).
Derrida, J. (2000) *Of Hospitality* (Stanford, CA, Stanford University Press).
Foucault, M. (1979) *Discipline and Punish: The Birth of the Prison* (New York, Vintage Books).
Freire, P. (2000) *Pedagogy of the Oppressed* (New York, Continuum).
Glissant, E. (1981) *Le discours antillais* (Paris, Seuil).
Graham, L. & Slee, R. (2008) An Illusory Interiority: Interrogating the Discourse/s of Inclusion, *Educational Philosophy and Theory*, 40:2, pp. 277–294.
Haney-Lopez, I. (2006) *White by Law: The Legal Construction of Race* (New York, New York University Press).
Harding, S. (1987) Is There a Feminist Method?, in: S. Harding (ed.), *Feminism and Methodology* (Bloomington, IN, Indiana University Press), pp. 1–14.
Heller, M. (1994) *Crosswords: Language, Education and Ethnicity in French Ontario* (Berlin and New York, Mouton de Gruyter).
Heller, M. (2006) *Linguistic Minorities and Modernity: A Sociolinguistic Ethnography* (London, Continuum).
Heller, M. (with the collaboration of Campbell, M., Dalley, P. & Patrick, D.) (1999) *Linguistic Minorities and Modernity: A Sociolinguistic Ethnography* (London & New York, Longman).
Ibrahim, A. (1999) Becoming Black: Rap and hip Hop, Race, Gender, Identity, and the Politics of ESL Learning, *TESOL Quarterly*, 33:3, pp. 349–369.
Ibrahim, A. (2004) One Is not Born Black: Becoming and the Phenomenon(ology) of Race, *Philosophical Studies in Education*, 35, pp. 89–97.
Ibrahim, A. (2005) The Question of the Question Is the Foreigner: Towards an Economy of Hospitality, *Journal of Curriculum Theorizing*, 21:2, pp. 149–162.
Ibrahim, A. (2008) The New *Flâneur*: Subaltern Cultural Studies, African Youth in Canada, and the Semiology of in-Betweenness, *Cultural Studies*, 22:2, pp. 234–253.
Ibrahim, A. (2009) Operating Under Erasure: Race/Language/Identity, in: A. Ryuko & A. Lin (eds), *Race, Language and Identity* (London & New York, Routledge), pp. 176–194.
Ibrahim, A. (in press) '*Hey, Whassup Homeboy?' Becoming Black: Hip-Hop Culture and Language, Race, Performativity, and the Politics of Identity in High School* (Toronto, University of Toronto Press).
James, C. & Shadd, A. (2001) *Talking about Identity: Encounters in Race, Ethnicity, and Language* (Toronto, Between the Lines).
McIntosh, P. (1998) White Privilege: Unpacking the Invisible Knapsack, in: P. Rothenberg (ed.), *Race, Class, and Gender in the United States* (New York, St. Martin's Press), pp. 165–169.

Mensah, J. (2002) *Black Canadians: History, Experiences, Social Conditions* (Halifax, Fernwood).

Mishra, V. (2005) What Was Postcolonialism, *New Literary History*, 36:3, pp. 102–119.

Mougeon, R. & Beniak, E. (1989) *Le Français Canadien Parlé Hors Québec: Aperçu Sociolinguistique* (Québec, Presses de l'Université Laval).

Mougeon, R. & Beniak, E. (1991) *Linguistic Consequences of Language Contact and Restriction: The Case of French in Ontario, Canada* (Oxford, Oxford University Press).

Nelson, C. & Nelson, C. (Eds.) (2004) *Racism Eh? A Critical Inter-Disciplinary Anthology on Race in the Canadian context* (Toronto, Captus University Press).

Ogbu, J. & Fordham, S. (1986) Black Students' School Success: Coping with the 'Burden of Acting White', *The Urban Review*, 18:3, pp. 98–116.

Rampton, B. (1995) *Crossing: Language and Ethnicity Among Adolescents* (London & New York, Longman).

Salih, T. (1991) *Season of Migration to the North* (Nairobi, Heinemann).

Simon, R. I. & Dippo, D. (1986) On Critical Ethnography Work, *Anthropology & Education Quarterly*, 17, pp. 195–202.

Spivak, G. (1999) *A Critique of Postcolonial Reason: Toward a History of the Vanishing Present* (Cambridge, MA, Harvard University Press).

StatCan.gc.ca (2008) Statistics Canada Website.

Todd, S. (2003) *Learning from the Other: Levinas, Psychoanalysis, and Ethical Possibilities in Education* (Albany, NY, State University of New York Press).

Winant, H. (2004) *The New Politics of Race: Globalism, Difference, Justice* (Minneapolis, MN, University of Minnesota Press).

Yon, D. (2000) *Elusive Culture: Schooling, Race, and Identity in Global Times* (Albany, NY, State University of New York Press).

Chapter 7

Audience Matters

Teaching Issues of Race and Racism for a Predominantly Minority Student Body

Julie E. Maybee

Editors' introduction

This 2011 essay by Julie Maybee discusses how to teach critical race theory (CRT) to predominantly minority university students. As such, the article provides a critical response to past research, by Zeus Leonardo and others, which typically focuses on teaching about white privilege to white students. As Maybee notes, Leonardo recommends an educational focus on white 'domination' rather than 'privilege', to center the harmful experiences and results of white supremacy for people of color, as 'privilege' sounds comparatively innocuous, showcasing merely positives for white people. However, this approach still foregrounds the educational experiences and needs of white students, while it also appears to presume that for students of color, white domination is an effective focal point. In this context, Maybee discusses her experiences as a white woman teaching ethnic and racial minority students about CRT and race and racism in the United States. As Maybee describes, CRT and related concepts of white domination and structural racism are not intuitive to most of her students. She thus reflects here on how race and racism are and are not experienced as such by black and other racial and ethnic minority youth in the United States, against the assumptions of many antiracist educators. Maybee observes that some of her students do not see themselves in the stereotypes of black Americans, but still accept those stereotypes, while they live in racial and ethnic enclaves which preclude their witnessing of racial exclusions and discrimination. The essay thus foregrounds the experiences of black and ethnic minority youth in learning about race and racism in higher education, with important implications for a broader understanding of how these phenomena operate in relation to varied members of society, going beyond simple black/white binaries.

Some of the literature about teaching issues of race and racism in classrooms has addressed matters of audience—questions about the racial or ethnic make-up of the student audience. Zeus Leonardo, for example, has used questions about audience to argue that teachers should use the language of white domination, rather than white privilege, in their classrooms when teaching about race and racism. While the discourse of white privilege speaks to a white audience, he argues, the discourse of white domination speaks to a minority audience, and is therefore more liberatory.

DOI: 10.4324/9781003346104-8

However, Leonardo's argument is largely based on thinking about an imaginary audience. Indeed, there is little discussion in the literature about teaching these issues to an audience that is in fact predominantly minority. In this paper, I address some of the specific challenges I have faced teaching theories of white domination to a predominantly minority student audience in New York City. In my experience, Leonardo is right that audience matters, but audience turns out to matter in ways that defy common assumptions—assumptions that Leonardo makes, and that I, too, had made before I began teaching these students. Seeing *how* audience has mattered, I argue, requires a close examination of the social positions of the students in their local contexts, given the history of racial and ethnic relations within the United States.

Leonardo argues that teachers who are interested in a critical pedagogy of race should aim their classes at an imaginary, predominantly minority audience—whether or not their audience is in fact predominantly minority—by using the discourse of white domination, rather than the discourse of white privilege. He suggests that using the language of white privilege in classrooms is flawed because it presupposes and serves the interests of an imaginary white audience. '[T]here is a difference', as he puts it, 'between analyzing whiteness with an imagined white audience against an imagined audience of color' (Leonardo, 2004, p. 141). Unlike the discourse of white privilege, he argues, the discourse of white domination takes its projected audience to be racial minorities (whether or not this is actually the case), and is therefore a more honest and liberatory pedagogy. The discourse of white privilege is perhaps best represented by the classic article by Peggy McIntosh, in which she examined ways in which she benefited from being white—benefits that were largely invisible to her, she said, before she began to compare her own whiteness to the various forms of privilege that men experience because of their gender (McIntosh, 1992). However, Leonardo argues, because talk of white privilege emphasizes supposedly invisible, unearned advantages of whites, it hides the fact that whites are the active agents of racial domination, and it obscures the real processes of racial domination that are ongoing and constantly reinforced and reestablished by whites, even today (Leonardo, 2004, p. 143). The discourse of white privilege also obscures the investment that whites have in the pedagogy of white supremacy, Leonardo argues. While people of color must create counter-discourses to maintain their humanity in the face of a system of white domination which functions in part by dehumanizing them, white students need the discourse of color-blindness or invisible racial privilege to maintain *their* sense of humanity (Leonardo, 2004, p. 144).There seem to be two ways in which whites are invested in the discourse of invisible racial privilege, for Leonardo. First, the white culture itself is founded on a *white* notion of humanity—a notion of humanity that is centered in or defined by and justifies the humanity (and humane-ness) of whites. Second, whites benefit from the discourse of color-blindness insofar as they get to go on ignoring the history of white atrocities that lead people of color to wonder whether whites are civilized or human at all. Because talk of white privilege hides the active role of whites in recreating the system of racial privilege and reinforces whites' sense of humanity, it provides a way of talking about race and racism that whites will find more palatable. Its projected audience is therefore whites. Talk of white privilege speaks to a white audience and 'white imagination' (Leonardo, 2004, p. 142). Leonardo's criticism of the language of white privilege, then, is grounded in an argument about the imaginary audience that is implied by that way of talking about race and racism.

Leonardo also addresses questions about teaching race and racism to real audiences, rather than just imaginary ones. He suggests, for instance, that there may be advantages to the discourse of white privilege when the audience is in fact white. The discourse of white privilege can make whites more receptive to the message, and it limits the guilt that can block critical reflection on the part of whites who end up worrying excessively about 'looking racist', rather than engaging in the project of understanding the structures of racism (Leonardo, 2004, p. 140). However, he argues, the discourse of white privilege reinforces white supremacy and white racial domination by hiding or leaving unspoken the *process of domination*, or the ways in which whites actively work at dominating people of color (Leonardo, 2004, p. 137). Moreover, Leonardo suggests, catering to the white point of view slows real racial progress. As Leonardo puts it, the discourse of white privilege caters to a worldview that 'refuses certain truths about race relations' and, as a result, 'proceeds at the snail's pace of the white imaginary' (Leonardo, 2004, p. 141). Even when the audience is in fact white, then, Leonardo argues, teachers should use the language of white domination rather than white privilege.[1]

When Leonardo turns his attention to teaching an audience that is minority, he makes what seems to be a perfectly reasonable assumption—an assumption that I, too, had made, when I first began teaching these issues to a predominantly minority student body. Leonardo suggests that minority students need little convincing about the reality of white domination (Leonardo, 2004, pp. 142–143, 150). The radical writings on white privilege are new or insightful only to white audiences who read mainly white authors. Contrary to those white audiences, he says, '[b]lack women know that their skin color does not match store-bought bandages' (Leonardo, 2004, p. 142). (One of the privileges mentioned by McIntosh is that her skin matches the color of supposedly 'flesh colored' bandages.) And, Leonardo suggests, 'Latinos know their language is not spoken by management in most business places, and Asians know that their history rarely achieves the status of . . . "official knowledge" in schools' (Leonardo, 2004, p. 142).[2] But, I would like to argue, while blacks, Latinos and Asians may know these truths in one sense, they do not necessarily connect these truths to systems of white, racial domination. That bandages are pinkish can be rationalized as merely a function of the fact that most consumers in the US happen to be white. The dominance of English can be rationalized as merely a function of the fact that the US is an English-speaking country. In other words, minority students do not necessarily *see* or *experience* these instances as signs of an embedded and intractable system of racial domination. The claim that racial domination is integral to the United States or built into its systems and institutions is something my minority students do not always see or want to believe. Of course, as Leonardo readily admits—and as he says Freire and Fanon have warned—oppressed people, as individuals, do not necessarily possess a correct or true understanding of racial oppression (Leonardo, 2004, p. 141). In my teaching of a predominantly minority student body, however, I have had to take seriously the *reasons* why my students resist claims about white domination, and I have had to think about teaching strategies that meet those reasons.

One might think that there is a simple explanation for the students' resistance to my teaching about white domination. I, after all, am a white woman. Housee has suggested that the ethnicity of the instructor matters. She argues that students of color object to having white lecturers teach race and racism modules because white lecturers, more or less by definition, cannot bring the lived experience of antiblack racism into the classroom (Housee, 2008, p. 418). My own experience suggests that Housee is right, but I believe that my whiteness nevertheless does not ultimately explain the students' resistance. During graduate school, I met and later married an African American man. Once I met my future husband and 'voted with [my] heart', I became a student of race issues in America from a new point of view. This education has been slow.[3] As other white people have pointed out, the road from being 'white' to being . . . something else—a path that is ultimately never 'finished' or 'done with', but always 'in process'—is fraught with misunderstanding and resistance (Allen, 2004; Leonardo, 2004; McIntosh, 1992),[4] and my own path was no different. The first course I ever designed was a course on philosophy and race, which was a reflection of a desire to share the lessons on race that I had been learning with my (mostly white) students. While the audience has changed, my proximity to my black husband and children means that, unlike most whites, I do in fact have personal experience with antiblack racism that I can bring to the classroom. At Lehman, I have always known and accepted that I would have to win the students over every semester—to earn their respect, as someone who has 'a *real* understanding of racism' (Housee, 2008, p. 417), and their trust, as someone who has the genuine interests of students of color at heart. Housee is right—my students of color do at first resist my teaching about race and racism. But while I do not tell the students about my family until later in the semester (some of my stories are a little hard to explain without the personal details),[5] I have plenty of stories about concrete examples of racism that I have personally observed. The students also come to know whose side I'm on, and that race and racism are not merely intellectual exercises for me, or not just 'the stuff of books' (Housee, 2008, p. 417).[6] I can thereby show the students, to use Housee's words, that I 'feel it' (Housee, 2008, p. 416). I talk openly about my process of learning about racism as a white person, as well as the ways in which I benefit from being white. I am very careful to admit that I do not experience race and racism *as* a person of color, and that I cannot *speak* as a person of color. Still, since students of color often use silence as a strategy of resistance toward white teachers (and toward white students in the class, though, in our classes, there are few white students) (Housee, 2008, p. 418; Wagner, 2005, p. 265), I can generally tell when I have won them over by their enthusiastic participation during classes.

Sadly, my whiteness may actually turn out to be an advantage. Once (or if) I succeed in convincing the students that I 'feel it', I may come to have a kind of heroic status. Unlike an instructor of color—who would be expected by students of color to 'feel it'—my 'feeling' racism may make me look extraordinary, special, or perhaps even 'heroic'. Although I certainly do not deserve such an image, I fear it may be another of the many, unfortunate benefits that accrues to whites.[7]

I was hired by Lehman College specifically to teach 'multicultural' philosophy, and I arrived at my new job eager to bring my teaching to a new audience. Using the standard racial categories from the national census, in the fall of 2006, the undergraduate student body at Lehman College was 47.9% Hispanic, 32.6% black, and 4.3% Asian/Pacific Islander. Only 10.3% of students were identified as white/non-Hispanic (Lehman College, 2007). Although I had had many good experiences at predominantly white institutions teaching issues of race and racism to students who took my courses by choice—even courses that were otherwise advertised as 'regular' philosophy courses—I had had more problems with students in lower-level, introductory, 'required' philosophy courses. As others have pointed out, whites have the strongest investment in race—psychologically and otherwise—and the most to lose economically and politically if the structure of racial advantage and disadvantage is dismantled. As Leonardo understatedly puts it, 'consequently, convincing them to appropriate racial analysis for their own lives *runs into difficulties*' (Leonardo, 2004, p. 143; emphasis added). As Leonardo suggests, whites (and hence white students) often have to be convinced of 'the first fact of racial analysis; mainly, that white domination is a reality' (Leonardo, 2004, p. 143 [cf. p. 150]). I was sure that teaching students at Lehman College would be a relief. At least, I thought to myself—as Leonardo suggests—I would not have to work to convince them that racism still exists. I set about designing a course in 'Contemporary Moral Issues' that revolved completely around issues of social justice—primarily around issues of race, but I also included readings on class and gender. The course is one course on a menu of required courses that all students have to take to get their degrees. The only required textbook for my class was Derrick Bell's *Faces at the Bottom of the Well: The Permanence of Racism* (1992)—one of the central, popular texts in critical race theory (CRT), which is perhaps the most influential branch of scholarship that explores the concept and practice of white domination. I managed to use it as a launching point for discussions of all the usual suspects in a course on applied ethics.[8] I was convinced that my new students would be just as relieved to be taught by someone who had learned to see some of the contours of race and racism as I would be to be teaching students who would not have to be convinced that racism still exists. But I was wrong. There were some students who were excited by my approach, but I encountered much more resistance from my new audience than I thought I would.

One way to gain entry into one source of my student's resistance to CRT is through existentialism. Existentialism has had its own turn as a theory of pedagogy. One of the tenets that emerged from existentialist pedagogy is the idea that teachers should start 'where the children are' (Kaelin, 1966, p. 171). E. F. Kaelin warns us against using this dictum to fall into what he disparagingly calls 'a disease known as "over-determination"' (Kaelin, 1966, p. 172). According to this 'disease', we start 'where the children are' by finding out a few things about their backgrounds, attaching a few categories to those backgrounds, and then using generalizations or stereotypes to draw some conclusions about what the students or their values are like. Because this process involves applying nearly-essentialist stereotypes or generalizations, this sort of existentialist pedagogy, Kaelin suggests, ironically starts out by raising a question about the lived humanity of our students, but ends up with an answer that 'is inhuman in that it has been essentialized out of its existence' (Kaelin, 1966, p. 172). As I will argue, many of my students come from racial and ethnic enclaves in New York City in which the Western European culture is not dominant, and in which they may not meet enough overt racism or ethnic discrimination to become acutely aware of white domination, and this fact sometimes makes it harder for me to motivate an interest in CRT and other theories of white domination.

Indeed, I first became aware of the importance of my students' cultural differences when I was teaching existentialism—not as a pedagogy, but as a philosophy.[9] There is actually a great deal of similarity between some of the claims made by CRT and some of those made by existentialism. Marvin Lynn has suggested that CRT is committed to five main tenets: (1) that the legal system is inherently unfair with respect to race, (2) that race is central to and racism is intransigent in American society, (3) that we should reject European and modernist pretenses to neutrality, objectivity, rationality and universality in favor of an emphasis on subjectivity, (4) that critiques of race and racism must rely heavily on the experiential knowledge of people of color, and (5) that the examination must be interdisciplinary (Lynn, 2004, pp. 155–156).Two, and perhaps three, of these tenets are arguably shared—though, of course, often without the emphasis on race—by many existentialists, namely, (3) that we should reject European and modernist claims of neutrality, objectivity, rationality and universality—at least in the forms in which those values were traditionally defended—in favor of subjectivity, (4) that we should rely heavily on experiential knowledge, on knowledge generated from the point of view of the existing person, and, even, perhaps, (5) that our studies must be interdisciplinary in today's sense.

Bernard Murchland has examined what he takes to be the main reasons why students at many institutions are readily attracted to courses in existentialism. Murchland argues that students (he does not distinguish the students by race) are attracted to existentialism because it deals with traditional questions—'questions about the emotions and values, about excellence and psychic integrity, about action and faith' (Murchland, 1977, p. 227). Murchland suggests that students enjoy the humanism of existentialism and its effective criticism of what he calls 'cognitive rationality' (Murchland, 1977, p. 228). Murchland argues that students are attracted, for instance, to Kierkegaard's emphasis on maturing the personality rather than cultivating the mind or intellect, along with his emphasis on passion, on conviction and commitment, on subjectivity, and on the moral ideals of a choosing, human being. As Murchland puts it, Kierkegaard's 'arguments for the primacy of subjectivity are a heady antidote to the cognitive restraints they experience in their own education' (Murchland, 1977, p. 231). Moreover, students 'readily transpose

Kierkegaard's battles against the rationalists into their own felt dissatisfaction with the bits and scraps of information that in most cases constitutes their educational experience' (Murchland, 1977, p. 231). According to Murchland, students are attracted to Nietzsche's emphasis on wholeness and self-creation, on the way in which we confer meaning on the world, on his tragic optimism in a world that is constantly in flux, and to his critique of the Socratic model of the person as a logical, calculating machine (Murchland, 1977, pp. 232–236). Murchland suggests that students are most attracted to Sartre's emphasis on the political implications of freedom—Sartre's interest in 'reducing the repressive circumstance of social life'—and on Sartre's theory of the emotions (Murchland, 1977, p. 237).[10] Murchland argues that existentialism appeals to students as a traditional humanism that gives voice to their interest in freedom as they are being prepared to be consigned to the corporate order, insofar as they are victims of 'enfeebled initiation rites', and insofar as they 'are not given adequate outlets for their emotions' or able 'to dream the large dreams appropriate to their age' (Murchland, 1977, p. 240). As Murchland puts it, '[e]xistentialism tells them, quite simply: be free and design a spiritually satisfying life' (Murchland, 1977, p. 240).

There is an aspect of existentialism that Murchland's analysis mentions but does not fully consider, however, that I think helps to explain the appeal of existentialism—at least to a predominantly white student audiences—as well as one of the difficulties that I have teaching existentialism to a predominantly minority student body. As Murchland mentions, Kierkegaard, Nietzsche and Sartre—along with other existentialists—were critics of 'our age', of Western culture, of the *culture* of 'cognitive rationality', to use Murchland's term (Murchland, 1977, p. 228). Kierkegaard is criticizing the lack of passion, commitment and so on that he takes to be part of the European culture that he lives in. Nietzsche's attack on the mono-theism of Socratic rationality is part of an attack on Western, European culture. Sartre's attack on the standpoint of 'seriousness' is also an attack on the dominant, European culture of his day. I think that young white students are attracted in part to this *cultural* critique, and to the alternative approach to life that it represents for them. It appeals to their adolescent and post-adolescent rebelliousness. In the same way that their rebelliousness leads them to adopt black music and the trappings of blackness as teenagers,[11] right before they go on to take their parents' places in the culture of whites and the system of whiteness,[12] so they enjoy a moment of rebelliousness—through existentialism—against the culture of 'cognitive rationality', right before they take their parents' places in that culture.

Because many of my students live in racial and ethnic enclaves in which the European culture of 'cognitive rationalism' does not dominate, I find I must begin my existentialism classes by teaching the culture of 'cognitive rationalism' *before* I teach existentialism. I start out with lectures about the standard targets of existentialist critique—Plato and Aristotle, Kant, and Hegel, for instance—and the (over)emphasis by these writers (so the existentialists charge) on universal concepts and on the eternalized, rational, anti-emotional human being. Eternal universalism, rationalism, and anti-emotionalism are not values that tend to be emphasized in African

American, African, Caribbean, or Latino cultures. Many of these cultures already resist the dominant white culture in ways similar to existentialism.[13] They value emotions and an attention to lived perspectives and experiences. They value wisdom over 'book learning', passion and empathy over disembodied disinterestedness, and engagement and commitment over objective disengagement. The students are often sympathetic to existentialism in the sense that they already share many of the anti-Western or anti-modernist values that existentialists support.[14] But, because they do not belong to the dominant Western culture, they have trouble seeing existentialism's force as a philosophy critical of Western culture. The students are therefore not attracted to it as an alternative approach to life, or as an expression of rebelliousness.

The fact that my students come from minority-dominated sub-cultures and ethnic enclaves may also explain in part why some students find it hard to entertain the tenets of CRT and theories of white domination. Students who live in racial and ethnic enclaves dominated by sub-cultures that shape their everyday lives and yet resist the values and norms of the European/American culture, may be less aware or conscious of the *dominance* of the European/American culture. Lehman College (as well as their earlier middle and high schools) may be one of the few sites in which they come face to face with the European/American culture, and, even here, because the student population is predominantly minority, it is unclear how acutely they may *feel* the dominance of the European/American culture when at Lehman.[15]

Indeed, some of my students report that they are not aware of much racism in their daily lives. For the same reason that the wages of whiteness (to use W.E.B. Du Bois' term) or white privilege are often invisible to whites—namely, because racism does not happen to whites—the disadvantages of being colored may often be invisible to minorities—because white privilege does not happen to people of color. Leonardo may be right to criticize a pedagogy grounded in discourses of white privilege, but it is also *true* that the privileges of whiteness are often invisible to whites. Whites do not go to the store and notice, for example, that employees are *not* watching them. For individual whites, not being followed around in the store is normal. Whites assume that everyone else gets the same treatment. It seems to me that individual people of color also often do not read their own treatment as a function of racism. My husband, for instance, assumed that everyone who purchased video games at a local Target store had to pay for the game first, and then pick the game up at customer service—until he found out that I had repeatedly been allowed to carry video games and other expensive video game equipment all over the store before paying at the cash register. Only after my husband and I traded stories about the way we were treated did he 'notice' that he had been '*targeted*' all right—almost certainly because of his race. Students who live in racial and ethnic enclaves in which all the customers are people of color may be even less likely to read the treatment they receive as racially coded. To the degree that a store targets members of racial minorities, in neighborhoods dominated by racial minorities, all of the customers may receive largely the same treatment. *All* of the post offices have bullet-proof plexi-glass between the customer and the postal agent. These students would have to be familiar with how 'other people live' and what post offices are like out in the suburbs to regard their own treatment as abnormal or strange.[16]

I readily admit that the claims of some of my students that they do not experience much racial oppression is hard to square with some of the social science research reporting that students of color in New York City are acutely aware of the ways in which they are stereotyped by race and gender (Lopez, 2002). Some of my students do report being racially profiled and treated as hoodlums by police officers and service personnel in stores (cf. Lopez, 2002).[17] Nevertheless, a significant number of students report having little awareness of overt racial discrimination. I cannot explain these claims, other than by reference, in part, to the ways in which the *racial* nature of racial discrimination is often hidden from the victims of that discrimination, especially, perhaps, for those people who live in certain racial and ethnic enclaves, as many of my students do. Nevertheless, the radically different reports I get from different students about their encounters with racism taught me that students of color are not a monolithic group, and forced me to abandon my hypothesis—and Leonardo's—that I would not have to convince at least some minority students of the existence and persistence of racism. The reports also made me think about *why* and *how* I had to convince those minority students to consider seriously theories such as CRT and the concept of white domination.

Some of the students' resistance is undoubtedly a function of what Leonardo calls 'whiteness' itself. 'Whiteness' is what Leonardo dubs the system of institutional, racial domination that is usually based on skin color (Leonardo, 2002, p. 32). If some of my students do not encounter white domination in their everyday lives very often, they do watch some English-language television and movies, and they are therefore subjected to some of the messages from the system of 'whiteness' that everyone else is exposed to.[18] But students will not necessarily recognize those messages as racial, because the messages are not coded as 'white'. As Bell, Leonardo and many others have observed, one of the ways in which whiteness dominates is that it dresses its messages up as universals. As Leonardo puts it, 'domination means that the referents of discourse are particulars dressed up as universals, of the white race speaking for the human race' (Leonardo, 2004, p. 139). Indeed, the fact that the messages of white domination are often hidden behind or dressed up as claims that are neutral, objective, rational and universal has led critical race theorists—like many existentialists—to call for the rejection of Western European or modernist claims of neutrality and so on, in favor of the subjective experiences of people of color. The trouble is, of course, that, as I discovered, the subjective experiences of people of color do not always agree with analyses of racism. Many students have little patience, for example, for the view defended by Robert Gooding-Williams in his article 'Disney in Africa and the Inner City: On race and space in *The Lion King*' (1995). Gooding-Williams argues that the original Disney movie, *The Lion King*, reinforces the European colonial mentality and racism in the US. He suggests that the movie supports the colonial mentality, for example, by reinforcing the European colonial tendency to view

Africa as a vast land with no people in it; and it reinforces racism by coding the 'bad guys'—the hyenas and the bad lion, Scar—as residents of inner-city neighborhoods. Because Scar and the hyenas are portrayed as evil, Gooding-Williams suggests, the movie reinforces the white 'blame-the-victim' message that people of color are responsible for their own plight and teaches young viewers to understand the conditions and exclusion of inner city residents as a function of the moral depravity of those residents themselves (Gooding-Williams, 1995). Many of my minority students think Gooding-Williams is (and I am, insofar as I agree with him) *crazy*. 'It's just a movie', they tell me, 'you are reading too much into it'.

Students sometimes have a similar reaction to the claims of CRT. For some of them, CRT's claim that racism is a permanent and intransigent feature of the United States is just crazy too. I have found that the best way to overcome this response on the part of students is to provide an argument for the claim. Critical race theory (CRT) was a response in part to critical legal theory, which had its roots in a Marxist-inspired, class analysis of the legal system.[19] While CRT rejects critical legal theory's (over)emphasis on class along with Marxist claims that racial subordination can be completely explained by class domination, there is an important element of the Marxist analysis and the analysis provided by critical legal theory that CRT does not reject. CRT is, like Marxism, a systems-focused theory. Just as Marx argued that class oppression was built into the system of capitalism, and therefore could never be addressed by piecemeal reform,[20] so CRT suggests that racial oppression is built into the very system and institutions of the United States, and will therefore not be addressed or eliminated by piecemeal reforms of the sort that we saw during the civil rights movement. Derrick Bell has suggested, for example, that the United States uses racism against blacks in various ways to survive as a nation. For instance, racism is used as a way to maintain a sense of unity (among non-blacks, of course) in an otherwise pluralistic population, and as a way to reduce tension during times of economic pressure, when blacks are scapegoated as the cause of economic problems that really have roots in the workings of capitalism. It is because Bell regards racism as integral to the social, political and economic system that he sees racism as a permanent feature of the US. Since the US needs racism to survive, he suggests, racism will never go away. Racism merely morphs or reinvents itself to meet new historical conditions or needs (Bell, 1992).[21]

I have found that highlighting the systemic approach of CRT and drawing connections between CRT and Marxism as 'systems theories' provides an argument for CRT that helps my students find CRT's claim that racism is a permanent feature of the United States and more general claims about systems of white domination more plausible. I think the connections to Marxism may be particularly helpful because, if some of my students may be less aware of racial subordination, many of them seem to be acutely aware of class subordination. Television and movies show day in and day out the consumer goods and lifestyle that the students' lack of money prevents them from having. Most of the students are also acutely aware of the lack of power that they have had as employees. They can therefore be highly sympathetic toward Marxist claims about the degree to which they are oppressed by their lack of economic power and resources in relation to the economically elite. I can sometimes use this sympathy and the connections between CRT and Marxism to motivate sympathy for claims about systems of white domination.

Nevertheless, as Leonardo remarks, some students of color can live out their lives in whiteness, or convinced by the messages of whiteness (Leonardo, 2002, p. 31). To the degree that my students absorb some of the hidden messages of whiteness from popular culture, they may well be committed to whiteness. Some of my students tell me they are committed, for example, to American individualism, which preaches that anyone in America can succeed though hard work and dedication and therefore fails to acknowledge the ways in which group-politics have been used by whites for centuries to disadvantage and exploit non-whites. Moreover, like many whites, as the discussion of Gooding-Williams above suggests, my students often accept the messages of popular (white) culture that racism is a thing of the past, or is limited primarily to radically racist, white groups such as the Ku Klux Klan (cf. Leonardo, 2004, p. 143). To the degree that my students are committed to these and other messages of whiteness, they often resist CRT's claim that racism or white domination is an institutional structure that is deeply embedded in, and a permanent feature of, the US. Even though *we* may say that their resistance is grounded in whiteness—because whiteness hides behind a discourse of objectivity and universality—the students themselves do not recognize their commitments to individualism or to the claim that racism is a thing of the past as instances of white domination.

The resistance to CRT on the part of some of my students can also be traced to factors that require us to think about the biographies of the students in even more detail. Many of my students are more conservative than you might expect. Some of the older African American students and students who are recent immigrants have little patience with economic or other 'excuses', so they say, for what they regard as the bad behavior of some blacks and Latinos. Some of my older black students, for example, complain about the laziness of young blacks who do not want to go to school or get jobs. These older students were often raised in the tradition of the intellectual activism of black scholars—W.E.B. Du Bois, Richard Wright, James Baldwin—as well as in the civil rights struggle for a better education for blacks. Although critical race theorists such as Bell are skeptical about the success of school desegregation in ending racism in education,[22] blacks fought for school desegregation because they were committed to improving educational opportunities for blacks. Whether or not desegregation worked, they were committed to education and intellectual pursuits. Some older students have little patience for what they say is the tendency of some young blacks to regard being an intellectual as 'acting white'. One student once asked, 'since when did being black mean having to be stupid?'. Even some younger students have little patience with what they see as complaints about racism. As one of my colleagues at Lehman put it to me, some students are 'tired' of complaints about and talking about racism. 'Get over it', is their attitude.[23] Of course, we must also keep in mind that the students at Lehman belong in one way to an elite group. They made it to college, after all. Because they made it—sometimes by having to work very hard and fight incredible odds—they may be less sympathetic toward those blacks and Latinos who do not.

Moreover, because our students often live in the same neighborhoods as some of the blacks and Latinos who engage in illicit activity, they observe and are sometimes the victims of that illicit activity. As a result, these students often have a strong 'law-and-order' attitude. Some of them wish the police would do a *better* job of controlling crime in their neighborhoods, and they have little sympathy for the people who commit the crimes. One of my older black students agreed that she was what I jokingly called an 'equal-opportunity bigot'. She did not have much love for white people, but she did not like those blacks who, she suggested, live up to the stereotypes of blacks held by whites—blacks who she thought were lazy, did not go to school or work, were criminals, had babies they did not look after properly, and so on. Since most of the black and Latino citizens in these students' neighborhoods are law-abiding, some of these students see the criminals in their neighborhoods as just criminals. For some of my students, claims about the effects of racism are just excuses offered by bleeding-heart liberals for the bad behavior of criminals who happen to be black and Latino.

Some recent immigrants who would be identified by whites as 'black' also often have little sympathy for some of the claims of CRT. These 'blacks' sometimes resist CRT's claims about the structural and permanent nature of racism in part, I think, because they do not think of themselves as 'black'. Some of these students come from cultures in which nearly everyone is black, and in which being 'black' is not necessarily a meaningful source of identity. 'Blackness' as a category is a *white* construction, and has meaning primarily for black people who confront whiteness.[24] For many of my students who are recent immigrants from the Caribbean or from Africa, the main categories of difference and identity are often cultural or religious, rather than pseudo-biological or racial. Students identify themselves as Jamaican, Haitian, Yoruba, and so on, rather than as 'black'.[25] Moreover, because some of my students now live in ethnic enclaves within the United States, their cultural or religious—rather than racial—identities may be reinforced, especially if some of them have not yet had to confront 'whiteness' on a daily basis within the US, and so may not have developed much of a 'black' identity.

Some of these immigrants also have dim views of American 'blacks' because they accept the stereotypes that whites associate with African Americans. Like other students, these students sometimes have to contend with a criminal element within the black and Latino neighborhoods where they live, which can reinforce those dim views. In part, their dim views of American 'blacks' may be due to the dominance of 'whiteness' in the mass media, where some of them learned about what African Americans are supposedly like. These students tell me that, before coming to the US, they had the opportunity to watch *The Lion King* as well as other products of the American mass media that portray African Americans in, shall we say, a less than flattering light. I once had a student in my class who found it difficult to relate to his Haitian-born father. Unlike his father, this student had none of the markers of being Haitian. He lacked, especially, his father's, reportedly thick, Haitian accent. My student reported that his father did not identify as black. For the father, African Americans were black, and he had a dim view of African Americans. But because my student lacked the markers of foreign-ness, he was treated as—and thought of himself as—an African American. He even rejected the use of his French- based, Haitian name and used only his initials.[26] This student's father's attitude and ignorance of the son's racial consciousness helps to illustrate that some black immigrants may not identify themselves as black, and, from that point of view, have difficulty entertaining CRT's claims about the embedded and permanent anti-black racism of the US. Some of my students are more like this student's father than they are like the son. They do not want to confront the persistence of racism because they do not want to be *black*—or, at least, they do not want to be black in the United States.[27]

These immigrant students' lack of sympathy with the claims of CRT may also derive from an optimism that they have about their life chances in the US. This optimism may be grounded in their hopes, dreams and desires as recent immigrants to the United States. Many of them came to the US for improved economic or educational opportunities, or to escape various sorts of oppressions in their homelands. They are optimistic that their life-chances in the US will be better than their chances would have been in their home countries,[28] and so they resist what they tell me is the pessimism of CRT's claims about the permanence and intransigence of racism. Many new Caribbean immigrants accuse black Americans of exaggerating the effects of racism in the US (Feagin & Feagin, 2003, p. 192). The optimism of these students may also be rooted in their real experiences within the US. Black and Latino immigrants—even in predominantly African American black neighborhoods in New York City—are hired more often by white employers than are African Americans, apparently because the white employers believe that these immigrants will view low-wage jobs as a good salary (Newman, 1998, p. 251). Foreign-marked blacks, such as my student's father, may be optimistic about their life chances in the US because their life chances really are more optimistic than are the life-chances of African American blacks. At the same time, once black immigrants have been in the US for a substantial period of time, they generally experience enough discrimination to lead them to give up their view that American blacks exaggerate the effects of racism (Feagin & Feagin, 2003, p. 192). As I have argued above, however, because many of my students live in ethnic enclaves, they may not experience enough discrimination—or at least experience enough treatment from whites that they 'code' as discrimination—to lead them to abandon their optimism.

Many immigrants—even those who appear to be black—may also resist the claims of CRT because being racist against blacks is 'as American as apple pie'.[29] As Toni Morrison noted in an interview in *Time* magazine, antiblack racism has provided generations of immigrants with their passage into being an American. What one immigrant had in common with another immigrant was contempt for blacks. Morrison tells the story of a 'smart little boy' she knew in fifth grade who had just arrived in the US and did not speak English. Morrison sat next to him in school and taught him to read. 'I remember the moment he found out that I was black—a nigger', she says. 'It took him six months; he was told. And that's the moment when he belonged, that was his entrance' (Angelo, 1989, p. 120; quoted also in Bell, 1992, p. 152).[30]

Many Latino students may resist the tenets of CRT because they do not want to be colored and because they, too, are optimistic about their life chances. Many come from families and cultures that are already racist. Many of my Latino students report that their parents value light skin and 'good' hair, and would object to their marrying someone darker than themselves. The desire among many Latino groups to lighten the family by marrying lighter-skinned spouses is well documented. Ricky Lee Allen describes the preference among Latinos for white racial traits as a kind of eugenics (Allen, 2004, p. 129). We ordinarily think of eugenics as involving sterilization, but the other side of sterilization is breeding. Allen's characterization implies that the desire on the part of some Latinos to breed white racial traits into their families is an anti-black eugenics of breeding.

In any case, Latino students have the same reasons for not wanting to be colored that everyone else in America has. As Lewis Gordon has argued, anti-black racism has set up a matrix of values in the United States according to which '(1) it is best to be white, and (2) it is worst to be black' (Gordon, 1997, p. 59). Gordon argues that these two messages create a logic that 'leads to obvious conclusions of rational action. Failing to become white, one can at least increase the distance between oneself and blackness' (Gordon, 1997, p. 59). The two principles thus lead to two corresponding imperatives of racial action: '(1) be white, but, above all, (2) don't be black' (Gordon, 1997, p. 63). Gordon calls the first principle *'the principle of white supremacy'*, and the second principle *'the principle of black inferiority'* (Gordon, 1997, p. 63). Gordon argues that these imperatives lead to a lived reality in which black people are encouraged to pass for mixed (Gordon, 1997, p. 59). But the same imperatives will also lead to a lived reality in which Latinos are encouraged to pass for white, or, at least, to distance themselves from blackness. Statistics suggest that this is precisely what may be happening. As Orlando Patterson has worried, already in the last census, 48% of those people who identified themselves as 'Hispanic' also identified themselves as 'white' (Patterson, 2001). Although 42% of Hispanics identified themselves as of an 'other' race, only 2% of Hispanics identified themselves as black (US Census Bureau, 2001).

The matrix of values that Gordon discusses is reinforced by how economic rewards are distributed in the US. Non-Hispanic whites outstrip both Latinos and blacks along measures of economic success such as average household income, but Latinos as a whole outstrip blacks economically. In 1999, for example, the mean income for non-Hispanic whites was $59,696, for Hispanics was $44,250 and for blacks or African Americans was $39,877 (US Census Bureau, 2005). The median household income for Puerto Rican ($30,129), Mexican ($31,123) and Cuban Americans ($38,312) all outstripped the median household income of blacks ($29,423) (Feagin & Feagin, 2003, p. 212; US Census Bureau 2005). Latino economic success over blacks occurs even though blacks outstrip Latinos in educational achievement. In 2000, for instance, 83.6% of whites, 52.4% of Hispanics or Latinos, and 73.2% of blacks had high school diplomas; 26.1% of whites, 10.4% of Hispanics or Latinos, and 14.3% of blacks had a college degree (US Census Bureau, 2003).[31] As a result, those Latino students who are light enough to have an unclear racial identity have plenty of motivation to deny being colored or black, and hence to deny that they have to worry about racism. Moreover, because Latinos in New York City are hired more often than African American blacks (Newman, 1998, p. 251), my Latino students may be optimistic about their life chances in a way that also discourages them from taking seriously the (as they see it) pessimistic claims of CRT.

This talk about optimism and pessimism reveals that many of my students also often resist CRT's claims about the permanence of racism because they do not *want* to believe it. There are discussions in the literature about ways in which white people—and, by extension, white students—want to, and try to, deny the existence and effects of racism (cf. Dlamini, 2002, pp. 59–60; Allen, 2004, p. 129f.). Aside from the fact that both white students and some of my black and Latino students may not experience racism in their everyday lives—or, at least, may not 'read' or 'code' events that they experience as instances racism (as I discussed above)—all of the students have some good reasons for denying that there is, as CRT claims, an embedded and permanent system of racial disadvantage in the US. Whites resist the claims of CRT to maintain their advantage and sense of innocence. But in one way the tenets of CRT are less threatening to whites than they are to students of color. To draw on a point Kwame Anthony Appiah made in a different context, while a white student who studies CRT can say 'if the critical race theorist we are studying is right, and *if I were black or Latino*, then I *would* be a target of a permanent, intractable structural racism', the black and Latino student must think, 'if the theorist we are studying is right, then I *am* a target of a permanent, intractable, structural racism (cf. Appiah, 1992, p. 42). Many black and Latino students do not want to believe that the sort of racism described by CRT is out there waiting for them, especially after they have worked so hard to go to college and hope to get a degree that will get them a better-paying job most likely in a white-dominated environment.[32] No one wants to believe that the future for which they have worked so hard is destined to be cloudy, no matter what he or she does.

The fact that my students are mostly women may also explain some of the resistance I see in my classes to the tenets of CRT. In the fall of 2006, 80.9% of Lehman's undergraduate students were women (Lehman College, 2007). Research has suggested that young, minority women in New York City are more committed to education and more optimistic about their life chances than are young minority men (Lopez, 2002). Nancy Lopez suggests that the optimism of these New York City women—and the pessimism of their male counterparts—is grounded in what Lopez calls their 'race-gender experiences'. Research has shown that minority women experience fewer difficulties in finding employment because white employers find them less threatening than their male counterparts, and because the women have wider social networks to rely on in the search for employment

(Lopez, 2002, p. 79). Lopez's own research also suggests that young minority women in New York City have better experiences in schools and with other institutions of 'authority' than their male counterparts, which may also account for their support of education and optimism about their life chances. Women are targeted by the police and by school authority figures in racially stereotyped ways less than are men, although they still face stereotypes that cast them as sexually promiscuous and available. Young minority women also develop independent identities at an early age, because they are often given roles of responsibility in family life that young men are not expected to perform. And these young women develop feminist practices by watching their mothers—who are by-and-large the heads of the households—succeed (Lopez, 2002, pp. 80–82). These factors may contribute to their support of education and optimism about their life chances, which may also explain why some of my students resist the—as they see it—*pessimistic* messages of CRT about the permanence of racism.

Nevertheless, many of my women students are aware of gender discrimination, and I can sometimes get them to entertain the tenets of CRT and theories of white domination through this avenue. To the degree that they are aware of the ways in which gender is an embedded social system that has shaped their lives in ways they did not choose, I can sometimes convince them to take seriously CRT's claim that race and racism are social structures that shape the life chances of people of color in ways that would not have been chosen, if there had been better options.

Ironically, I can often reach students who find the claims of CRT overly pessimistic through an existentialist motif. Bell encourages just such a response in the book I used for my 'Contemporary Moral Issues' class, *Faces at the Bottom of the Well*. As many existentialists might preach, liberation and freedom do not come from some ultimate or final victory, but from the process of struggle. What defines us and makes us free is the commitment to identities, to causes, to the process of self-creation. We do not need to win, to win. Bell emphasizes that those who accept CRT will find their fulfillment not in some elusive victory, but in the struggle for racial justice itself (Bell, 1992, pp. 46, 98). He describes being surprised when he was a civil rights lawyer in the south by how many blacks were willing to take significant risks to support the desegregation of schools in the face of white threats of economic and other violence. When he asked Mrs Biona Mac-Donald where she and other black families 'found the courage to continue working for civil rights', as Bell puts it, Mrs MacDonald responded, in part, 'I lives to harass white folks' (Bell, 1992, p. xii). As Bell explains, she did not expect to win. Instead, Mrs. MacDonald found fulfillment and meaning in the struggle itself, and Bell encourages his readers—and I encourage my students—to do the same.

For some students who resist CRT's claim that racism persists and is an integral feature of the US, the study of CRT proves to be a life-changing experience. I have met many young people of color who are ashamed because they believe that the history of slavery and racism prove that members of minority groups are inferior, and I have found motivation in a desire to break that shame. The teacher does not have to be me, and does not have to be white, but I try to be one person who teaches students of color what I have fought to instill in my own children: a sense of history and pride in the struggle, and an ability to see through the propaganda. For those students who previously saw the economically disadvantaged condition of blacks only through the lens of white stereo types as rooted in laziness and irresponsible behavior, entertaining the thought that the condition of blacks is rooted in and caused by systems and structures of racism can be liberating. What they had previously taken to be a source of racial shame is recast for some of these students as a source of racial pride and anger. After all, CRT's insistence on the intractable permanence of racism is only one side of the theory's program. Critical race theorists also stress the way in which blacks and other people of color have been, as Ricky Lee Allen puts it, 'the ingenious survivors of 500 years of white supremacy and, as a result, the upholders of true humanity' (Allen, 2004, p. 127). In my classes, I repeatedly highlighted a passage in Bell's book in which one of his white characters points out that 'slavery . . . tried to dehumanize blacks, and failed, and didn't try to dehumanize whites, but succeeded' (Bell, 1992, p. 94 (cf. p. 46)). Bell does not provide an argument for this claim, but I had my students construct one as a philosophical exercise. I think that some of my students' are resistant to the tenets of CRT because they are ashamed of belonging to a race that has been oppressed. Because the positive program of CRT recasts this shame as a source of pride and cause for anger— anger that must be employed to fight back against white domination—these students can ultimately find the tenets of CRT liberating.[33]

Notes

1 Leonardo's position is controversial. First, a good deal of the literature suggests that one should not focus on white supremacy too quickly when teaching issues of race and racism to 'privileged' (in this case, white) learners, but rather that talk of white supremacy should 'constitute the final cognitive task for privileged learners, not the first' (Curry-Stevens, 2007, p. 49). Curry-Stevens (2007), for instance, argues against Leonardo that introducing the concept of white supremacy too early will exacerbate resistance to the topic by white students. Second, much of the literature on white privilege does connect it to systems and structures of racial domination (as Blum [2008, p. 315] remarks), suggesting that talk of white privilege is intended to include the concepts of white domination or supremacy. Finally, the fact that talk about white privilege is often connected to a self-examining pedagogy which urges whites to come to terms with their own complicity in racism (an aspect of the 'white privilege' literature criticized by Niemonen, 2007), and that whites often resist this pedagogy (see, e.g. Warren & Hytten, 2004), might lead one to conclude that the discourse of 'white privilege' is not intended to make racism more palatable to a white audience. At the same time, Leonardo is not alone in suggesting that 'white privilege' pedagogy leaves out a more substantive discussion of the processes of white domination. Lawrence Blum has argued more recently that talk of white privilege should include structural analyses—based on social analysis and research—of how specific racist systems work (2008, p. 315). Jack Niemonen makes a similar argument in his critique of anti-racist education (2007, p. 168). (Niemonen's characterization of anti-racist education, however, is at times unfair.)

2 There may well be a certain amount of racist sentimentality, first, behind my (and Leonardo's) assumption that the students would have a monolithic response—especially if the teaching is provided by white instructors (Blum [2008, pp. 316–318] also criticizes the 'white privilege' literature for its tendency to treat non-whites as a monolithic group)—and, second, behind my failure to fully consider my effects as a white teacher on the students. As I suggest below, however, I always assumed that I would have to win the respect of the students, but I have changed my techniques for doing so over the years, primarily because I overcame the first sentimentalist assumption, namely, that students of color would have a monolithic response to (my) lessons about white domination.

3 I often think of what the black defendant, Carl Lee Hailey (played by Samuel L. Jackson) tells his white attorney, Jake Tyler Brigance (played by Matthew McConaughey) in the 1996 movie *A Time to Kill*. 'See, Jake', Carl says, 'you think just like them, that's why I picked you; you are one of them, don't you see? . . . You are my secret weapon because you are one of the bad guys. You don't mean to be, but you are. It's how you was raised.' I had always been a student of race issues in America. My connection to my husband led me to learn about race from a different point of view and to be more consciously aware of race. One does not un-learn the early, largely unconscious lessons about race over night.

4 As Janine Jones points out, the 'goodwill white . . . simply may not *want to believe* or simply *cannot believe*—evidence to the contrary—that race is relevant' to various situations (2004, p. 67). One of the most difficult lessons I learned was to see race as operative in—as relevant to—situations in which I would not have seen it before.

5 When I first started teaching at Lehman, I used to tell the students at the beginning of the semester about my family situation, but I discovered that it created as much resentment as it did good will. I was particularly troubled by the gendered nature of the response—my news tended to alienate primarily women students, while it fostered good will among the men. Many women made clear that they resented my having taken one of the 'brothers' (especially a fairly successful one), while I feared the men liked the vicarious possibility of being the object of white (and hence more valued) women's attention. (I must admit, however, that I never discussed this issue directly with any of the men students.) The gendered nature of the response was particularly problematic because most of the students at Lehman are women—a factor I discuss further below. I did not blame the women for feeling resentful, or the men for being influenced by racist patterns that value white women over women of color (if that was what was indeed behind their responses), but I decided it was better to avoid these responses by earning the students' respect on my own terms first.

6 Elsewhere (Maybee, 2001), I have admitted that being married to a black man does not by itself make a white woman a 'race traitor'. As I suggest there, some black men are no doubt happy to marry white women in an attempt to escape their blackness, and some white wives are no doubt willing to oblige this attempt. I also examine some of the limits under which a white woman married to a black man can be considered to have a black identity. I also argue, however, that political commitment to the antiracist struggle should be given more weight in thinking about racial identity—for both spouses.

7 Barbara Applebaum (2004, pp. 69–70), drawing on an example originally offered by Hytten and Warren (2003, p. 87), argues that judgments of who is good and who is bad are affected by racism, such that antiracist work by a white person tends to be viewed by whites as more praiseworthy than does antiracist work by a black person. My experience suggests that this same pattern of valuation may be found

in the judgments of people of color as well: they, too, may be affected by the racist assumptions of the larger culture such that they view antiracist work by a white person as more praiseworthy (heroic) than they would the antiracist work of a person of color.

8 For instance, one chapter in Bell's book led from a discussion of Anthony Appiah's article 'Racisms' (1990), to a discussion of Kant's deontological theory of morality. I used Bell's book as a springboard to a discussion of John Stuart Mill's utilitarianism. I was also able to use it as an entry into Charles Mills' book, *The Racial Contract* (1997), which I then used to introduce the contract theory of morality. There is also a passage in Bell's book that I used as an entry into a discussion of moral relativism.

9 To the degree that I did not take seriously that the new context in which I was teaching would make a difference to how I should teach existentialism, I was reenacting my own status as a racially privileged person—a status which meant that my whiteness prevented me from seeing that my students of color might have a different response to existentialism from the one that predominantly white students had had at the other institutions at which I taught. I am grateful to an anonymous reviewer for this point.

10 Murchland also discusses the appeal of certain existentialist novelists, but I will not discuss that here.

11 Tricia Rose suggests that difference, attraction to the forbidden, and rebellion help to explain the attraction of young white teenagers and adults to rap music as well as to earlier forms of black music, such as jazz, rock 'n' roll, soul and R&B (Rose, 1994, p. 5).

12 Zeus Leonard distinguishes between white people, whiteness and white culture in 'The Souls of White Folk: Critical pedagogy, whiteness studies, and globalization discourse' (2002).White people are just individual white people. 'Whiteness' is a racial discourse or perspective, or worldview, usually based on skin color, that is 'supported by material practices and institutions' (p. 32). Individual white people can be anti-white to some extent. Whiteness is not a culture. White culture is the collection of cultural events that white people participate in. It is 'an amalgamation of various white ethnic practices' (p. 32).

13 The suggestion that African Americans have a distinctive and separate culture from the dominant white culture in the United States has been defended, for example, by Patricia Williams (1987), and Patricia Hill Collins (1990). Bonnie Mitchell and Joe Feagin (1995) have defended the idea that African Americans have what they call an 'oppositional culture' in relation to the dominant Anglo-Protestant culture in the US. Sandra Harding (1987) has noticed a coincidental similarity in values and ethics between African and feminist moralities, which she argues are both opposed in similar ways to the dominant, Western, male moral system. She suggests that the similarity between African and feminist moralities may be rooted in the fact that both Africans and women have been oppressed by and have had to oppose the dominant European male culture. Edna Bonacich (2000) has suggested that minority students from Chicano and other cultures resist the assimilationist structure of universities in the United States in part because they regard the values of the dominant, Western, white culture as alien and ultimately sick. Teresa A Martinez argues, for example, that Gloria Anzaldúa's concept of 'mestiza consciousness'—like W. E. B. Du Bois' concept of 'double consciousness'—marks out a significant form of oppositional culture and consciousness for Latinos, though Anzaldúa's conception goes beyond Du Bois' by referring to sexuality and gender as well as culture (Martinez, 2002)

14 Cf. Bonacich, 2000; Collins, 1990; Harding, 1987.

15 Kwame Anthony Appiah discusses the degree to which race is experienced or has meaning for contemporary Africans and for African Americans in ethnic enclaves in *In My Father's House* (1992, pp. 5–9).

16 Lewis Gordon points out that one unique experience that biracial people have over either blacks or whites is that biracial people are familiar with the 'innermost private lives' of both some white and some black families. They know what 'other' people do in their homes (Gordon, 1997, p. 66).

17 Interestingly, many of these students are white or lighter-skinned. White or light-skinned students report being targeted by police because the police assume that the white or light-skinned students must be up to something illegal, since they evidently do not *belong* in the Bronx.

18 Latino students may have an advantage over other minority students in this regard. Because they have access—especially in New York City—to Spanish-language television and movies, they may be less exposed to the messages of the system of whiteness than are those students who must use English as the predominant language through which they get their information and entertainment.

19 This connection is made clear, for instance, in 'Divining a Racial Realism Theory', chapter five of Derrick Bell's *Faces at the Bottom of the Well* (1992), the book I used for my 'Contemporary Moral Issues' class.

20 See, for example, Karl Marx 'Economic and Philosophical Manuscripts: First Manuscript, Wages of Labour' (Marx, 1963, pp. 77f).

21 Bell suggests that the legal victories over school desegregation, for instance, are an example of what he calls 'bogus freedom checks' given by whites. Even where whites were forced by desegregation laws to integrate black students into schools, they simply found new ways of segregating blacks from whites within the same buildings—by so-called 'ability groups' (see for instance Bell, 1992, pp. 18–19). Bell uses this response on the part of whites to show how racism does not end but simply changes shape under different historical conditions. Leonardo has suggested that whites' past willingness to accept the Irish into the 'white race' and the possible future acceptance of Asians into the 'white race' are also symptoms of the flexibility of racism to accommodate changing historical conditions (Leonardo, 2002, pp. 41–44).

22 See note 12 above.

23 I am grateful to Gary Schwartz for this characterization.

24 See note 13 above.

25 Kwame Anthony Appiah discusses the cultural and religious origins of contemporary African identity in *In My Father's House* (1992, pp. 173–177). The tendency of first-generation black immigrants from the Caribbean to distance themselves from American blacks and stress their national or ethnic identities as Jamaican, Haitian and so on has been well documented. See Waters (1994, p. 796).

26 This father and son thereby exhibited the tension in identity that Mary C. Waters has documented between many first-generation black immigrants and some second-generation black immigrants. The student exhibited the type of identity-pattern Waters characterizes as 'black American-identified'. These second-generation youth identified with other black Americans as black, and did not see their 'ethnic' backgrounds as important to their identities. 42% of the youths in Waters' study exhibited this identity. 30% of the youth exhibited a strong 'ethnic' identity and, like the father, distanced themselves from American blacks and did not want others to see them as American blacks. 28% of the youths had a third 'immigrant' identity. These youths, most of whom were recent immigrants themselves, had accents and clothing styles that marked them as immigrants. Like the 'ethnic'-identified youths, they had a strong ethnic identity as Jamaican or what have you, but they did not distance themselves from American blacks. Waters theorizes

that, because they bore the markers of an immigrant, they did not have to make a 'choice' about what sort of American they are (Waters, 1994, pp. 802–803). Second-generation youth who lack the markers of being foreign, by contrast, face a dilemma. They are aware of their parents' negative attitudes toward American blacks and of the advantages of being a foreign-born black, but they are also aware that other people will identify them as black (Waters, 1994, p. 798). They must therefore choose between being identified as American black, or working to actively assert their ethnic identities (Waters, 1994, p. 796).

27 Feagin and Feagin report that many Caribbean and African immigrants want to be black and are proud of being black, but just do not want to be black in the United States, where assimilation (as a black American) means 'moving from a positive image to a less than positive one' (Feagin & Feagin, 2003, p. 192).

28 E. Chukwudi Eze reminds us, for instance, of the sad irony that, '[t]oday . . . Africans come to Europe and America to find—ironically—a place of refuge, a refuge always precarious because of racism and discriminatory immigration laws' (Eze, 1998, p. 219).

29 As an anonymous reviewer for this journal reminded me.

30 As mentioned above, part of Bell's argument for the structural and permanent nature of CRT is precisely that racism is used as a way to maintain a sense of unity in an otherwise pluralistic population in the US.

31 As Feagin and Feagin have pointed out, the educational attainment gap between blacks and whites has narrowed much further than has the economic gap between blacks and whites (Feagin & Feagin, 2003, p. 185), which indicates that blacks are not being fully rewarded economically for their educational achievements.

32 I have encountered similar resistance to feminist criticisms of the profession of philosophy from women graduate students in PhD programs in philosophy when I try to talk to them about sexism in the profession of philosophy. They do not want to believe that there are structures of sexual advantage and disadvantage in the profession of philosophy. They want to believe that, if they work hard enough, they will be welcomed and recognized by the profession. They see me as a poor, bitter and twisted (old?) woman. For a discussion of sexism in the profession of philosophy, see my 'Politicizing the Personal and Other Tales from the Front Lines' (2002) as well as other articles in that collection.

33 I would like to thank Jane Gordon (Temple University) and the anonymous reviewers for this journal for helpful criticisms and comments on drafts of this paper. A very early version of this paper was delivered at the Ohio Valley Philosophy of Education Society's Annual Conference in Dayton, Ohio (September 2007).

References

Allen, R. L. (2004) Whiteness and Critical Pedagogy, *Educational Philosophy and Theory*, 36:2, pp. 121–136.

Angelo, B. (1989) The Pain of Being Black, (Interview with Toni Morrison), *Time*, 133:21 (May 22), pp. 120f. Available at: www.time.com/time/community/pulitzerinterview.html (accessed 11 May 2009).

Appiah, K. A. (1990) Racisms, in: D. T. Goldberg (ed.), *Anatomy of Racism* (Minneapolis, University of Minnesota Press), pp. 3–17.

Appiah, K. A. (1992) *In My Father's House: Africa in the Philosophy of Culture* (New York, Oxford University Press), pp. 3–17.

Applebaum, B. (2004) Social Justice Education, Moral Agency, and the Subject of Resistance, *Educational Theory*, 54:1, pp. 59–72.

Bell, D. (1992) *Faces at the Bottom of the Well* (New York, NY, Basic Books).

Blum, L. (2008) 'White Privilege': A Mild Critique, *Theory and Research in Education*, 6:3, pp. 309–321.

Bonacich, E. (2000) Racism in the Deep Structure of US Higher Education: When affirmative Action Is Not Enough, in: A. Aguirre, Jr. & D. V. Baker, *Structured Inequality in the United States: Discussion on the Continuing Significance of Race Ethnicity and Gender* (Upper Saddle River, NJ, Prentice Hall), pp. 67–76.

Collins, P. H. (1990) *Black Feminist Thought: Knowledge, consciousness, and the Politics of Empowerment* (Boston, MA, Unwin Hyman).

Curry-Stevens, A. (2007) New Forms of Transformative Education: Pedagogy for the Privileged, *Journal of Transformative Education*, 5:1, pp. 33–58.

Dlamini, S. N. (2002) From the Other Side of the Desk: Notes on Teaching about Race When Racialized, *Race, Ethnicity and Education*, 5:1, pp. 51–66.

Eze, E. C. (1998) Modern Western Philosophy and African Colonialism, in: E. C. Eze (ed.), *African Philosophy: An Anthology* (Malden, MA, Blackwell), pp. 213–221.

Feagin, J. R. & Feagin, C. B. (2003) *Racial and Ethnic Relations* (Upper Saddle River, NJ, Prentice Hall).

Gooding-Williams, R. (1995) Disney in Africa and the Inner City: On Race and Space in The Lion King, *Social Identities*, 1:2, pp. 373–379.

Gordon, L. (1997) *Her Majesty's Other Children: Sketches of Racism from a Neocolonial Age* (Lanham MD, Rowman and Littlefield).

Harding, S. (1987) The Curious Coincidence of Feminine and African Moralities: Challenges for Feminist Theory, in: E. Kittay & D. T. Myers (eds), *Women and Moral Theory* (Totowa, NJ, Rowman and Littlefield), pp. 296–315.

Housee, S. (2008) Should Ethnicity *Matter* When Teaching about Race and Racism in the Classroom? *Race, Ethnicity and Education*, 11:4, pp. 415–428.

Hytten, K. & Warren, J. (2003) Engaging Whiteness: How Racial Power Gets Reified in Education, *Qualitative Studies in Education*, 16:1, pp. 65–89.

Jones, J. (2004) The Impairment of Empathy in Goodwill Whites for African Americans, in: G. Yancy (ed.), *What White Looks Like: African-American Philosophers on the Whiteness Question* (New York, Routledge), pp. 65–86.

Kaelin, E. F. (1966) The Existential Ground for Aesthetic Education, *Philosophy of Education: Proceedings of the Annual Meeting of the Philosophy of Education Society*, 22, pp. 170–177.

Lehman College (2007), Office of Institutional Research 'Fact Book'. Available at: www.lehman.edu/provost/provostoffice/oir.htm (accessed September 2007).

Leonardo, Z. (2002) The Souls of White Folk: Critical Pedagogy, Whiteness Studies, and Globalization Discourse, *Race, Ethnicity and Education*, 5:1, pp. 29–50.

Leonardo, Z. (2004) The Color of Supremacy: Beyond the Discourse of 'White Privilege', *Educational Philosophy and Theory*, 36:2, pp. 137–152.

Lopez, N. (2002) Race-Gender Experiences and Schooling: Second Generation Dominican, West Indian, and Haitian Youth in New York City, *Race Ethnicity and Education*, 5:1, pp. 67–89.

Lynn, M. (2004) Inserting the Race into Critical Pedagogy: An Analysis of Race-Based Epistemologies, *Educational Philosophy and Theory*, 37:2, pp. 153–165.

Martinez, T. A. (2002) The Double-Consciousness of Du Bois and the 'Mestiza Consciousness' of Anzaldúa, *Race, Gender and Class*, 9:4, pp. 158–176.

Marx, K. (1963) [1844] Economic and Philosophical Manuscripts: First Manuscript, Wages of Labour, in: *Early Writings*, T. B. Bottomore trans. (New York, McGraw-Hill, 1963), pp. 77f.

Maybee, J. (2001) Who Am I: The Limits of Shared Culture as a Criterion of Group Solidarity and Individual Identity, *Radical Philosophy Review*, 4:1&2, pp. 39–53.

Maybee, J. (2002) Politicizing the Personal and Other Tales from the Front Lines, in: A. M. Superson & A. E. Cudd (eds), *Theorizing Backlash: Philosophical Reflections on the Resistance to Feminism* (Lanham, MD, Rowman and Littlefield), pp. 133–152.

McIntosh, P. (1992) 'White Privilege' Unpacking the Invisible Knapsack, in: P. S. Rothenberg (ed.), *Race, Class and Gender in the United States*, 4th edn. (New York, St. Martin's Press), pp. 165–169 [This article has been reprinted in several other volumes as well, sometimes in longer or shorter versions].

Mills, C. (1997) *The Racial Contract* (Ithaca, NY, Cornell University Press).

Mitchell, B. & Feagin, J. (1995) America's Racial-Ethnic Cultures: Opposition within a Mythical Melting Pot, in: B. Bowser, G. Auletta & T. Jones (eds), *Toward the Multicultural University* (Westport, CT, Praeger), pp. 65–86.

Murchland, B. (1977) The Teaching of Existentialism, *Philosophy Today*, 21: Fall, pp. 227–240.

Newman, K. S. (1998) What Scholars Can Tell Politicians about the Poor, in: P. S. Rothenberg (ed.), *Race, Class and Gender in the United States*, 4th edn. (New York, St. Martin's Press), pp. 249–252.

Niemonen, J. (2007) Antiracist Education in Theory and Practice: A Critical Assessment, *American Sociologist*, 38:2, pp. 159–177.

Patterson, O. (2001) Race by the Numbers, *New York Times Op-Ed Page*, 8 May.

Rose, T. (1994) *Black Noise: Rap Music and Black Culture in Contemporary America* (Hanover, NH, Wesleyan University Press).

US Census Bureau (2001) Overview of Race and Hispanic Origin, *Census 2000 Briefs* (c2kbr01–1.pdf), (www.census.gov/prod/cen2000/) (March).

US Census Bureau (2003) Educational Attainment 2000, *Census 2000 Briefs* (c2kbr-24.pdf), (www.census.gov/prod/cen2000/) (August).

US Census Bureau (2005) Household Income 1999, *Census 2000 Briefs* (c2kbr-36.pdf), (www.census.gov/prod/cen2000/) (June).

Wagner, A. E. (2005) Unsettling the Academy: Working through the Challenges of Anti-Racist Pedagogy, *Race, Ethnicity and Education*, 8:3, pp. 261–275.

Warren, J. T. & Hytten, K. (2004) The Faces of Whiteness: Pitfalls and the Critical Democrat, *Communication Education*, 53:4, pp. 321–339.

Waters, M. C. (1994) Ethnic and Racial Identities of Second-Generation Black Immigrants in New York City, *International Migration Review*, 28:4, pp. 795–820.

Williams, P. (1987) Alchemical Notes: Reconstructing Ideals from Deconstructed Rights, *Harvard Civil Rights and Civil Liberties Review*, 22:1, p. 412.

Chapter 8

Rethinking *the* History of Education for Asian-American Children in California in the Second Half of the Nineteenth Century

Kyung Eun Jahng

Editors' introduction

While most of the essays in this collection focus on the black/white race binary, this 2013 essay by Kyung Eun Jahng uses critical race theory (CRT) and Foucauldian theory to trace racism against Asian-American children in the late-nineteenth century in the western United States. As Kyung notes, recently Asian-Americans have been framed in the United States as 'model minorities', but such positive (though still problematic) treatment does not extend to early periods of American history. Instead, Asians, mostly described collectively as 'Mongols', 'Orientals', and Chinese, were framed as racially deficient, dangerous, unlawful, and infectious to an unnamed, unremarked-upon white population. Asians at that time were not provided citizenship rights, given their apparently inferior and deviant racial status, and they were educated, if at all, in segregated schools, so that white students could be 'safe' and 'free' to develop apart from Asians (as well as apart from Native American 'Indians' and black children). This essay elegantly intertwines perspectives from CRT and Foucauldian analyses of history with a critical examination of policy documents and other discourses at vogue in the United States in the late-nineteenth century, to document and trace the racialization and racism faced by Asian-American people and children in the society and its institutions, particularly schools.

Introduction

This article intends to rethink the taken-for-granted images and narratives of Asian-American children as a model minority by questioning *the* history of education for Asian-American children in California in the second half of the nineteenth century. Here, what I mean by '*the* history' is not so much the master narrative as a disinterested recounting of the past events claiming neutral objectivity. The purposes of the article are twofold. First, through different theoretical and conceptual frameworks, it questions a series of knowledge given by historical texts—what has been believed to be factual and therefore truthful. Secondly,

DOI: 10.4324/9781003346104-9

different interpretations of the given historical texts reveal the possibility that the image and narrative of Asian-American children, such as a model minority, which we have today, are not transparent. Rather than historicizing the education for Asian-American children, it applies conceptual tools drawn from Foucault and critical race theory to the analysis of historical contexts in order to uncover hidden practices and rationality embedded in the educational policy during the time. This makes the history ahistorical, uncovering different histories regarding education for Asian-American children.

Focusing on public education systems of California during this period, I discuss the discourses[1] inscribed in California public school law. Since most historical research regarding minority education has examined dominant ethnic minority groups such as Hispanic or African-Americans, relatively little attention has been given to the topic of education for Asian-American children, particularly in the field of history. Inspired by a Foucaultian ethos and critical race theory, this article takes a reconceptualist approach to the analysis of historical documents, including California public school laws, speeches and reports of a governor-elect and a superintendent, and a report of the board of supervisors, from the 1860s to the 1880s. In this article, the philosophical and theoretical interrogation of education for Asian-American children covers education on what is now the continental USA, with a particular focus on California, where most of the early Asian immigrants resided (Takaki, 1989). This selection is also based on the presumption that discourses are specific to space and time (Foucault, 2007b). In other words, a discourse dominant in California may be different from that in New York.

Considering that history is, in nature, a set of historians' interpretations of a series of past events, I selected Foucault's key ideas as a window of interpretation through which to look at California's education systems of the second half of the nineteenth century, since Foucault has not been employed in this topic. Foucault's philosophical reflections on history unearth normalizing and dividing practices that embody the mode of living and thus raise different histories characterized by 'the contingency, singularity, interconnections, and potentialities of the diverse trajectories of those elements which compose present social arrangements and experience' (Dean, 1994, p. 21).

Foucaultian ideas are useful in questioning 'what governs statements' and how the statements 'constitute a set of propositions' (Foucault, 1980, p. 112) that are socially acceptable. The important thing here is the regime of power—the effect of power on the set of statements. Drawing on Foucault, I search for different regimes of power inscribed in the statements in the historical documents. Regarding this, Foucault (1980) writes:

> [t]he history which bears and determines us has the form of a war rather than that of a language: relations of power, not relations of meaning. History has no 'meaning' . . . it is intelligible and should be susceptible of analysis down to the smallest detail—but this in accordance with the intelligibility of struggles, of strategies and tactics. (p. 114)

Therefore, my Foucaultian approach attempts to identify rationality inscribed in the power relations circulating through the educational systems.

In addition, I employed critical race theory (CRT hereafter) to interrogate racism institutionalized through the public school law as I view CRT as an application of Foucault's non-hegemonic ideas. In my article, racism is an important discursive regime which is the effect of power (Foucault, 1980). Therefore, CRT, which originally emerged from critical theory in law, is a useful tool for 'examin[ing] and challeng[ing] the ways race and racism implicitly and explicitly impact on social structures, practices and discourses', particularly in relation to legal history (Yosso, 2005, p. 70). The following are its presumptions. Racism is not a separate individual act, but is institutionalized and structured, legally and culturally affecting everyday life while being closely related to property rights. Defining race as a major social problem (DuBois, 1989), CRT centers race and racism as a knowledge and form of oppression that shapes the experiences of people of color and stabilizes social structures legitimized by dominant discourses (Ladson-Billings & Tate, 1995; Lo´pez, 2000; Teranishi, 2002; Yosso, 2005). Taken together, CRT allows me to explain how the intersection between race and property is deeply ingrained in the education of Asian-American children. While CRT allows for effectively reading legal texts with a particular focus on racism and thus explaining the impact of the social structures that legitimize it, Foucault enables me to reread the texts in order to excavate power relations underlying the social structures. I did not conduct an extensive historical search but limited my analysis to some important events that could contribute to problematizing the present knowledge that we believe to be true: the image and narrative of Asian-American children as a model minority.

As I note that 'everything is political' (Foucault, 2007a), this article is intended to evoke the immanence of political/power relations everywhere in society. Therefore, I deny that the reality of the past is neutrally presented in my writing. Rather, the description given here involves a multitude of interpretations densely loaded with values and perspectives. Acknowledging different interpretations of past events is a way of rethinking the images and narratives of Asian-American children and interrogating *the* history through the revelation of different histories related to their education. Thus, this article challenges the now ever-present notion of Asian-American children as a model minority by situating it in a different historical context in which race and racism intersecting with other forms of oppression (Ladson-Billings & Tate, 1995) subordinated the children as a homogeneous object.

Education for Asian-American Children Through a Foucaultian Lens

Racializing Discourses: The Qualification for Attendance in Public Schools

In the nineteenth century, 'the nation was signified as a unified "race", a word impregnated with Northern European values about civilization and the civilized people of a presumed human type of shared descent' (Popkewitz, 2008, p. 38).

That is, race was a category that identified what was normal and what was non-normal (Hall, 1997). The racialization of Asian-American children casts them out from the unified, racially homogeneous space called the nation. That is, dividing children by racial categories (Hall, 1997) disenfranchises them from their right to be citizens of the nation.

During the early stage of Asian immigration, there was a large influx of Chinese laborers that began from the California Gold Rush in the 1840s and the Transcontinental Railroad construction in the 1860s and increased afterwards. The Chinese in the field of agriculture replaced white laborers and started to monopolize the labor market at the plantation farms since they were considered cheap laborers (Chan, 1986; Wong & Chang, 1998; Jung, 1991). This led to increasing antipathy towards the growth of Chinese laborers and the prevalence of an anti-Chinese sentiment (McKenzie, 1927) although, according to Miller (1969), the animosity was disseminated by those, such as American travelers, traders, and missionaries, who visited China before 1849. The Chinese, as cheap laborers, thus 'served as a caste at the bottom' (Chan, 1986, p. 287). According to Hendrick (1977), this social climate considerably affected Asian-American children's education.

Having said that, the analysis of the California school law in this article reveals the deficit theory inscribed in the education for Asian-American children, which fabricated the images of Asian-American children. Deficit theory posits that children of color should be blamed for their school failure and are thought of as at-risk. 'It overlooks any strengths and promise of the student so labeled, while drawing attention to the presumed personal and familial shortcomings of the individual' (Valencia, 2010, p. xvii). This deficit thinking is embodied in an act of oppression that legitimates school segregation and compulsory ignorance laws, keeping minority groups of children illiterate (Ryan, 1971; Valencia, 2010).

In the same manner, education for Asian-American children was inscribed with deficit thinking. They were viewed as deficient and incapable, as seen in the Amendment of California school law:

1864 Amendment of California School Law

Negroes, Mongolians, and Indians shall not be admitted into the public schools; provided, that upon the application of the parents or guardians of ten or more such colored children, made in writing to the Trustees of any district, said Trustees shall establish a separate school for the education of Negroes, Mongolians, and Indians, and use the public school funds for the support of the same; and provided, further, that the Trustees of any school district may establish a separate school, or provide for the education of any less number of Negroes, Mongolians, and Indians, and use the public school funds for the support of the same, whenever in their judgment, it may be necessary for said public schools.

(California Statutes, 1864, p. 213)

1866 Amendment of California School Law

Children of African or Mongolian descent, and Indian children not living under the care of white persons, shall not be admitted into public schools, except as provided in this Act; provided, that upon the written application of the parents or guardians of at least ten such children to any Board of Trustees or Board of Education, a separate school shall be established for the education of such children; and the education of a less number may be provided for by the Trustees in any other manner.

(California Statutes, 1865–1866, pp. 395–398)

According to the above documents, Mongolian children, which referred to Chinese, Japanese and Korean, were not qualified to attend public schools unless they were 'living under the care of white persons'. Although an unsaid group of children, white children, was not forcibly restrained, colored children, including Asian-Americans, were legally defined as deficient in that they were in need of the special care of white persons. Thus, deficit theory was closely associated with racializing practices in education (Valencia, 2010). Children were differently conceived/treated and categorized on the basis of race. According to Delgado (2000), a black/white binary makes unknown the fact that Asian-Americans are dispossessed of properties that whites enjoy. Although Asian-Americans insisted that they were white, their claims were not accepted; they were not allowed to possess whiteness.[2] The idea of white/black binary thus served as a basis for dividing people (Delgado, 2000) and envisioning their in/capability and in/eligibility for the right to have properties. Race was a significant factor in stabilizing Asian-American children's unequal and disempowered state (Teranishi, 2002).

Difference was not acceptable; it was deemed non-normal. More exactly, the difference actually meant their biological inferiority (Menchaca, 1997). According to Wu (1982), during the nineteenth century, Asian people were regarded as morally degenerate, unmotivated and biologically inferior. The following Governor-Elect Leland Stanford's inaugural speech in 1862 also shows the image and narrative of Asian-Americans during that period.

There can be no doubt that the presence of numbers among us of a *degraded* and *distinct* people must exercise a *deleterious* influence upon the *superior* race, and, to a certain extent, repel *desirable* immigration. It will afford me great pleasure to concur with the Legislature in any constitutional action, having for its object the repression of the immigration of the *Asiatic* races.

(Melendy & Gilbert, 1965, p. 118)

In this speech, difference was viewed as 'degraded and distinct'—deviant from normality. Here, Asian-Americans are described as damaging the superior race—whites—and interrupting desirable immigration. In other words, they were positioned as opposed to a superior race or desirable immigrants and were defined as damaging the reputation of the whites. According to Ladson-Billings and Tate (1995), 'to damage someone's reputation is to damage some aspect of his or her personal property' (p. 60). For this reason, they might be conceived as less desirable immigrants. Such an inferiority paradigm underlying the image and narrative of Asian-Americans—discourse describing them as intellectually inferior, immoral barbarians—was deeply rooted in the system of reasoning inscribed in the educational regulations. Given the alleged qualities of Asian-American children, they were consequently disqualified from public education (Low, 1981, p. 109).

According to Hendrick (1977), 'whites feared racial amalgamation with Asians more than with [African-Americans]' (p. 29). While a hostility towards non-whites was expressly held in segregation taking place in their education, African-Americans, who also suffered from social inequality and inordinate discrimination, were permitted to be citizens of the USA and were conceded many (though of course many that were violated nonetheless) legal rights like other citizens. By contrast, Asian-Americans were given neither American citizenship nor any legal rights to have any property (Ladson-Billings & Tate, 1995). Rather, they remained in separate schools, whereas *some* African-Americans attended desegregated schools from 1880 to the end of the century (Wollenberg, 1976; Hendrick, 1977, p. 29).

While Asian-American children could attend separate schools in the 1860s, there was no recognition of their presence or the necessity for their education in the school law of California in the next decade. The following school codes do not include the term Mongolian or Asian:

Section 1669. The education of children of African descent and Indian children must be provided for in separate schools.

(Senate Journal, 1874, p. 683)

Section 1670. Upon the written application of the parents or guardians of such children to any Board of Trustees or Board of Education, a separate school must be established for the education of such children.

(Assembly Journal, 1874, pp. 1085–1086)

In the above school law of California, there was no recognition of Asian-American children. According to Wu (1982), during the early Asian immigration period, the importance of schooling for Asian children was not adequately recognized. Their absence from the educational policy implies the inscription of social values in the children. The fact that Asian-American children were unmentioned in the school policy indicates that their existence bore no significance in the society.

In the following decades, the signifiers of Asian-American children started being used again (Okihiro, 2001). When it comes to the issue of language, the naming words such as Chinese and Japanese are not silent signs. As Goodwin (2010) argued, the social category Asian and Pacific Islander masks differences between ethnic groups and within ethnic groups. Her deconstruction revealed diversity contained in, yet hidden by, the label. The label further infuses a particular nature into the subject (Popkewitz, 2008), reflecting social values, beliefs and meanings, and creating stereotypes (Hall, 1997). It is inscribed with a set of statements that say what Asian-Americans are like and should be—discourses (Lee, 1996). That is to say, identifying Asian-American children as a monolithic group of Asians is a practice that embodies a discourse of 'Asianness' and objectifies them within the discourse. Currently, the discourse on Asianness encloses the premise of the model minority myth that says an Asian-American child is a high-achieving math and science genius. As Pang et al. (2011) refuted this model minority myth by disclosing 'the significant achievement gaps between white Americans and their Asian American and Pacific Islander peers in reading and math' (p. 378), my analysis in this article makes the same attempt by showing that the way Asian-American children are racialized is contingent upon historical and social contexts.

Appiah (1996) used the term 'racialism' to describe how race, as a prescriptive category, assumes 'certain fundamental, heritable, physical, moral, intellectual, and cultural characteristics' for those who belong to the racial group (Appiah, 1996, p. 54). In this respect, race is not just a label but a set of knowledge—a discourse that constructed the members of the racial group. Likewise, an Asian race involved a racial/racist discourse, the discourse of Asianness as previously mentioned, that made up Asian-American children.

Foucault (1990) spoke of 'the complex and unstable process whereby discourse can be both an instrument and an effect of power, but also a hindrance, a stumbling block, a point of resistance and a starting point for an opposing strategy' (p. 101). He further acknowledged that discourses accompany other discourses, even the ones standing in opposition. Discourses involve a multiplicity of tactics that sanction, deny and go across a multitude of the in-between. This tactical process is unstable and obscure (Foucault, 1990).

In this manner, the discourse of Asianness provoked another discourse that ran counter to it, when it was used to identify all Asian children under the grouping. What is said about Asian-American children, about any notion of a good Asian-American student, encompasses what is not like Asian-American children, that is, what is not the nature of Asian-American children. Therefore, the grouping/naming under a homogenizing racial category is a strategy that operates the discourse of Asianness (Hall, 1997); race is a discursive category that 'organizes the great classificatory systems of difference' (Hall, 1997, p. 6). This is well manifested in the use of the terms Asian, Oriental and Mongolian in the policy and law documents related to education in the nineteenth century, as presented in Section 1662 of the Political Code of 1880, which reads as follows:

> Every school, unless otherwise provided by law, must be open for the admission of *all children* between six and twenty-one years of age residing in the district, and the Board of Trustees, or City Board of Education, have power

to admit adults and children not residing in the district, whenever good reasons exist therefor. Trustees shall have power to exclude children of *filthy* or *vicious* habits, or children suffering from *contagious* or *infectious* diseases and also to establish *separate* schools for children of *Mongolian* or Chinese descent. When such separate schools are established Chinese or Mongolian children must not be admitted into any other schools.

(*Statutes and Amendments to the Codes*, California, 1885, pp. 99–100)

Here, the terms Mongolian and Chinese refer to all Asian heritage groups of people (Hwang, 2006). Juxtaposing Asian-American children to those who have filthy or vicious habits or suffer from contagious or infectious diseases denotes that they can have a contaminating influence on whiteness. The nature of Asian-American children is thus envisioned and embodied in the educational law. At the same time, it makes unthinkable other sets of knowledge about them.

In addition, grouping Asian-American children into a monolithic category 'Mongolian'—dividing Asian-American children and whites (Hall, 1997)—makes it easier to control and rule them. Isolating their bodies in separate schools is a spatial practice that places them in a different space (Popkewitz, 1998). Here, the separate school to which they went became a locus where dividing practices were implemented. As a body was a site of control (Foucault, 1990), segregating their bodies from a space for public education was a way of regulating them as transcendental subjects that were controlled and manipulated by certain criteria of or for a normality that envisioned what is normal or non-normal. Such segregation meant that Asian-American children were different/non-normal and were not therefore did not qualify for legal rights—an opportunity to enjoy the same quantity and quality of education (Teranishi, 2002) allowed to white children (Hendrick, 1977).

The nineteenth century was marked by social reform movement and rapid economic growth. In education, Horace Mann secularized education to make it more practical for promoting citizenship education. The birth of modern schooling (mass public schooling) during this century was the outcome of transformative movements that 'linked the governing patterns of society and the inner governing "mentalities" of the individual' (Popkewitz, 2001, p. 160). Public school as a modern institution was a site in which the segregating practices of a governing society embodied the systems of ideas that located Asian-American children outside of reason and normalcy.

In California school law, race was the salient category that was used to distinguish those attending public schools from those who were not permitted to go to the public schools (Lo'pez, 2000). Asian-American children were dispossessed of the right to use 'social, cultural, and economic privileges' whereas whites had the right to enjoy them (Ladson-Billings & Tate, 1995; Gillborn, 2006). Asian-Americans not only had no right to possess whiteness as property (Leonardo, 2007), but also have been invisible throughout history. For instance, they have been never mentioned as pioneers who shaped the American land, though they helped to build the transcontinental railroad (Chan, 1986; Takaki, 1989; Jung, 1991).

Given that race has been one of the primary categories used for dividing practices in America (Hall, 1997), racialization is an artificial process of 'otherness' as 'American, as the home of the chosen people, was a radical "otherness" in which the nation's citizens were the "racially elect"' (Popkewitz, 2008, p. 48). According to Takaki (1989), early Asian immigrants 'wore a racial uniform' (p. 13) disqualifying them from naturalization (Woo, 1994); ethnocentrism, prejudice and racism transformed them into strangers. Asian-Americans are still considered 'forever foreigners' who will never be able to become American citizens with legal rights to have properties (Ladson-Billings and Tate, 1995; Tuan, 1998). This entails the inclusion/exclusion couplet that puts colored/racialized people into the 'other' category, producing knowledge about the state of the normal and the non-normal, which naturalizes their inferior status (Foucault, 1980).

Segregated Schooling

Asian-American children were not included in the list of those who were protected before the law in the late nineteenth and early twentieth century. Under the episteme in which aspects other than race were excluded in expressing Asianness, the segregated schooling for Asian-American children was enacted by order of law. Therefore, segregated schooling, for them, was unquestioned at that time. It is, therefore, evident that segregated schooling for Asian-American children was produced in that particular period by a political rationality constructed through a prevailing discourse that controlled and regulated non-white people as inferior races (Wu, 1982). The discourse of Asianness was strongly grounded in and underpinned by another predominant discourse, namely Social Darwinism, which held that social policy should weed out weak and unfit genes from the population (Spencer, 1860).

Segregation by race *per se* had a connotation that it was natural to treat people unequally or differently on the basis of their race. Therefore, segregated schooling for Asian-American children was deemed reasonable based upon the reasoning that hierarchizes a population by comparative norms. However, it is now unthinkable, considering their current model minority image and narrative that corresponds to the norms of a white, middle-class culture (Lee, 1996; Lee & Kumashiro, 2005). Even the 'equal opportunity for all' in education secured by the democratic principles on which the US Constitution is based was differently interpreted in this earlier epoch. At present, democratic rationality is based on the concept of individual freedom and equal opportunity for all (equal education for all children) regardless of background. However, in the nineteenth century, democratic rationality was different. Although Thomas Jefferson, the third president of America, wrote that 'all men are created equal' in the Declaration of Independence, the equal opportunity for all was exclusively applied to white males, excluding in its coverage slaves, Native Americans, poor people, immigrants and women.

The concept of equality was not part of the Constitution until the Fourteenth Amendment was ratified in 1868. In spite of the passage of the Fourteenth Amendment, racial segregation continued. The decision made in *Plessy v. Ferguson* ruled 'separate but equal'. According to this decision, racial segregation was allowed unless separate facilities were unequal. The concept of equality was interpreted in different ways at different times. A particular interpretation of equality embedded in the law at a particular time ruled ways of policing the education of Asian-American children.

While Asian-American children were indirectly mentioned through statements about separate schools for children of color, white children were not mentioned as rules of exception (Hendrick, 1977). For example, when the law ordered Asian-American children to be supervised under white guardians, there was nowhere that mentioned white children in the statements. What was unsaid about Asian-American children regarding their education (e.g. integrated, equal education for all children without any discrimination) was unthinkable and unimaginable (Hendrick, 1977). Rather, the requirement of surveillance by white adults in order to receive a normal education insinuates that intervention was necessary for them as a means of guiding or correcting them to reach the state of normality from which they were thought of as deviant.

Segregation was also a political strategy to protect the security of white people from imagined threat by Asians (Lee, 1996), as their numbers were rapidly growing to a mass that became an object of fear, as Superintendent Moulder (1885) asserted:

> Without such [separate education] action I have every reason to believe that some of our classes will be inundated by Mongolians. Trouble will follow.
> (*Evening Bulletin*, 1885, p. 2)

This short statement indicates that the special management of their education was legitimized for the purpose of protecting white children. Segregated schools for Asian-American children thus functioned as a 'social medicine' (Foucault, 2000a) that publicly aimed at curing and fixing problems arising from the *inundation* of Mongolian children in their school and society. But, in actuality, its function was not so much to, in an aseptic sense, protect white people from the desegregating effects of the mass of children of color, as it was to sacralize their own spaces, to divide them for *regular* public schools (legitimate educational institution) and their community boundaries, to crystallize their status and position, and facilitate ruling/regulating 'other' people's children through legalized segregation and alienation (Lo´pez, 2000). Whenever Asian power was believed to be menacing to whites, an antagonistic attitude towards Asians as well as an act of alienating them worsened so as to keep the *status quo* of American society from changing (Thompson, 1978; Delgado, 2000). Apparently, segregating Asian-American children from public education was a discursive practice implemented on their bodies by dint of the mechanism of spatial division (Foucault, 2007a).

In a similar vein, in the current educational system, the model minority myth provides a backdrop for resegregating Asian-American children from whites and other minority groups (Lee, 1996). It is a camouflage that appears to glorify Asian-American children for their alleged high academic achievement without paying attention to their within- and between-ethnic-group differences (Lee, 1996; Lee & Kumashiro, 2005; Lew, 2006; Zhao & Qiu, 2009).

Institutionalized Discourses Constituting Asian-American Childhood

Legal documents of California public school systems disseminated judicial knowledge that inscribed and circulated the discourses of Orientalism and Mongolianism, as presented in the following segment of the report by the board of supervisors of San Francisco:

> Meanwhile, guard well the doors of our public schools, that they do not enter. For however hard and stern such a doctrine may sound, it is but the enforcement of the law of self-preservation, the inculcation of the doctrine of true humanity, and an integral part of the enforcement of the iron rule of right by which we hope presently to prove that we can justly and practically *defend ourselves from this invasion of Mongolian barbarism.*
>
> (Farwell, 1885, p. 62)

In the nineteenth and early twentieth century, the word Mongolian was the term used to refer to people of Korean, Chinese and Japanese descent (Hwang, 2006). The resemblance of the physical features, especially an epicanthic fold (a fold of the skin of the upper eyelid), between those with Down syndrome and Asians, led Down syndrome to be often called Mongolism (Medicine Net, 2002).[3] The term Mongol was also often associated with the meanings of 'idiot' or 'retarded' person (Medicine Net, 2002). In this sense, the image and narrative of the Mongol were closely tied to those of Asian-American children.

Johann Friedrich Blumenbach named an Asian race Mongolian (Blumenbach, 1865). He wrote that '[the Mongolians] are for the most part of a wheaten yellow, with scanty, straight, black hair, and have flat faces with laterally projecting cheek- bones, and narrowly slit eyelids' (Blumenbach, p. 304). He put the Mongolian race as a secondary one after the Caucasian race in his invented division of people into five races. As alluded in the above-mentioned linkage between Mongolian and Down syndrome, the general discourse of 'Asian-Americans' was degenerated into an inferior race. According to Blumenbach (1865), Christoph Meiners (1747–1810), a German philosopher, was the first person to use the term Mongolian. It is noteworthy that he was a supporter of polygenism—a belief that human beings originated from more than one ancestry and that each race has a different origin; the *polygenesis theory* was a grounding work for advocates for slavery (Luse, 2009).

Likewise, the terms Asians and Orientals were interchangeably used to refer to all Asians. This is also evidenced in Superintendent Moulder's report (1886) as follows:

> Independently of this consideration the duty which the teachers owe to the children committed to their charge should prompt them to active efforts to save *the rising generation* from *contamination* and *pollution* by a race reeking with the *vices of the Orient*, a race that knows neither truth, principle, modesty nor respect for our laws. The *moral and physical ruin* already wrought to our youth by contact with these people is fearful. Let us exhaust all peaceful methods to stop its *spread*.
>
> (Circular No. 56, 1886)

This segment of the superintendent report testifies that the Orient was situated as opposite to the rising generation as he referred to the Orient as Asia here in this report. The Orient is associated with vice, contamination and pollution. This connection is inscribed with comparative reasoning that Orientals as Asians are less human beings than the rising generation, which means 'white' children since Orientals here are considered to know neither truth, principle, modesty nor respect for laws. Accordingly, the notion of Orient(al) does not just indicate a geographical space or a racial category. Rather, it enunciates the quality of Asian-American children as featuring vice, contamination and pollution. The sentence 'Let us exhaust all peaceful methods to stop its spread' implies that Asian-American children's vice was contagious (spread) to white children for it could morally and physically ruin white children even by contact. By comparative style of reason, Asian-American children as a whole were positioned as 'them' who did not know 'our' laws and were deemed to do harm to 'us' by spreading vice and contaminating 'our' morality and physical conditions.

According to Said (1994), 'theses of Oriental backwardness, degeneracy, and inequality with the West most easily associated themselves early in the nineteenth century with ideas about the biological bases of racial inequality' (p. 206). The notion of Orient(al) described in this statement resonates with that of Asian-Americans expressed in the above superintendent report segment.

Obviously, race was at the center of the discourses on Orientalism and Mongolianism. Since Asian-American children lived in and through these racial discourses, they were described, identified and divided on the basis of their discursively defined race (Lo´pez, 2000). Such racialization placed them into the 'other' category, which is different from the group of people who were not named colored. In the same manner, scientific and biological knowledge circulated through the discourse on Mongolianism sanctioned the separating practice for Asian-American children and warranted their inferiority—abnormality.

Throughout reviewing the California school law statutes in the nineteenth century, I noticed that the notion of a model minority was absent from the discourse on Asian-American childhood during this period. Asians were represented as Chinese, who were regarded as an inferior race (Wu, 1982; Wong & Chang, 1998; Hwang, 2006), which refutes the prevalent discourse about Asian-American children as a model minority that is currently considered to be ever-present (Lee, 1996; Lee & Kumashiro, 2005; Lew, 2006).

In this manner, Asian-American children were constructed as different from unnamed children through segregated schooling. Fear of the increase in their number led to their differentiation and construction as easily malleable and controllable subjects (Delgado, 2000). Lee (1996) pointed out that 'a racial group's perceptions of their own social, economic, and political positions informed their attitudes toward Asian/Asian Americans and Asian American success' (p. 136). Likewise, whites might lose a sense of security due to the large influx of Chinese immigrants during the nineteenth century. Given the 'ebbs and flows of the favoritism and nativist treatment' (Perea, Delgado, Harris, & Wildman, 2000; cited in Delgado, 2000, p. 301), Asians taking jobs away from whites were then disfavored as whites 'occasionally select a particular minority group as a favorite, usually a small, non-threatening one' (Delgado, 2000, p. 299).

The norms indicating the general characteristics of *normal* 'American' children enclosed Asian-American children as the 'pathological others' (Popkewitz, 1998, p. 43), naming them Mongolian barbarians, as stated in the above report by the board of supervisors of San Francisco. The image of barbarian linked to the notion of Asia/Asianness was invented as a repercussion against Persian expansionism (Hall, 1991). The expansion of the Persian identified as Asian advanced condemnation of Asia as void of the nature of human beings such as order and normalcy. Based on the racist norms framing educational policies, Asian-American children were excluded from public education since they were not regarded as normal. This was a way that they were deprived of 'the right to use and enjoy what schools can offer' (Ladson-Billings & Tate, 1995).

The education law thus constructed Asian-American children by enunciating the social meanings and values embedded in their race and defining both 'privileges and disadvantages justified by' racial discourses (Lo´pez, 2006, p. xv). The contents explaining race are constructed in relation to their contemporary social structure (Leonardo, 2007). Accordingly, education is a reflection of social, political, and economic forces, as well as a mechanism through which a set of knowledge securing the self-interests of a dominant group is enacted (Ladson-Billings & Tate, 1995; Teranishi, 2002; Yosso, 2005; Gillborn, 2006).

Conclusion: Power Relations

This article has discussed discourses embodied by California education systems in the nineteenth century. California public school laws and other official documents have been re-examined through a Foucaultian encounter with critical race theory. As a result, I have pointed out how power relations are deeply rooted in the early education for Asian-American children and how the images of Asian-American children and their education were informed by race and racism. The political effect generates shifting dominancy in discourses regarding minority children (from dangerous, deficient barbarians to a high-achieving model minority) and their education and changing concepts of equality (or equal education).

Although the present dominant image of Asian-American children is a model minority, the search for different histories discloses that there existed other images and narratives of the children. Even the qualification for attendance in regular education in California was mandated and naturalized by public school 'law and prohibition' (Foucault, 1980, p. 121). This is how sovereign power, defined as the power of domination, is imposed by state laws. By educational law, Asian-American children were not allowed to possess intellectual property such as an opportunity to learn at school (Teranishi, 2002). Even when they were sent to separate schools, the property value such as the quality and quantity of the curriculum would be disreputable (Ladson-Billings & Tate, 1995; Gillborn, 2006).

Here, the notion of governmentality (Foucault, 1991) fills in the 'missing link' (Lemke, 2000, p. 2) between technologies of domination and technologies of the self. In the modern state, sovereign power is not the only type of power exercised on the population (Foucault, 1991). How the state governing brings about the effect of governing of the self is explained by governmentality. Asymmetrical power relationships manifested in the California school laws are transferred to micro-practices of power that function as dividing, classifying, and categorizing mechanisms for Asian-American children. Therefore, self-governing takes place while they internalize the rules and principles produced by discourses that envision certain images of the children. The self-governing practices of the subjects were not specifically discussed in this article since I focused on the educational policy. However, in the court case *Tape v. Hurley* (1885), the fact that Chinese-American parents sued the San Francisco Board of Education when their daughter was denied admission to school for her Chinese ancestry indicates their resistance to the constraints. 'Resistance comes when one senses not only one's dependence on these constraints, but also one's tendency to give in to them' (Hoy, 2005, p. 100), as Foucault insisted that 'where there is power, there is resistance' (Foucault, 1990, p. 95). Similarly, Ladson-Billings and Tate (1995) argued that racism affects an individual's psyche through legal and cultural sanctions/constraints. Subjects, as historically constituted forms, are shaped through practices driven by the will to truth. The way that subjects position themselves in relation to the racializing rule and put it into practice is formed in relation to political and social realities (Rabinow, 2000; Foucault, 2000b).

Focusing on the effects of segregated schooling on the images and narratives of Asian-American children, this article has revealed that Asian-American children currently described as a model minority were stigmatized as non-normal/

abnormal aliens constructed by shifting discourses. Placing race at the central axis of power relations (Omi & Winant, 1986; Leonardo, 2007) allowed for different interpretations of the past events, which was a way of interrogating *the* history through the revelation of different histories in the education for Asian-American children.

Notes

1 Foucault (1972) defines the discourse as 'the group of statements that belong to a single system of formation' (p. 107).
2 See Lo´pez (1996), at 79–109, 203–12 (discussing cases showing that Asians were not regarded as white race, including *In re* Saito, 62, F. 126 (C.C.D. Mass. 1894) [holding that Japanese are not white]; *In re* Ah Yup. 1 F. Cas. 223 (C.C.D. Cal. 1878) (No. 104) [holding that Chinese are not white]).
3 For more details, please refer to the article titled 'Down Syndrome was not discovered by Dr. Down' on the Medicine Net website. The article on this website discusses how the disabling condition of Down syndrome was attributed to inferiority of Asians by being called 'Mongolism'

References

Appiah, K. A. (1996). Race, culture, identity: Misunderstood connections. In K. A. Appiah & A. Gutmann (Eds.), *Color conscious: The political morality of race* (pp. 30–105). Princeton, NJ: Princeton University Press.
Assembly Journal (20th Session) (1874), pp. 1085–1086.
Blumenbach, J. F. (1865). *The anthropological treatises of Johann Friedrich Blumenbach* (T. Bendyshe, Trans. & Ed.). London: Longman, Green, Longman, Roberts, & Green.
California Statutes (1864), p. 213.
California Statutes (1865–1866), pp. 395–398.
Chan, S. (1986). *This bitter-sweet soil: The Chinese in California agriculture, 1860–1910*. Berkeley, CA: University of California Press.
Circular No. 56 (April 1, 1886). *In San Francisco. Circulars and memoes of the school superintendents*, July 6, 1875 to January 7, 1929.
Dean, M. (1994). *Critical and effective histories: Foucault's methods and historical sociology*. London: Routledge.
Delgado, R. (2000). Derrick Bell's toolkit—Fit to dismantle that famous house? *New York University Law Review*, 75, 283–307.
DuBois, W. E. B. (1989). *The soul of black folks*. New York: Bantam (Original work published 1903).
Evening Bulletin (March 4, 1885), p. 2, col. 5.
Farwell, Williard B. (1885). *The Chinese at home and abroad together with 'the report of the board of supervisors of San Francisco on the condition of the Chinese quarter of that city'* (pp. 58–62). San Francisco: A.L. Bancroft & Co.
Foucault, M. (1972). *The archaeology of knowledge*. London: Tavistock.
Foucault, M. (1980). *Power/knowledge: Selected interviews & other writings, 1972–1977*. New York: Pantheon.
Foucault, M. (1990). *The history of sexuality: An introduction* Vol. 1. Westminster, MD: Knopf Doubleday.

Foucault, M. (1991). Governmentality. In G. Burchell, C. Gordon, & P. Miller (Eds.), *The Foucault effect: Studies in governmentality with two lectures by and an interview with Michel Foucault* (pp. 87–104). Chicago, IL: University of Chicago Press.

Foucault, M. (2000a). The birth of social medicine. In J.D. Faubion & P. Rabinow (Eds.), *The essential Foucault: Selections from the essential works of Foucault 1954–1984: Power* (pp. 134–156). New York: New Press.

Foucault, M. (2000b). The ethics of the concern of the self as a practice of freedom. In J.D. Faubion & P. Rabinow (Eds.), *The essential Foucault: Selections from the essential works of Foucault 1954–1984: Ethics: Subjectivity and truth* (pp. 281–301). New York: New Press.

Foucault, M. (2007a). *Security, territory, population: Lectures at the College De France, 1977–78* (G. Burchell, Trans.). New York: Palgrave MacMillan.

Foucault, M. (2007b). The force of flight. In J. W. Crampton & S. Elden (Eds.), *Space, knowledge and power: Foucault and geography* (pp. 169–172). Burlington, VT: Ashgate Publishing.

Gillborn, D. (2006). Critical race theory and education: Racism and anti-racism in educational theory and practice. *Discourse: Studies in the Cultural Politics of Education, 27*(1), 11–32.

Goodwin, A. L. (2010). Curriculum as colonizer: (Asian) American education in the current US context. *Teachers College Record, 112,* 3102–3138.

Hall, E. (1991). *Inventing the barbarian: Greek self-definition through tragedy.* Oxford: Oxford University Press.

Hall, S. (1997). *Race, the floating signifier.* Northampton, MA: Media Education Foundation.

Hendrick, I. G. (1977). *The education of non-whites in California, 1849–1970.* San Francisco, CA: R & E Research Associates.

Hoy, D. C. (2005). *Critical resistance. From poststructuralism to post-critique.* London: MIT Press.

Hwang, V. (2006). *Brief of Amici Curiae Asian Pacific Island legal outreach et al. in support of all respondents in the six consolidated marriage cases.* San Francisco, CA: Asian Pacific Islander Legal Outreach.

Jung, J. D. (1991). *A study of Korean immigrants in America, 1872—present.* Unpublished thesis. San Jose State University.

Ladson-Billings, G., & Tate, W. (1995). Toward a critical race theory of education. *Teachers College Record, 97,* 47–68.

Lee, S. J. (1996). *Unraveling the model minority stereotype: Listening to Asian American youth.* New York: Teachers College Press.

Lee, S. J., & Kumashiro, K. K. (2005). *A report on the status of Asian Americans and Pacific Islanders in education: Beyond the 'model minority' stereotype.* Washington, DC: National Educational Association.

Lemke, T. (2000). *Foucault, governmentality, and critique.* Paper presented at the Rethinking Marxism Conference, University of Amherst, MA, September 21–24, 2000. Retrieved February 6, 2011, from www.andosciasociology.net/resources/Foucault$2C+Governmentality$2C+and+Critique+IV-2.pdf.

Leonardo, Z. (2007). The war on schools: NCLB, nation creation and the educational construction of whiteness. *Race Ethnicity and Education, 10,* 261–278.

Lew, J. (2006). *Asian Americans in class: Charting the achievement gap among Korean American youth.* New York: Teachers College Press.

Lo'pez, I. F. H. (2000). Institutional racism: Judicial conduct and a new theory of racial discrimination. *Yale Law Journal, 109*, 1717–1884.

Lo'pez, I. F. H. (2006). *White by law: The legal construction of race.* New York: New York University Press.

Low, V. (1981). *The Chinese in the San Francisco public school system: An historical study of one minority group's response to educational discrimination,* 1859–1959. Unpublished doctoral dissertation, University of San Francisco, San Francisco, CA.

Luse, C. (2009). *'The offspring of infidelity': Polygenesis and the defense of slavery. Unpublished doctoral dissertation.* Atlanta, GA: Emory University.

McKenzie, R. D. (1927). *Oriental exclusion: The effect of American immigration laws, regulations, and judicial decisions upon the Chinese and Japanese on the American Pacific coast.* New York: American Group, Institute of Pacific Relations.

Medicine Net (2002). Down syndrome was not discovered by Dr. Down. Retrieved February 25, 2009, from www.medicinenet.com/script/main/art.asp?articlekey=945

Melendy, H. B., & Gilbert, B. F. (1965). *The governors of California: Peter H. Burnett to Edmund G. Brown.* Georgetown, CA: Talisman Press.

Menchaca, M. (1997). Early racist discourses: The roots of deficit thinking. In R.R. Valencia (Ed.), *The evolution of deficit thinking: Educational thought and practice* (pp. 13–40). New York: Falmer.

Miller, S. C. (1969). *Unwelcome immigrant: The American image of the Chinese, 1785–1885.* Berkeley, CA: University of California Press.

Okihiro, G. Y. (2001). *The Columbia guide to Asian American history.* New York: Columbia University Press.

Omi, M., & Winant, H. (1986). *Racial formation in the United States: From the 1960s to the 1980s.* New York: Routledge.

Pang, V. O., Han, P. P., & Pang, J. M. (2011). Asian American and Pacific Islander students: Equity and the achievement gap. *Educational Researcher, 40,* 378–389.

Perea, J. F., Delgado, R., Harris, A. P., & Wildman, S. M. (2000). *Race and races: Cases and resources for a diverse America* (2nd ed.). St. Paul, MN: West Group.

Plessy v. Ferguson. Judgement, decided 18 May 1896. Records of the Supreme Court of the United States: Record Group 267: Plessy v. Ferguson, 163, 15248. National Archives.

Popkewitz, T. S. (1998). *Struggling for the soul: The politics of schooling and the construction of the teacher.* New York: Teachers College Press.

Popkewitz, T. S. (2001). The production of reason and power: Curriculum history and intellectual traditions. In T. S. Popkewitz, B. M. Franklin, & M. A. Pereyra (Eds.), *Cultural history and education: Critical essays on knowledge and schooling* (pp. 151–183). New York: RoutledgeFalmer.

Popkewitz, T. S. (2008). *Cosmopolitanism and the age of school reform: Science, education, and making society by making the child.* New York: Routledge.

Rabinow, P. (2000). Introduction. In J.D. Faubion & P. Rabinow (Eds.), *The essential Foucault: Selections from the essential works of Foucault 1954–1984: Ethics: Subjectivity and truth* (pp. xi—xlii). New York: New Press.

Ryan, W. (1971). *Blaming the victim.* New York: Pantheon Books.

Said, E. W. (1994). *Orientalism.* New York: Vintage Books.

Senate Journal (20th Session) (1874), p. 683/

Spencer, H. (1860). The social organism. *Westminster Review, 17,* 90–132.

Statutes and Amendments to the Codes, California (26th Session) (1885), pp. 99–100.

Takaki, R. T. (1989). *Strangers from a different shore: A history of Asian Americans.* Boston, MA: Little, Brown and Company.

Tape v. Hurley, 66 Cal. 473 (1885).

Teranishi, R. T. (2002). Asian Pacific Americans and critical race theory: An examination of school racial climate. *Equity & Excellence in Education, 35,* 144–154.

Thompson, R. A. (1978). *The yellow peril, 1890–1924.* New York: Arno Press.

Tuan, M. (1998). *Forever foreigners or honorary whites? The Asian ethnic experience today.* Piscataway, NJ: Rutgers University Press.

Valencia, R. R. (2010). *Dismantling contemporary deficit thinking: Educational thought and practice.* New York: Routledge.

Wollenberg, C. M. (1976). *All deliberate speed: Segregation and exclusion in California schools, 1855–1975.* Berkeley, CA: University of California Press.

Wong, S., & Chang, S. (Eds.). (1998). *Claiming America: Constructing Chinese American identities during the exclusion era.* Philadelphia, PA: Temple University Press.

Woo, D. (1994). *The glass ceiling and Asian Americans.* Federal Publications. Paper 129.

Wu, W. F. (1982). *The Yellow Peril: Chinese Americans in American fiction, 1850—.* Hamden, CT: Archon Books.

Yosso, T. J. (2005). Whose culture has capital? A critical race theory discussion of community cultural wealth. *Race Ethnicity and Education, 8,* 69–91.

Zhao, Y., & Qiu, W. (2009). How good are the Asians?: Refuting four myths about Asian-American academic achievement. *Phi Delta Kappan, 90,* 338–344.

Chapter 9

The Anti-Black Order of No Child Left Behind

Using Lacanian Psychoanalysis and Critical Race Theory to Examine NCLB

Connie Wun

Editors' introduction

In this 2014 essay, Connie Wun examines the United States educational policy No Child Left Behind (NCLB) from the perspectives of Lacanian psychoanalysis and Critical Race Theory. As Wun points out, Lacanian psychoanalysis demonstrates how people experience loss and anxiety as their cultivation of a coherent and comprehensible sense of self depends on their use of external representations and symbols. As the symbolic and language exist within relationships, this means the subject is constituted through an external language structure. Yet Wun observes here the deficiencies of this theory of identity formation in relation to experiences of racism. As Wun notes, for Black children not only does language and the symbolic distort their sense of self, but pervasive anti-Black racism further characterizes them as deficient, abnormal and transgressive. Related white fantasies characterize Black people more generally as savage and evil, with significant impacts on the development of Black children. In connection with these theories, NCLB is on its surface 'colorblind' or racially neutral. However, through its focus on inequalities, the disaggregation of student data by race for accountability purposes leads ultimately to a fixation on Black children as problematic. Lacking effective affirmative supports in relation to Black students' unequal outcomes, interventions are conducted by schools upon Black children themselves. These interventions do not necessarily benefit the children academically, but they facilitate stigmatization, tracking and suspending of Black students and shifting increasing numbers of Black children into special educational needs programs. Thus, as this essay shows, in the implementation of NCLB, Black bodies continue to be cast as problematic others in need of fixing or working against, given the social and ideological context of NCLB's creation.

Introduction

Contemporary US educational reform efforts, including legal mandates, largely focus on addressing racial inequalities in schooling policies and practices and their subsequent effects. During a period in which an array of governmental institutions is being refashioned ostensibly to meet the demands of an increasingly complex

DOI: 10.4324/9781003346104-10

economic and political context, the No Child Left Behind Act of 2001 (NCLB) has altered the entire public US educational system.[1] This article argues that this mandate, in spite of claims to redress inequalities in education, has shaped and continues to shape the racial subjectivities of Black youth as the problematic other.[2] Drawing from Lacanian psychoanalytic theory, I argue that in addition to identifying and measuring a racial achievement gap, one of the structural implications of NCLB is that it paradigmatically configures and fixates on Black youth as problematic others within the United States' Symbolic order.

I argue that combining elements of both critical race theory in education and Lacanian psychoanalysis will provide much needed insight into the connection between educational policy and the racial formation of Black students. NCLB serves as a prime example of this constitutive relationship. Considering NCLB and its revered emphasis on racial disparities, the theoretical synthesis seeks to challenge and shed light upon the underlying racial suppositions of the seemingly benevolent policy.

First, I look at contemporary discourses surrounding race in education, then complete an overview of Lacanian psychoanalytic theory of identity formation, with particular attention to the function of the Symbolic. Next, I explore racial critiques of Lacanian psychoanalysis. I end by analyzing NCLB as part and parcel of a Symbolic order structured by anti-Black fantasies. Combining Lacanian psychoanalysis with critical race theory will help us to critically examine the relationship between educational policy and racial formations.

Race in Education

Critical race theory emphasizes the social, political and historical implications and contexts of race and racism in the USA, centralizing the perspectives of people of color (Ladson-Billings & Tate, 1995). This approach has made useful interventions into public discourses, originally appropriated from the field of legal research. Since 1995, this theoretical framework has provided much needed insight into the lived experience of race and racism through the use of 'counternarratives'. These first hand accounts of racialized experiences subvert mainstream knowledge because the latter has rarely acknowledged institutional investments in race and racism. Counter-narratives by racial minorities not only help subjects to 'name one's own reality' but they provide alternative, sometimes contradictory perspectives to Eurocentric or White American views. In addition to centralizing marginalized accounts of the effects of race and racism, critical race theorists recognize the larger social and historical landscape that informs these experiences.

Social policies, however, have increasingly incorporated these narratives about disenfranchisement and inequality to further educational reform agendas that extend, rather than challenge, the logic of racism in the US educational system. For instance, data on racial disparities in schools have been used to support NCLB, which researchers have argued does not rectify but, instead, exacerbates inequalities. Although stressing the importance of counter-narratives from marginalized students is a critical challenge to the history of racial subjugation in education, the fact that these narratives can be incorporated institutionally, or worse co-opted, may be a red herring, necessitating critical discussions.[3] Perhaps in lieu of narrating from the position of the racialized subject to demonstrate the effects of racism, an approach that centers on the formative role of the state and its policy mandates in shaping these racial identities may be more helpful.[4] More directly, I advocate for an analysis of the constitutive relationship between racial fanta-sies, state policies and racial formations. Fantasies, Verhaeghe (1999) explains, are the means by which reality—including our perceptions and relationships—is constructed. That is, they do not merely operate as escape mechanisms from dif-ficult worlds. On the contrary, they shape worlds. In this sense, it is important for policy pundits and scholars not only to evaluate the effects of policy on racial groups *per se*, but also to critically analyze the racializing effects and racial motiva-tions behind educational policy.

Scholars should analyze not only the material effects of racism and race, but also the effects of racial ideology. Leonardo (2005) writes about the pervasive role that 'racial ideology' plays in shaping subjectivities and social relationships (p. 406). Every subject is informed and constituted through the inescapable ideology of racism. Emphasizing the role of racial ideologies challenges race-conscious scholars to examine race as part and parcel of racial ideology, beyond reason, unconsciously adopted and performed. This type of emphasis does not discount the empirical data on racial inequalities in education, but explores how race is not only a social or historical construct, but one inscribed by language and projections.

Traditional discourses on race and schooling draw from concepts of race that are often based upon fossilized conceptions of race, what David Marriott (2007) calls, 'racial imagos' (p. 208). When one looks at the ideological machinations of critical race theory in education, racial subjects are presumed to pre-date racist acts. However, Marriott's attention to 'racial imagos' challenges this approach to move beyond materiality and to analyze the centrality of racial fantasies, par-ticularly the anti-Black fantasies which he argues are inextricably haunted by the history of slavery. Adding Lacanian psychoanalysis to theories of race and educa-tional policy may help to elucidate how racial fantasies and legal mandates inform one another and their effects.

Usefulness of Lacanian Psychoanalysis

The question of the human subject, including how she came to be, her under-standing and experiences in the world, of others, and her self is central to psycho-analytic theory. Lacan (1975) demarcates the psyche into three structures that control the human subject's life and desires: the Imaginary, Real and Symbolic (trans. Miller, p. 8). According to Lacan (2006), a human subject is informed by a traumatic loss that occurs once she enters through language (trans. Fink, pp. 413–414). In the earlier stages of Lacan's career, he drew explicitly from Freudian psychoanalysis. He theorizes that particularly in a child's earliest stages, an infant's internal world is characterized by less control and sense of self and others. Images found through what Lacan calls the Mirror stage enable the child to imagine some coherence, an identity. However, as she increasingly identifies with these images that she sees in the mirror and the ways others identify her, she separates herself from this internal world that is less coherent and less available for representation. This separation is a form of loss, provoking narcissistic anxiety with demands to be reconstituted into or returned to the imagined place of wholeness and completion—even if amorphous (2006, pp. 76–81). In other words, the subject and by extension those in the social world are always seeking to address the loss, an effect of language bisecting her primordial being. She is always striving to fulfill the fantasy of wholeness.

The paradox for the human subject is that while she uses language to identify and understand her internal and external worlds, it is this medium that alienates her from her self. Language affords her the ability to articulate her internal world, needs and desires. It is the main vehicle for relaying and relating to others. Yet this medium is incapable of capturing the full capacity or the tenor of her psychic and affective world—the way these two spaces intermingle, clash and coincide with one another. As we shall see later in the article, for the Black subject,[5] language authorizes her suffering particularly as the social world constructs itself around her negation—negating her existence, her agency, her ability to be other than the projections set onto her. Put differently, she is positioned as the other whose suffering is necessary and illegible for White civil society.

Through the Imaginary the subject projects the fantasies of loss and completion upon an Other. It is also here that the subject finds her own coherence through images and projections. The fixation on a nostalgic wholeness and the accompanying anxieties from primordial lack are projected onto the subject's sense of self and relationship to counterparts. These images inform her ego and enable the subject to imagine herself as coherent and whole. In linguistic terms, her subjectivity attaches to signifiers for comprehension. However, this illusion of coherence wrapped around the ego obviates a fundamental recognition that the subject is not whole. Her identity and existence are related to other signifiers; moreover, she is also a screen for projections. That is, she operates as a screen for others' fantasies of her—a role institutionally reserved for Black students under NCLB—projections of others' own unresolved anxieties, the Real.

The Real is the underlying traumatic loss incapable of articulation. It is a part of the subject's entrance into civilization, a necessary effect of coming into existence through language and into society. The traumatic Real resurfaces as numerous upheavals despite and because of the reoccurring yet futile attempts to repress it. Despite its evasiveness, the Real is at the core of subjectivity. It is an underlying current of trauma that cannot be articulated, but is associated with the subject's death drive and pleasure principle. The Real informs the subject's emotional gravitation towards death or that which is imagined to satiate the need to return to a primordial cohesiveness. The death drive and pleasure principle are motivated by the Real and the anxious pursuit of wholeness. It is this seemingly abysmal presence of the Real that motivates efforts to project and eject anxieties and trauma onto others through social, political and intimate relationships and discourse. The attempt is to imagine wholeness without the presence of the Real lodged within.

The Symbolic functions as a substitute for the evasiveness of the Real—the trauma, its complexities, and its foundational relationship to our subjectivity. It is the matrix by which subjects and the social order manage the Real. In other words, we manage the Real by eluding it through the Symbolic order, which governs and organizes our desires, social relationships, knowledge and means of communication. It operates as the set of rules, regulations, laws and contracts that govern subjectivities and intersubjective relationships. The Symbolic is *the* organizing system by which people come to see, understand and represent reality.

Words are defined and understood in relation to other words. Lacan provides an example of the word 'tree' (2006, p. 416). One knows the word and the idea of a tree in relation to an endless list of what it is not: 'car', 'person', 'bathroom'. This relationship between words is endless and constitutes the structure of language that shapes and exists within what Lacan identified as the Symbolic. This order governs the unconscious and human subjectivity.

> The 'subject' is nothing other than what slides in a chain of signifiers, whether he knows which signifier he is the effect of or not—each of them is an element.
> (Lacan, 1998, p. 50)

In other words, she exists within a relationship to other signifiers. One of the most important significances of this theory is that the subject is constituted through this linguistic structure. The subject and others are defined and known based in large part on the Symbolic as actualized through law (and policies) that precedes the subject—ordering language, its available significations, representations and images.

Racial Subjects Critique of Psychoanalysis

Even with its usefulness in conceptualizing human subjectivities, psychoanalytic scholars have often failed to account for race, racism and its effects. For example, although both Brown, Atkinson and England (2006) and Todd (2003) offer important discoveries into the applicability of psychoanalysis to educational theory, they deracialize the pedagogical subject and her learning environment. Either race generally fails to enter into the discourse or it is conveniently forgotten. Because psychoanalysis, Lacanian in particular, is considered a critical intervention into contemporary theories about human subjectivity, their psyches and experiences, the exclusion of race from this theoretical framework is even more problematic. For instance, theories surrounding how the subject exists through the Symbolic have rarely questioned the role that race, what Leonardo (2005) identifies as the racial ideology, plays in informing the unconscious. Scholars such as Hortense Spillers are increasingly placing the idea of race as the paradigmatic structure that exists before language, and subsequently informs language.

According to Spillers (2003), the first violence is not language but race. The *signifierness* of race covers the individual before language and its differential laws take hold of the speaking human organism (Viego, 2007, p. 18; italics in original). In *Black skin, white masks*, Frantz Fanon offered a well-known and important critique and intervention into the field and practice of psychoanalysis. He questioned its applicability to and usefulness for the colonized subject's condition and experiences. In particular, psychoanalysis did not attend to the particularities of the colonial subject's social condition and psychic world. For instance, psychoanalysis failed to account for the Black subject's experience with neurosis and phobia, which were not contingent upon transgressions as they were for the deracialized psychoanalytic subject. In this sense, whereas Freudian psychoanalysis theorized that childhood traumatic events contributed to neurosis, Fanon argued that a Black child's neurotic reaction is an effect of living in a White world that imprisoned her as a racial imago. A Black child raised in a 'normal family' is rendered abnormal upon and with the slightest contact with the White world (1967, p. 143). Thus, he takes Freud's psychogenic argument and replaces it with a sociogenic one.

According to Fanon, Black bodies are imagined, characterized and ossified as the White world's phobogenic object. Regardless of whether she commits transgressions, demonstrates evil, ugliness or actually possesses the overwhelming sexual prowess that the world fantasizes of her, she incites fear. These fantasies, similar to the system of signifiers, precede her.

Fanon (1967) argued that psychoanalysis did not account for this existence or the cultural mechanisms that enabled these fantasies. He argued that 'books, newspapers, school texts, advertisements, movies and radio' (p. 131) helped to circulate Manichean fantasies of anti-Black images. Psychoanalysis did not account for the effects of these draconian productions and the social forces that objectify and fetishize Black racial subjects. He used his own experience with a young White boy and his fantasy of being eaten: 'Mama, the [black man] is going to eat me up' (Fanon, 1967, p. 93). The Black subject is constantly inscribed by civil society's fantasy and articulations that she is not only antithetical to humanity but a threat to it.

In 'Bonding over phobia', David Marriott (2007) also criticizes psychoanalysis' relationship to race, racism and anti-Blackness in particular. He draws from Fanon and explores the fetishization and fixation on Black subjects in an anti-Black world. According to Marriott, Blackness is an 'instinctual component of the white psyche, linked inextricably to the psychic processes in which aggressive drives associated with phobic anxiety and fear become psychically effective through a racial subject or delegate' (2007, p. 427). In other words, these aggressive drives and anxieties exist before the Black subject. Based upon Marriott's analysis, these anxieties are activated and projected onto the Black subject even before she arrives on the scene. She becomes locked in as the screen for the projection of White phobic anxieties. Marriott astutely examines the collective White or more precisely the anti-Black unconscious that permeates society, shaping subjectivities.

Marriott (2007) highlights the discursive effects of anti-Black racial fantasies on Western society.[6] For some racial subjects, historical contexts and political climates have shaped the racial fantasies that inform how a subject is racialized. For instance, according to the theory of racial formations, there are political, economic and social contexts that govern how race is understood, constructed and contested (Omi & Winant, 1986). Marriott argues, however, that the ossification of Black subjects as phobogenic objects is atemporal. That is, there is a collective anti-Black unconscious that undergirds Western civil society and is not contingent upon specific contexts or periods. An anti-Black culture precedes the Black subject and her unconscious desires. These fantasies of her savagery, deficiency and evilness are part and parcel of an impenetrable racist culture equipped with violent institutions and apparatuses to reproduce them. True to the function of the unconscious, these fantasies are articulated in and permeate the Symbolic, through law in ways that are inescapable.

The penetration of the anti-Black unconscious into the Symbolic also shapes how Black youth relate to themselves and each other. He demonstrates this through a close reading of two historic case studies: Kenneth and Mamie Clark's doll study from the famous *Brown v. Board (1954)* case and Erik Erickson's study of a young Black girl who attempts to scrub Blackness off her skin and paints an already white piece of paper white again. He argues that the outcomes of these studies demonstrate that these Black children internalized the Manichean racist tropes associating Blackness with ugliness and negativity. According to Marriott, not only do the anti-Black unconscious and Symbolic exist to create psychic fissures in Black children, thereby creating split selves, but these split selves are necessary to the formation and coherence of White civil society. The psychic states of these children were inextricably connected to the social world, one largely shaped by White anxieties and anti-Black fantasies. These racial fantasies of the threatening Black figure thwart the possibility of Black subjectivities independent from anti-Black fantasies. This condition is what he calls the 'essence of blackness' (Marriott, 2007, p. 226).

Fanon, Spillers and Marriot offer challenges to psychoanalysis in ways that draw attention to this specific condition. They argue that an anti-Black unconscious is central to White society. These others are not only an effect of a racial hierarchy, but also imbued with racial fantasies that are necessary to the production of the illusion of a coherent and complete White society. Imagining Black figures as intrusive, dangerous, parasitic and different is part and parcel of the fantasy for a complete White society. It can take multiple forms.[7] This fantasy that they need to protect themselves against Black figures is in part what enables the community to come together. Thus, not only is there a collective unconscious, but that collective is fastened together by the anti-Black unconscious.

This does not mean that subjects do not resist. The resistance to being imprisoned by these fantasies and projections may be a part of what precipitates the compulsive reproduction and circulation of these fantasies. I would argue that resistance to anti-Blackness—whether actively performed or not—can also operate as justifications for conscious and unconscious efforts to survey, further imprison and punish Black subjects. The reproduction and circulation of these are not only ideological. They are institutionalized, circulated and reproduced through various conduits, and none with more discursive effects than through law.

NCLB: The Fixation and Fantasies

Drafted and implemented during President George W. Bush's administration, No Child Left Behind was the reauthorization of President Lyndon B. Johnson's Elementary and Secondary Education Act of 1965 (ESEA). Ostensibly crafted to address educational disparities, the policy mandated that federally funded schools be governed by an accountability system equipped with standards, measurements and yearly progress reports. NCLB's Statement of Purpose explains its intent, '[c]losing the achievement gap between high and low-performing children, especially the achievement gaps between minority and nonminority students, and between disadvantaged children and their more advantaged peers'.[8] Proponents of NCLB hailed the policy for bringing to national attention the issue of educational inequalities. The policy man dated disaggregating student data by income, race and language to monitor student, school and district performance. While there is some praise for this attention, I argue that NCLB has manifested itself as a part of a larger structural framework that fixates on Black bodies as problems.[9]

For example, the law requires that the performance of schools be determined by 'annual measurable objectives' (AMOs), which indicate the minimum percentage of students necessary to meet the proficiency level of reading and mathematical assessments. These measurement objectives also disaggregated data to assess the specific performance of limited English language learners, students with disabilities, major race and ethnic groups, and economically disadvantaged students. Schools are measured by the progress of these subgroups. Studies have shown that some of the subgroups identified by NCLB overlap such that Blacks often fit into a couple of the categories including race and ethnic majority and economically disadvantaged students (Kim & Sunderman, 2004). Thus, NCLB has popularized and institutionalized national attention on Black youth as problems to be solved. They operate as the premise for conversations on the failing educational system. The paradox is that while NCLB is supposed to be a beneficent policy, one designed to ensure accountability to historically marginalized youth, it is undergirded by an anti-Black fetishization—one that renders Black bodies as perennially deficient.[10]

The Discursive Effects of No Child Left Behind

As current policies, particularly NCLB, shed light on the problem of racial disparities, they also affect schooling experiences, particularly for marginalized youth, and the formation of racial subjectivities. Schools that failed to consistently meet

Adequate Yearly Progress (AYP) would be placed in Program Improvement (PI) and potentially sanctioned or reconstituted. Despite its claims to addressing inequalities, there have been growing criticisms of NCLB and its effects on marginalized youth. Scholars and researchers argue that the subsequent effects of NCLB on the educational environment, particularly for marginalized students, have not met the purported aims of the federal mandate.

Darling-Hammond (2007) has argued that this punitive dimension of NLB, although meant to hold schools and faculty accountable, further stigmatized already marginalized schools that often serve poor students of color. She also argued that qualified teachers would be less willing to work in sanctioned districts or schools—further punishing already underperforming schools. In addition to stigmatizing schools, researchers argue that the policy inadvertently tracks students (Heilig & Darling-Hammond, 2008). For instance, some schools may categorize underachieving students, mostly Black students, as special education students to circumvent rigorous standards and subsequent penalties.

NCLB has also affected how teachers directly teach their students. Au (2007) argues that to accommodate NCLB standards, teachers have increasingly narrowed their pedagogical and curricular focuses. Educational practices have become increasingly tailored to focus on reading, science and math standards. According to King and Zucker (2005),

> [T]he core academic subjects of reading, mathematics, and science are given priority at the expense of the time and resources dedicated to the instruction of other subjects in the curriculum, including social studies, physical education, foreign languages, and the arts.

In other words, academic courses are tailored to accommodate NCLB, often limiting the types of subjects that marginalized youth are taught. In this sense, according to the researchers, NCLB has helped to restructure schools such that teachers and classes primarily 'teach to the test' at the expense of other potentially important subjects.

Researchers are also beginning to find that the national rates of suspensions and expulsions have increased since the implementation of NCLB. According to the Advancement Project (2011), since the passage of NCLB, the role of police in schools has expanded and the 'school to prison pipeline' has grown. Their study argues that the shift toward high-stakes testing, school measurement and evaluation has contributed to the development of harsh school discipline policies and the criminalization of youth of color in schools. The report asserts that NCLB has not only facilitated an environment that narrows the curriculum and stigmatizes its students, it has also propelled schools to progressively filter out students who fail to meet rigidly ascribed school standards. According to a recent report issued by the Department of Education Office of Civil Rights, from 2009 to 2010, while Black youth make up 18 percent of the student population, they constitute 42 percent of the referrals to law enforcement, 35 percent of school-related arrests, 35 percent of the population of students suspended once, 46 percent of those suspended more than once and 39 percent of all students expelled. Students with disabilities, who are also disproportionately Black,[11] represent 12 percent of students in the sample, but nearly 70 percent of students physically restrained by adults (CRDC, 2012). These numbers provide some insight into the ways that the current public education system manages its Black students.

Taken together, these critical reports have helped to challenge NCLB and its claims to reform educational disparities in public education. Evaluating the mandated reforms is beyond the scope of this article. Although I have referred to the work that policy analysts and scholars have done to examine the disparate effects of NCLB, the objective of this article is to highlight the paradigmatic and structural implications of this educational policy and its fixation on marginalized youth for the purpose of 'closing the achievement gap'.

Despite its beneficent claims to equalizing educational opportunities and outputs, the race-conscious mandate, according to Leonardo (2007), is an instrument of Whiteness. The color-blind educational policy may claim intentions to redress racial inequalities, but its underpinnings and outcomes demonstrate otherwise. Contrary to the articulated claims of closing the achievement gap, NCLB naturalizes social inequalities. For instance, although schools do not receive adequate funding to meet NCLB mandates these students are blamed for failing to meet the standards because theoretically they were given ample opportunities to succeed. In addition, students who fail to meet the policy's racialized academic standards are stigmatizated and further alienated (Leonardo, 2007). Despite an apparent commitment in its language, the Act is unable to meet its goals of addressing and redressing racial disparities. This, I argue, is not a paradox or indicative of the policy's failure. Instead, it is a symptom of its fantasies of Black youth as deficient, Other, and perennially behind.

In lieu of providing a structural critique including the racism of US educational policies, NCLB fixates on marginalized students as problems. Even if the language of the policy is essentially to provide equal opportunities and high standards for historically neglected students, the emphasis is that these students are academically deficient, if not fetishized as such. Here, Lacanian psychoanalytic theory may help to investigate the formation of the racialized subject (and its society) through educational policy as a violent act (Gillborn, 2005). Given that racial fantasies and language shape subjectivities and inform law, I argue that NCLB is a formative signifier that shapes how Black students are recognized within the law, social institutions and language. It almost goes without saying that these students will be stigmatized, as Leonardo discussed in his essay (Leonardo, 2007). However, given the power of language to shape human subjects, their sense of each other and themselves, imagining Black students as deficient and problematic produce effects that extend beyond stigma. I argue that NCLB helps to constitute the Black subject to reify the illusion of a complete society premised upon anti-Blackness.

It is important to recall Lacanian psychoanalysis' theory of language existing before its subjects. While current academic standards and measurement systems may highlight important educational disparities, the anti-Black world fantasizes the existence of the deficient, evil, problematic Black other. NCLB institutionalized these fantasies of the phobogenic other. This does not mean that achievement gaps are not a fact or that educational disparities do not exist. It is important, however, for race-conscious scholars to analyze more than empirical evidence for what informs these mandates, their discourses and their effects.

As part of the formative Symbolic the Act has marked these students as problems for the entire educational system to be refashioned around. Studies show that this restructuring is failing to rectify the problem. In fact, as mentioned earlier, some studies show that NCLB has not only been unsuccessful in redressing educational inequalities, but also created more disparities, especially in the areas of school discipline and punishment. This may be because the problem lies not with the students, schools, teachers or funding, but with the pre-existing anti-Black fantasies that shape the Symbolic, the law and its institutions.

Lacanian Psychoanalysis and Critical Race Theory in Education

Some scholars have used psychoanalysis to understand race and racial subjectivities (Cheng, 2001; Eng, 2001; Eng & Kazanjian, 2003; Lane, 1998; Viego, 2007). Willy Apollon (1996), a Lacanian clinician, writes that colonialism prevents colonized subjects from developing their own use of the system of signifiers; they are denied their own phallic law. According to Apollon, the bane of colonialism is that the colonized subject is precluded from making her own meaning from the system of signifiers. Colonization's Symbolic refuses colonized subjects access to their own meaning making. The effects of this denial are undertheorized in deracialized psychoanalytic theory but counter-narratives in critical race theory do attempt to create an alternative world. However, critical race scholars must not only speak to the experiences of subjugation, but also challenge how the Symbolic violently creates its subjects, including people of color, making our identities and counter-narratives possible.

Returning to the field of education, if it is true that Black students are being marked and shaped by the NCLB mandate and its surrounding discourse on race and racism, then educational scholars must pay attention to how NCLB and the prevailing discourse on the achievement gap produce more than inequalities. NCLB not only shapes educational practices or increases disparities, but also reproduces the image of Black subjects as problems.

Although the important reforms and varied machinations including new school performance waivers may function to curtail some of the more explicit forms of disparities, the mandate at large has signifying effects. Drawing from Lacanian theory, NCLB is part and parcel of the Symbolic—*the* matrix that produces subjectivities and relationships to self and others. NCLB may be a colorblind policy reifying Whiteness (Leonardo, 2007), but it is undergirded by a particular form of racism, anti-Black racism which positions Black in the collective unconscious as the permanent Other, regardless of if they demonstrate otherwise. As Fanon, Marriott and Spillers remind us, Blackness existed as problems before she came onto the scene and before the test scores were available. This is not to say that supporters of NCLB have malevolent intentions. Instead, anti-Blackness is ubiquitous and inescapable, particularly when it has been couched in benevolent terms. NCLB is a means by which anti-Blackness is written into law.

Discussion

What is the traumatic truth being suppressed through the Symbolic of educational policies that imagined deficient Black children and shaped all its educational practices accordingly? Perhaps the truth of the current educational agenda reflects the fantasies of racialized subjects who must exist as the object of the White nation and anti-Black fears. I place NCLB at the level of the Symbolic, the register that allows subjects to elide what operates at the level of the Real, the register where phobic anxieties, tensions and abjection live. Psychoanalysis recalls the investments in repressing traumatic events and histories. Marriott (2007) astutely argues that Black subjects have become screens for the White psyche to project its phobic anxieties; that is, Black bodies operate as receptacles for layers of society's anxieties (p. 220). This is more than scapegoating. This is about how a society externalizes its phobic anxieties onto others, characterizing them as deficient, criminal, behind, low-achievers, marginal, minority and disadvantaged. While Black students may lack resources—as an effect of institutional and structural biases—there is an investment in this disparity that scholars in education and critical race theory must investigate. How would policy analysts and scholars think of educational reform if—as Fanon and Marriott remind us—Black students do not necessarily need to actually transgress or demonstrate inefficiency because they are already fantasized as threats and deficient before proving otherwise? NCLB has refashioned an entire educational system, including discourses framed in large part around the specter of the deficient Black youth. Combining critical race scholarship with Lacanian psychoanalysis may help us to better understand this particular problem and the fantasies that these youth are problems to be solved.

Notes

1 For a comprehensive study of NCLB, see Henry Giroux (2003).
2 For this article, I argue that Black and Latino youth are subjects of anti-Black fantasies.
3 This author is aware that the sovereignty of the state enables it to appropriate and integrate various perspectives to accommodate its political agenda.
4 Drawing from Althusser, Leonardo (2005) has identified this production as a form of interpellation.
5 While there are a multitude of Black communities, subjectivities and cultures, throughout this article I use the singular form of Black subject. I do this because I am addressing the White gaze, which conflates and homogenizes Black subjectivity.

This is one of the critiques that I have of both psychoanalysis and Whiteness which disavows the possibility for complex, Black human existence.

6 The emphasis on anti-Blackness does not mean that other forms of racism do not exist. I am using Fanon and Marriott's terms to better understand the pervasiveness of the Manichean ideology that shapes subjectivities, desires and experiences.

7 For example, she imagined as that which always takes from White society, extracting any multitude of resources (e.g. material items, mental labor, jobs, welfare, educational resources space).

8 www.law.cornell.edu/uscode/uscode20/usc_sec_20_00006301-000-.html

9 This author recognizes that schools, teachers and the educational system have been implicated in perpetuating the achievement gap. However, my argument is that these students were seen as problems to be fixed or failing students to begin with. The system and its agents failed to bring them, these problematized children, up to par with their peers. I also recognize that other students of color are negatively impacted or fixated upon by NCLB. Anti-Black fantasies also govern and discipline those who have some perceived proximity to Blackness.

10 It may be true that marginalized youth fall behind their peers in reading and mathematics, yet the focus is not on rectifying institutional poverty or the generational effects of structural racism. Instead, the language of NCLB is to hold schools and teachers accountable to an achievement gap that exists between particular groups.

11 According to the study, Black students represent 21 percent of students with disabilities. Forty-four percent of students with disabilities are subjected to mechanical restraints.

References

Advancement Project. (2011). *Test, punish, and push out: How "zero tolerance" and high-stakes testing funnel youth into the school-to-prison pipeline*. Washington DC: Advancement Project.

Apollon, W. (1996). Postcolonialism and psychoanalysis: The example of Haiti. *Journal for the Psychoanalysis of Culture and Society*, *1*(1), 43–51.

Au, W. (2007). High-stakes testing and curricular control: A qualitative metasynthesis. *Educational Researcher*, *36*(5), 258–267.

Brown, T., Atkinson, D., & England, J. (2006). *Regulatory discourses in education: A Lacanian perspective*. Oxford: P. Lang.

Cheng, A.A. (2001). *The melancholy of race*. Oxford and New York: Oxford University Press.

Darling-Hammond, L. (2007). Evaluating no child left behind. *The Nation*. Retrieved from www.thenation.com/doc/20070521/darling-hammond/3.

Eng, D.L. (2001). *Racial castration: Managing masculinity in Asian America*. Durham, NC: Duke University Press.

Eng, D.L., & Kazanjian, D. (2003). *Loss: The politics of mourning*. Berkeley, CA: University of California Press.

Fanon, F. (1967). *Black skin, white masks* (C. Lam Markmann, Trans.). New York: Grove Press.

Gillborn, D. (2005). Education policy as an act of white supremacy: Whiteness, critical race theory and education reform. *Journal of Educational Polity*, *20*(4), 485–505.

Giroux, H. (2003). *The abandoned generation: Democracy beyond the culture of fear*. New York: Palgrave Macmillan.

Heilig, J.V., & Darling-Hammond, L. (2008). Accountability Texas-style: The progress and learning of urban minority students in a high-stakes testing context. *Education Evaluation and Policy Analysis, 30*(2), 75–110.

Kim, J., & Sunderman, G.L. (2004). *Large mandates and limited resources: State response to the No Child Left Behind act and implications for accountability.* Cambridge, MA: The Civil Rights Project at Harvard University.

King, K., & Zucker, S. (2005). *Curriculum narrowing.* San Antonio, TX: Pearson Education.

Lacan, J. (1975). In Miller, J. (Ed.), *Seminar XXII of Jacques Lacan, R.S.I., 1974–1975* (J. Stone Trans.). Paris, France: Editions du Seuil.

Lacan, J. (1998). *On feminine sexuality: The limits of love and knowledge, 1972–1973.* New York: W.W. Norton.

Lacan, J. (2006). *Ecrits: The first complete edition in English* (B. Fink trans). New York: W.W. Norton & Co.

Ladson-Billings, G., & Tate, W.F. (1995). Toward a critical race theory of education. *Teachers College, 97*(1), 47–68.

Lane, C. (Ed.). (1998). *The psychoanalysis of race.* New York, NY: Columbia University Press.

Leonardo, Z. (2005). Through the multicultural glass: Althusser, ideology and race relations in post-civil rights America. *Policy Futures in Education, 3*(4), 400–412.

Leonardo, Z. (2007). The war on schools: NCLB, nation creation and the educational construction of whiteness. *Race, Ethnicity, and Education, 10*(3), 261–278.

Marriott, D. (2007). *Haunted life: Visual culture and black modernity.* New Brunswick, NJ: Rutgers University Press.

Omi, M., & Winant, H. (1986). *Racial formation in the United States: From the 1960s to the 1980s.* New York: Routledge & Kegan Paul.

Spillers, H.J. (2003). *Black, white, and in color: Essays on American literature and culture.* Chicago, IL: University of Chicago.

Todd, S. (2003). *Learning from the other: Levinas, psychoanalysis, and ethical possibilities in education.* Albany, NY: State University of New York Press.

US Department of Education Office for Civil Rights. (2012). *Civil rights data collection.* Washington DC: US Department of Education Office for Civil Rights.

Verhaeghe, P. (1999). *Does the woman exist? From Freud's hysteric to Lacan's feminine* (M. du Ry, Trans.). New York: Other Press.

Viego, A. (2007). *Dead subjects: Toward a politics of loss in Latino studies.* Durham, NC: Duke University Press.

Chapter 10

Interview With George Yancy, African-American Philosopher of Critical Philosophy of Race

Michael A. Peters

Editors' introduction

This 2019 article is written in the form of an interview between *Educational Philosophy and Theory* Editor-in-Chief Michael A. Peters with George Yancy, a Professor of Philosophy at Emory University and one of the leading American scholars on critical philosophy of race and whiteness studies. In the article, Peters discusses with Yancy his recent infamy in relation to his publications on race and whiteness in the United States (including a 2015 essay, 'Dear White America' and a 2018 book, *Backlash: What Happens When We Talk Honestly About Racism in America*); how he defines and understands race and racism in theory and reality; and the historical and ongoing challenges with discussing race broadly in society. The essay highlights concern with being able to communicate and express concerns about race and racism as a scholar, as well as challenges with joining academia and becoming a professor in the largely white field of philosophy, within a white supremacist society. In relation, Yancy addresses his own personal struggles against racism throughout his career as a case in point. The interview also connects race to a variety of problematic circumstances in the society more broadly, such as the election and fanfare around Donald Trump, and the viciousness of anti-Black backlash experienced by people of color throughout American history. This interview provides a dynamic dialogue about race in 2019 and the challenges faced by scholars of color as well as those courageous enough to fight against ongoing anti-Black rhetoric and violence.

George Yancy is professor of philosophy at Emory University. He is one of the leading scholars in the US on critical philosophy of race and critical whiteness studies. Yancy received his BA (cum laude) in philosophy from the University of Pittsburgh, his first MA from Yale, and his second MA in Africana Studies from New York University. He obtained his PhD in philosophy from Duquesne University with distinction. Yancy has authored, edited, and co-edited over 20 books. Some of his recent books are *Black Bodies, White Gazes: The Continuing Significance of Race in America* (Rowman & Littlefield, 2017), *On Race: 34 Conversations in a Time of Crisis* (Oxford University Press, 2017), and *Backlash: What Happens When We Talk Honestly about Racism in America*

DOI: 10.4324/9781003346104-11

(Rowman & Littlefield, 2018). Yancy is known for his controversial and widely discussed interviews and articles published in *The New York Times'* philosophy column, The Stone. Three of his books have won Choice Outstanding Academic Book Awards and he has twice won the American Philosophical Association Committee on Public Philosophy's Op-Ed contest.

Michael Peters: It's great to have this opportunity be able to interview you. You are not only an important scholar but also something of a 'celebrity,' if this means receiving huge media attention and lots of hate mail. Your new book *Backlash* has occasioned much comment but before getting you to talk about your most recent book can I ask you about your professional career. You are no stranger to controversy. Your 2015 essay 'Dear White America,' published in The Stone, *The New York Times* philosophy column, caught the attention of many in America who found your views unpalatable and they reacted badly, evenly violently. First of all, can you use this incident to explain your views on race and the controversy that followed?

George Yancy: Yes, well, you are right about the 'celebrity.' The article 'Dear White America' was one of those philosophical pieces that touched a raw nerve in white America; it went viral. The article received over two thousand comments. You know, despite the many publications that precede that article, when I am introduced to people they will often say, 'Yeah, you wrote that piece "Dear White America."' However, that 'celebrity' came with a price. But first, here is my understanding of race. To put things succinctly, race is a social construction. Like marriage, it isn't a natural kind, but a social kind. By this I mean that the concept of race doesn't have a referent in the natural world. There is no *thing* to which the concept of race points. So, it is a concept that is ontologically empty. Yet, it is a concept that exists. Its emergence in the world came from Western Europe. It is a concept that is socially and historically produced and shaped by colonial desire, bad faith, domination, psychological projection, and ontological and epistemic logics that are Manichean in nature, where whiteness has come to constitute what I term the transcendental norm. In short, whiteness, by its very nature, is binary and hierarchical. Whiteness is the thesis (that is, it establishes itself as such) and 'racialized' groups that are not white are deemed 'different,' 'deviant,' that is, the antithesis. Despite the fact that race is not a natural kind, it has tremendous *social* ontological power; the concept is a powerful organizing social vector that functions as if it cuts at the very joints of reality. The concept of race constitutes our institutional spaces, our political forms of arrangement, our perceptions, our bodily comportment in space, our organization of lived space and lived experience. In fact, the state itself is a site of racial power. So, let's get one point clear. While the concept of race is unreal qua natural kind, the concept of race has served to create rigid social binaries and used to oppress, to dehumanize, to murder, to render disposable. That is what we mean by racism. Historically, within the context of North America, this is what I mean by white racism. In our contemporary moment, it can be argued that race continues to advantage white people globally, continues to render their lives worth living, and axiologically supreme vis-'a-vis people of color.

These were some of the stated and unstated assumptions that were embedded within my article 'Dear White America.' My objective was to write a letter of love to white Americans to get them to tarry with the concept of what it means for them to have inherited, even if unintentionally, white privilege, which I see as a certain kind of immunity. The most controversial part of the letter was that I asked white people to dwell within the uncomfortable space of accepting the impact that their whiteness has on Black people and other people of color and how that implicates them within processes of racist iteration. So, I wanted white people to understand that they are positioned through a social web of racial differential power that has a negative impact on people of color. I wanted them to think about how their whiteness constitutes a relational site of oppression, and how white racism is an opaque structure that delimits how they understand their own racism. At *no* point did I say that *all* white people are racist. I argued for a contextual perspective, a relational dynamic view that argues that white racism is not to be limited to a neoliberal conception of the self and a thin causal argument about how 'mean white people' directly and consciously harm people of color. I introduced an ontology that speaks to forms of complicity that relationally place white people in positions of both psychic opacity regarding an awareness of the limits of their own racism and structural embeddedness within whiteness. Given this, how can we continue to speak of 'white innocence'? I don't think we can.

The controversy that followed the publication of 'Dear White America,' and, hence, that sense of 'celebrity' that followed, consisted of tons of really nasty and hate-filled mail sent to me by white people, threats of physical violence, death threats, and the use of unconscionable racist epithets. I was called 'nigger' hundreds of times. My sense is that I held up a disagreeable mirror to white America and they refused to see themselves within it. But James Baldwin has warned that when people continue to hold on to their innocence long after that innocence has gone that they turn into monsters. I like this point because it speaks to the fact that to maintain that 'innocence,' white people will prefer the monstrous over honesty. The lack of innocence is too hard to bear and the response to those who insist upon the lack of white 'innocence,' well, they become the targets of that massive denial. That is what I became. I became a target of white denial. I became the so called anti-white monster who dared to tell the truth. You know, there is a price to be paid for telling the truth, especially when it involves uncovering what has been covered over. Yet, this is the history of white America. It is a history of spinelessness when it comes to facing the truth about its continued systemic white racism. So many white people would rather hide behind a hypocritical 'innocence.'

Michael Peters: A very clear explanation of whiteness and racism. Your treatment at the hands of those offended by your letter is horrendous and it must have been very scary for you and potentially dangerous for you and your family. I wonder whether I can draw you out on a couple of points. 'Dear White America' seems to me a pedagogical device and that social change is related to truth telling.

This seems to me an exemplary role for a philosopher but why should White America depend on a Black philosopher for truth and responsibility? Truth seems so much at a premium in Trump's America of systematic lying and distortion. Can you comment on this issue.

George Yancy: It was very scary, especially when one needs the protection of university police, which is what I needed after so many threats. And they continue. As recently as this interview, there was a message sent to me that said, 'Kill yourself.' You are correct. The letter was designed as a pedagogical device to cultivate a sense of white self-criticality, to augment white consciousness, to encourage white people to identify ways in which they suffer from an epistemology of ignorance and bad faith. In this sense, pedagogy ought to be dangerous, because it can function as a process of loss and fundamental transformation, which can be a very dangerous process, especially as it means losing assumptions and embodied habits that help to buttress hegemonic systems. Within this context, pedagogy is a site of parrhesia or courageous speech regarding white privilege and power. Michel Foucault described parrhesia as a process of truth-telling in the face of possible death, as a form of risking the possibility of death. I have no desire to die because of what I say, but I do want to bear witness to the truth, to speak truth in the face of so much deception, simulacra, and hyper-reality. This is what Socrates did, what Martin Luther King Jr. did, and what Audre Lorde did. It seems to me that truth-telling is part of the *raison d'tre* of what it means to be a philosopher, especially within our contemporary moment in North America. Your point about dependency vis-à-vis truth and responsibility is a good one. There are times when I abhor the idea that white America depends upon me or Black people, more generally, to teach them about *their* racism and the importance of *their* responsibility to own *their* racism. It is unfair. It is like asking women to do the lion's share of the work of teaching men about their sexism, our sexism. So, women, though oppressed, are supposed to be our liberators as well? This is a move still dictated by the logics of male hegemony. Such a requirement would be an unjust form of labor. In my case, I don't want white people do be dependent upon me, but open. I want them to do the hard work of being open to be wounded by the truth that they are not innocent. In short, I see myself as a contemporary philosophical gadfly. Baldwin had this in mind when he talked about forcing our white brothers and sisters, with love, to see themselves as they are. So, it's about *Alethea*, which is the Greek word that means to be unconcealed. I want to reveal whites to themselves—unconcealed and naked. And while white people are the target of the truth-telling, there is something existentially far larger: it is the process of speaking truth so that I might live another day, so that my Black sons will not be killed by a white lie that says that they are 'criminals' because they are Black. The presupposition here is that the act of truth-telling functions to liberate us all, because our lives are haptic, what I call an ontology of no edges.

This way of reframing sociality in terms of an ontology of no edges as opposed to an ontology that undergirds neoliberalism is so important within the madness that is North America under the 'leadership' of Donald Trump. Within Trump's fictional and alternative world, the precious lives of undocumented immigrants are disposable, a 'blight' on white America's growing white nationalist isolationism. It is that white nationalist lie that is now the unabashed meta-narrative that is being fed to a predominantly white base that doesn't give a damn about truth or fact. Appearance is what matters and obfuscation helps to relieve the guilty of their guilt. Trump peddles masks and aspires for a system of control as threatening as *1984*. I should have seen it coming as many white supremacist websites that 'discussed' my article had images of Trump smiling like an emoji figure. The face of Trump was juxtaposed right there next to all sorts of electronic forms of racist berating and dehumanization of me. In short, the image of Trump 'validated' the racist responses to me. Hence, the responses that I continue to receive regarding 'Dear White America' have the sound and fury of white authoritarianism and neo-fascism. And like under Nazism, if we are not careful, democratic freedom will not simply suffer, but it will die. And truth-tellers will be faced with more than the condemnation to drink hemlock. If we are not careful, Trump will outlaw truth and convince many that it is for their own good. In Trump's ideal world, 2+2 will *no longer* equal 4, but 5. And to critique whiteness will be labelled a 'thought-crime.' The threat of *1984* is upon us, the stench of dystopia is in the air.

Michael Peters: I also wonder about your ability to withstand such viciousness. As it is Black philosophers are not numerous—an aspect also of White America, or what I have called White Philosophy. It has been such a white discipline (policing the canon) even for those known as pragmatists fall short of recognizing the context and history of America. Would you please tell us something of your background and why you turned to philosophy, traditionally a white discipline even if the politics had remained buried until very recently.

George Yancy: You are correct. The last that I checked, Black people constitute about 1.1% of the profession. And there are far fewer Black women professional philosophers than Black men. So, there is the intersectional problem. You know, when the threats ushered in, I was very delighted that The Committee on the Status of Black Philosophers provided me with a great deal of support. The American Philosophical Association (APA) did as well. In fact, it was an historic moment that they came out in support of a high profile public philosopher who was being bullied. Of course, not all Black philosophers think alike. I'm sure that there were some who would rather I had not written the letter. Some may have even found themselves in the position of having to protect their white colleagues against my act of truth-telling. But your point is important as it does raise the issue of the continued paucity of Black people within the professional field of philosophy. It is, as you know, not just a question of numbers, but a question of the normative whiteness of the field, the ways in which the term 'universal' is still deployed to deny philosophical importance to issues regarding race, racism, whiteness. The normative whiteness of the field continues to attempt to reside within the ethereal clouds of ideal theory, where ideas are treated as 'ahistorical.' And while pragmatism sees philosophy as a site for engaging in processes of critical confrontation with problems that human beings confront, recognizing the importance of this-worldly issues and the importance of critical intelligence, I would welcome more white philosophers who identify as pragmatists to grapple with the issue of whiteness, their whiteness, more frequently and with deep vigilance. At the end of the day, not only does the canon continue to be policed, but Black bodies continue to be policed within the conceptual space of the profession, especially as issues that grow out of a broad and diverse 'Black experience' are not deemed *philosophically* relevant. Within this context, Black students turn away from philosophy because they don't see themselves reflected within the field; neither within the phenotypic whiteness of the field nor within the conceptual space of the field.

I initially turned to philosophy (discovered it really) at 17-year-old with absolutely no knowledge about how the field is governed by white epistemic orders, though I do remember seeing the faces of all white men when shown who represented the history of Western philosophy. Of course, Western philosophy governed and fashioned itself as philosophy qua philosophy. So, I was naïve, but I was still enthusiastic that there was this field that critically engaged questions regarding the meaning of human existence, whether or not God exists, the nature of beauty, justice, truth. I was an unusually curious young boy. I would bug my mother almost daily about the existence of God and the meaning of death. And I did all of this while living within the ghetto, a place where young Black people were to die, and where we were certainly not to emerge as philosophers. Yet, there I was reading about Plato, Spinoza, Bertrand Russell, et al. I was a young Black boy living in poverty reading the grand thoughts of white men. But there was a certain unspoken conceptual violation perpetrated. Why did I believe that I was the only Black philosopher in the world at that young age? Who had failed me? My white teachers had at no point mentioned the existence of Black philosophers. It was my good fortune, though, to have been introduced to a brilliant African-American scholar by the name of James G. Spady. He introduced me to an invisible canon that included Black philosophers. I then found myself at home within philosophy in a very different way. There began to emerge an understanding that philosophy is inextricably linked to non-ideal conditions. Philosophy was no longer by definition white, pure, and abstracted from the deep racial horrors of everyday Black existence.

I recall when I became interested in African-American philosophy, a white philosopher-mentor of mine warned: 'Be careful that you don't get pegged.' This was very revealing. At no point did he warn me about being pegged a Kantian or Hegelian or Platonist. You see, African-American philosophy, like the Black body, was marked as 'different,' as 'ersatz.' My white philosopher-mentor had already been seduced by the so-called universality of the Western philosophical experience or the white North American philosophical experience. Embedded within that notion of 'universality' is white narcissism, a form of white nativism. One might ask here: Is there a difference between the white ideological assumptions of philosophy and Trump's rhetoric regarding making America great (that is, white) again? I think that both are torn from the same racist and ideologically toxic cloth, the same white hubris. And both attempt, as Henry A. Giroux might argue, to hide beneath a destructive form of neoliberal hegemonic common sense.

These days, philosophy for me is no longer simply a site of wonder, but a site of suffering. While that might sound counterintuitive to many, it isn't for me. Philosophy dares to engage questions that speak to who and what we are, how we have failed ourselves, and what we might become. It dares to challenge power structures that are firmly in place, it dares to demask, which also includes removing the masks that I hide behind. You see, that can be painful, that involves suffering as we begin to learn about ourselves and our complicity regarding the suffering of others. Thinking philosophically makes me lose sleep. It forces me to face forms of responsibility that I would rather not see. In this way, African-American philosophy or Black philosophy or Africana philosophy must weep as it dares to face the tragic, dares to grapple with those experiences that are painfully concrete and that are implicative of who we are as finite human beings. My book *Backlash* grows out of this suffering. I characterize it as the most raw/candid book on racism written by a professional philosopher. Writing out of this experience, doing philosophy from within the muck and mire of the embodied impact of lived racism, engages the process of rethinking philosophy as a site of tarrying within the messiness of life. Like the Blues, philosophical thought tarries with pain and suffering, but doesn't become defeated by the pain and the suffering. The Blues singer begins in a place and time of suffering; it is a location. So, African-American practice and performance of philosophy begins from *somewhere*, and it lays bare the lie that philosophy begins from *nowhere*.

Michael Peters: The narrative of your background makes compelling reading and your statement 'philosophy for me is no longer simply a site of wonder, but a site of suffering' is very moving. Ok so let's turn to your new book *Backlash: What Happens When We Talk Honestly about Racism in America* (2018). The blurb reads

> When George Yancy penned a *New York Times* op-ed entitled 'Dear White America' asking white Americans to confront the ways that they benefit from racism, he knew his article would be controversial. But he was unprepared for the flood of vitriol in response.
>
> The resulting blowback played out in the national media, with critics attacking Yancy in every form possible—including death threats—and supporters rallying to his side. Despite the rhetoric of a 'postrace' America, Yancy quickly discovered that racism is still alive, crude, and vicious in its expression.

Can you elaborate on this and maybe also talk about the way in which the election of Trump has damaged any progress—I'm thinking about Charlottesville as an example but there have been dozens of incidents including police shooting of Black folk.

George Yancy: Sure. A white female colleague of mine actually said to me that I was being disingenuous when I said that I had not anticipated the level of white racist vitriol that I received. In many ways, she perpetuated some of the same toxic discourse. In this case, she accused me of lying. By the way, there were also white readers who actually said that I lied about the racist discourse directed at me, a barrage of discourse that left its bodily impact on me. One cannot be called a 'nigger' hundreds of times without it negatively impacting one's psyche. It is like a blunt object. Yet, I had not anticipated the sheer number of times that I was called a 'nigger,' a 'monkey,' a 'hoodrat,' a 'piece of shit,' a 'coon,' a 'racist pig,' a 'race baiter,' told to 'kill myself,' told to 'go fuck myself,' warned that I might end up on a cold slab, that my mouth needs to be shut permanently, accusations that I wrote 'Dear White America' so that white women would perform fellatio on me (no kidding here). That is the *sickness*, and so much more, that white America threw at me, vomited out of their white twisted imaginary. So, despite my understanding of white American history, I was not fully prepared. Perhaps there is this nagging urge, even if grossly misleading, to believe that white America is better. So, for me, any talk of a 'postrace' America is a lie. As Paul Gilroy has argued, we need to discern the actual *racial* work that a 'postrace' discourse performs. 'Postrace' discourse serves to maintain whiteness precisely by postulating a fictive notion of 'post' regarding race. Sorry, but we are in the belly of the beast of American white supremacy and Trump is the Freudian psychoanalytic impulsive id of its unabashed expression.

So, for me, Trump is not an anomaly. He is the expression of a subterranean sedimentation of white supremacist beliefs unleashed while occupying the 'highest' political office in the United States. And his racism didn't just begin during his morally inept characterization of what took place in Charlottesville, VA. However, it was explicitly on display and the nation and the world got to witness it. Trump claimed that there was blame on both sides when it came to judging the actions of white supremacists and those who opposed them. He also said that there were very fine people on both sides. Needless to say, white supremacists were proud of Trump's moral equivocation. And for those who are unaware of Trump's history, keep in mind that back in the early 1970s a federal lawsuit was brought again him for allegedly discriminating against African-Americans regarding renting from one of his properties. This is consistent with the racist xenophobe that we have come to know. Also keep in mind that after five teenagers of color (Black and Latino) were arrested in 1989 and imprisoned for the alleged crime of assaulting and raping a white woman, Trump took out ads in a few major New York newspapers calling for the death penalty to be returned. Fourteen years later, based upon DNA evidence, all five were found innocent. To my knowledge, Trump has not as of yet publically accepted their innocence. In short, such bodies, for Trump, are always already guilty. For Trump, the Sartrean credo regarding people of color works in reverse: essence precedes existence. We are fixed in our essence vis-à-vis 'criminality.' Even as he was running for president he referred to Black people in problematic and fixed terms, claiming that we live in our poverty, that our schools are no good, and that we have no jobs. This is the stuff of white racist stigmatization of Black spaces as dysfunctional. After all, he asks Black people, 'What the hell do you have to lose?' In short, Trump positioned himself as the 'white savior figure,' apparently the only one capable of healing the self-imposed pathology that Black people have brought upon themselves. Or think about the racist perpetuation of Trump's Birther lie regarding Obama's place of birth. This was and is an affront to North America's first African-American president and those, especially Black people, who voted from him. Or think about Trump's reference to 'shithole' countries in Africa, especially in opposition to Norway. This is Trump at his white racist symbolic best. Within this context, how different is Trump's rhetoric from Hitler's support of Nordicism? The expressed preference for those from Norway can't be easily extricated from myths regarding the existence of a 'master race.' After all, we know Trump's position on undocumented immigrants as being 'animals' and Mexicans being 'rapists.' And we know that NFL players (mostly Black) who decide to take a knee against racial injustice are called 'sons of bitches.' And recently, we know that those who ought to be deemed our neighbors, those for whom we ought to extend our mutually shared humanity, are being dehumanized and traumatized through violent processes of familial separation, where parents are being sequestered from their precious children under Attorney General Jeff Sessions' zero tolerance policy regarding those entering the US illegally. Sounds very much like the horrible Japanese internment camps in the US and the history of fear of the 'Yellow Peril.'

Let me be clear, these actions read like the potential nightmare of a *final solution*. And the Nazi reference is intended here. That is how dire I read Trump's neo-fascism, his xenophobia, his white nativism. Indeed, I also read Trump through several concepts articulated by Giroux where he sees a form of pathological nationalism, uninhibited militarism, the identification of 'enemies' as ideological tools of national unification, and a politics of disposability under Trump. I have every reason to agree with Giroux. Think here of the disposability of Black bodies by the state or proxies of the state. On June 19, 2018, 17-year-old Antwon Rose, in East Pittsburgh, PA, was in a vehicle stopped by police. Rose, unarmed, ran from the car and was shot 3 times and died later. This is a narrative all too familiar when it comes to Black lives; they don't matter in white America. Why do I say this? Think here of the history of the slave trade, the diseased infested hold of slave ships, states of traumatic un-freedom, phenomenological trauma, geographic dislocation and psychological disorientation, the violent rape of Black women's bodies, Black codes, the violent disruption and surveillance of Black bodies within public (white) spaces, convict leasing, Black bodies used as capital, castrated Black bodies, white myth-making, lynched Black bodies, Jim Crow, the new Jim Crow, mass incarceration, macro and micro-racist aggressions, environmental racism, the school-to-prison pipeline. That is America to me! So, when I think about young Rose, I think about that shameful and anti-theological history. In the case of Rose, where was the hesitation? Where was the benefit of the doubt? Where was that sense of Rose being treated as a Thou? How is it that running away from a police officer is a 'threat' to that police officer's life, a threat that would 'justify' shooting, in this case, Rose, who probably had his back facing the officer as he ran? America has always been a place where Black bodies have faced and been targets of white state violence. Indeed, as David Theo Goldberg would argue, America, in its state formation, is a racial formation. But when I think about the recent death of Rose, I cannot divorce such actions from Trump's militarism, his rhetoric of 'fire and fury,' the violent imagery that he used during his run for the presidency, and his statement, while president, that police officers shouldn't be 'too nice' when arresting people. What is that callous statement but a stamp of approval for the violent treatment of Black and Brown bodies, those who are disproportionately locked behind bars? So, for me, Trump is an existential threat to Black and Brown people, and he is an enemy of what is left of our fragile American democratic experiment.

This brings us back to *Backlash*. The book is a philosophical text that communicates a profound sense of suffering and does so without flinching. I think that is rare for a traditional philosophical text. Yet, it also communicates a fundamental truth about North America; it is a nation that is racist to its very core. That is hard for the white demos to hear and let alone to accept. The actual inclusion of so much of the white racist vitriol within the book also makes *Backlash* a rare philosophical text that encourages its readers to remain on the proverbial ground, situated within the sickness that floods much of white consciousness in North America. That brings me back to the theme of suffering. White America has not suffered. And by this I don't mean that white America has not seen its share of disasters. But white America has not faced its continued refusal when it comes to treating Black people as human beings. On the whole, white America doesn't give a damn about my call to suffering and certainly not a national form of healing. Yet, there will be no national healing until white America weeps long into night for its crimes against Black people. *Backlash* demands that white America see itself as it is. Its future depends upon seeing itself in our (Black) disagreeable mirror. That mirror is terrifying. It has to be, because that is the history of white America. We return, then, to masks or, more accurately, unmasking or demasking. For love can also be terrifying, especially when it asks of us to remove those masks, as Baldwin has prophetically stated, that we fear we cannot live without and know we cannot live within. That is what *Backlash* is about; it is about a form of love as a dangerous practice where white people learn how to live without masks.

Chapter 11

Teaching Whiteness
A Dialogue on Embodied and Affective Approaches

Jane Chi Hyun Park and Sara Tomkins

Editors' introduction

This essay by Jane Chi Hyun Park and Sara Tomkins, published in 2021, describes the experiences of two women teachers with different racial and cultural backgrounds, Korean American and white Anglo Australian, involved with teaching a class 'Representing Race and Gender' to undergraduate students at the University of Sydney. The class and the essay focus particularly on the challenges of teaching about whiteness and white privilege in relation to the teachers' own racial backgrounds and that of their students. After giving some context to the course and its development and explaining the relationship between the two authors as educators and colleagues, Park and Tomkins focus on their pedagogy and practices during the week in which they focus on whiteness and their aftermath. In particular, the paper explores affect and embodiment in their classroom experiences, discussions of white guilt and 'whitesplaining', and the roles of various students, including students of colour in the classroom, noting the different experiences of students based on their racialised backgrounds, as well as on who their teacher is and their teacher's pedagogy and background. This article is noteworthy for taking an intersectional approach to the challenges faced in Australia related to race, ethnicity, gender, religion, and other issues, and for its strong narrative style which creatively bends the rules for academic article publication, particularly through its use of a dialogical format.

Introduction

This paper provides a critical reflection of our different experiences—as Asian American and Anglo Australian women—teaching a second-year undergraduate course at the University of Sydney called 'Representing Race and Gender'. Using scholarship on feminist pedagogy and whiteness, we discuss the strategic ways in which we have referenced and performed our own embodied identities to encourage students to apply concepts about race and gender to their own lives. In particular, we focus on how we have taught material on whiteness and white privilege to students of various racial, ethnic, and cultural backgrounds and how they have responded to the same material when it is taught by a white or non-white woman. Through this shared reflection, we consider how the pedagogical

DOI: 10.4324/9781003346104-12

practice of acknowledging our identities and lived experiences in the classroom has contributed to the development of critical racial consciousness in our students.

The paper consists of three sections: the first provides necessary context on the course and the instructors; the second, an overview of the readings and primary text for the week on whiteness; and the third, a simulated dialogue between the instructors on various issues that consistently have come up during this week.

We want to emphasise that this paper presents a highly individual case study for 'teaching whiteness'—one that has emerged from a specific cultural, geographical, and temporal context (a Gender and Cultural Studies department in one of the leading research universities in Australia from 2013 to 2018) and that reflects the confluence of the unique personalities, communication styles, and life experiences of the two lecturers. We hope that some of the strategies we discuss below will prove interesting and potentially useful to readers who likewise teach or are interested in teaching similar, affectively and politically charged university courses that centre issues of difference around race, gender, sexuality, and disability using an intersectional framework.

However, we would strongly caution against incorporating these strategies into one's own teaching practices without considering seriously the particular aims of the course, the needs and expectations of the students, and one's own unique style and personality as an instructor. In other words, the highly anecdotal and experience-based case study below should not be taken as a teaching model but rather as an invitation for readers to reflect on their own embodied identities and experiences in the classroom, to consider how they might be read by their students and what strategies would work best to communicate clearly, honestly, and compassionately with them.

Course Background and Instructors

According to the course description, Representing Race and Gender (hereafter, RRG) 'introduces students to cultural theories about race and ethnicity and uses these theories to examine representations of racial minorities across a range of media such as film, literature and performance within multiple national contexts'. Lectures, tutorials, and assignments are geared toward getting students to analyse power dynamics in cultural narratives that foreground racial and ethnic difference mostly in Australia and the US. The course usually attracts around 100 students every semester. In general, the cohort is politically progressive, feminist, queer, and queer-friendly.

When RRG ran for the first time in 2013, it was allocated a classroom with capacity to seat 30 students maximum. Instead over 100 students enrolled, and the course has continued to be popular and well received by students within and outside the major—in large part because there are so few courses like it. Until very recently, this was the only course in the Department of Gender and Cultural Studies that addressed scholarship on race and ethnicity. Based on the curricular importance and ongoing popularity of RRG, a first-year unit, 'Introduction to Diversity' and a third-year unit, 'The Cultural Politics of Difference' were introduced in 2018 and 2020, respectively, as part of a pathway for students interested in pursuing 'Diversity Studies' within Gender and Cultural Studies. The majority of students who enrol in this course are invested in social justice and are aware of the need to acknowledge the existence of racism within an intersectional framework. Students of colour in particular are hungry for scholarship that acknowledges the structural racism most of them have faced throughout their lives and teachers who treat this scholarship—and their experiences—with sensitivity and compassion.

Jane, a Korean American senior lecturer, developed the course in 2013 and has coordinated, lectured, and tutored on the course since then. She had previously conducted research and taught courses in the United States on media representations of people of colour with a focus on Asian Americans. Upon arrival in Australia, she noticed the lack of such courses in the department as well as the Faculty of Arts.

When Sara began tutoring for RRG in 2015, she was finishing her dissertation on black-Jewish relationality in Jewish American comedy under Jane's supervision. She and Jane have a long history of working together. Jane supervised Sara's honours thesis and they kept in touch while Sara worked on her MA in American Studies before beginning her PhD in the department. In addition to tutoring on the course, Sara coordinated and lectured for RRG in 2016.

Week on Whiteness

We have chosen to focus on the week on whiteness to illustrate some of the broader issues we encounter while teaching this class. This topic falls in week 3, after weeks on race and experience and racial stereotypes. The whiteness week is a necessary foundation for the rest of the semester which goes on to centre people of colour through our choices of topics, readings, and films.

In this week students watch the Australian film *Romper Stomper* about young, Neo-Nazi youth who attack Vietnamese youth (Wright, 1992) then analyse the racial, class, and gender dynamics in the film using concepts from the required readings—extracts from *White* (Dyer, 1997) and *White Nation* (Hage, 1998) as well as the article 'White Privilege: Unpacking the Invisible Knapsack' (McIntosh, 1988/2004). Due to space constraints, we will not discuss the film and readings in detail, though we will engage with relevant concepts.

We begin the tutorial by unpacking the list of white privileges in McIntosh's (1988/2004) classic article. Items on this list include 'I can if I wish arrange to be in the company of people of my race most of the time' and 'I can go shopping alone most of the time, pretty well assured that I will not be followed or harassed' (McIntosh, 1988/2004, p. 99). While this list is dated and assumes a racial optic specific to the United States, it remains a useful teaching tool to open up class discussion (see Croll, 2014, p. 78; Haltinner, 2014).

We ask students to go through the list of 46 items and tick what applies to them. Then we ask them to raise their hands to indicate their results mostly yeses, mostly noes, or a mix of yes and noes. This visually striking part of the activity leads to some valuable conversations around ideas such as conditional whiteness and the privileges and losses associated with being white-passing. Finally, we ask students to reflect critically on the usefulness of this activity in the classroom space, which often (though not always) is dominated by white women. We discuss the possibilities and constraints of such a space to decentre whiteness by making it visible (Dyer, 1997, p. 4). Sometimes this involves directly asking students if they think this activity allows us to critique white privilege or if it reinforces it and marginalises non-white students.

We have continued to use the McIntosh list to help counter the problem of abstraction, an ongoing issue in the course especially pronounced in the whiteness week. For instance, in discussions of *Romper Stomper*, abstraction often takes the form of students locating racism in the Neo-Nazi youth gang members. These principal characters embody what Hage (1998, p. 93) conceptualises as 'bad white nationalists' (those with explicitly racist views) rather than the target audience of the film who resemble the peripheral 'good white nationalist' characters (those who 'tolerate' racial and cultural difference so long as it does not threaten their white privilege, which remains unacknowledged). Hage's key argument is that these two forms of white nationalism are not separate but rather, exist on a continuum. Both are different expressions of a dominant 'white will' that, within the system of Australian multiculturalism, *manages* and speaks for Indigenous and other non-white, non-western peoples and cultures (Hage, 1998, pp. 78–116). Despite students reading Hage's critique, many inadvertently reproduce it during discussions of *Romper Stomper*.

Unsurprisingly, this week on whiteness is a loaded one for both of us, for different reasons. Through a dialogue format, in the next section, we examine how we conduct our discussions and students' responses. We also consider key issues that have emerged in relation to this topic, making reference to specific aspects of classroom dynamics.

Affective and Embodied Approaches

Sara: Of all the topics in this course, the week on whiteness is the one I feel most comfortable teaching. While I have research expertise on other topics in the course, this feels like the only topic where I have bodily authority. Key to my perspective on teaching this course is my own experience of whiteness as an undergraduate student. I took a similar class to RRG as a nineteen-year-old, and it was the first time I had ever been exposed to any critical material around race. I discuss my history directly with my students because, following Daniela Gachago (2018, p. 140), I believe being a white academic ally means 'being hyperaware and upfront about who we are, our own intersectional subjectivities' and how this impacts our teaching and research. My background has allowed me to anticipate how white students might come to the course material and to develop pedagogical scaffolding that is contextually specific to Australian approaches to race.

It has also informed how I react when students make mistakes and express ignorant or explicitly racist views in class. I try to engage with them in these moments in an intellectually and interpersonally generous way while ensuring my responses are not catering to white fragility, both the students' and my own.

Robin DiAngelo (2011, p. 54) conceptualises this idea of white fragility as a 'state in which even a minimum amount of racial stress becomes intolerable, triggering a range of defensive moves. These moves include outward display of emotions such as anger, fear and guilt, and behaviors such as argumentation, silence and leaving the stress-inducing situation'. She cites an 'entitlement to racial comfort' as one of the key factors that inculcates white fragility, which in the classroom informs my efforts to push myself and white students outside our racial comfort zones in order to begin the work of genuinely grappling with racism and the ways we are implicated in it (DiAngelo, 2011, p. 60). Whenever I feel concerned about striking a balance between discomfort as a pedagogical strategy and ensuring my students' well-being, I am reminded of DiAngelo's (2011, p. 61) point about not confusing comfort with safety. That is, even as I want the classroom to be a space of learning and care, I also do not want it to be a space where white people's experiences and emotions are being valued over those of non-white people (Froyum, 2014). That said, the ignorance, micro-aggressions, and racism that come out during this course land very differently on Jane and students of colour than it does on me and the white students. For academics of colour, especially women, the white fragility of students often generates a range of challenging responses from passive aggressive resistance to their teaching and authority right through to outright hostility and confrontation (see Bermúdez & Camacho, 2019; Evans-Winters & Hines, 2020). Due to this, the emotional labour of teaching RRG falls disproportionately on Jane.

Jane: I have historically approached this week with fear and dread. No matter how positive my teaching evaluations or how friendly the classroom vibe, I invariably feel like a wise old mouse teaching a class of eager kittens with a few scared and angry young mice scattered among the group. This feeling stems not only from the increasingly dehumanising constraints of the corporate university and the institutionalised racism of the Western academic system but also my own internalised need to address and please white people, and the high functioning anxiety that underlies constantly having to perform my racial and gendered difference in a friendly, non-threatening way—in the classroom, as a 'teaching moment'.

Nonetheless, I firmly believe in the power of using my identity and experiences, a pedagogical strategy I have elsewhere discussed as 'embodied inter-referencing' (Park, 2019), to facilitate both cross-cultural conversations between white and non-white students and inter-cultural conversations among students of colour who identify as such. Given the miniscule numbers of non-white female scholars and university teachers in the Faculty, I am highly visible—in positive ways as a role model for students of colour and negative ones as a public target.

This was highlighted last year when a newspaper reporter secretly infiltrated Introduction to Diversity, a first-year unit that I had developed with the help of Sara and was convening for the first time. This anonymous reporter took a photo of me and my dog who I had brought to class, and published it in a defamatory article ridiculing my work as 'peddling pc nonsense'. Still reeling from the trauma of this event, I had to give a lecture on white privilege in this class on the very afternoon that I learned about the news article. It was one of the most difficult lectures I have had to deliver in my almost twenty years of teaching. It was also my best lecture yet on the topic of whiteness, precisely because my anger overrode my usual fear. I spoke frankly about the emotional challenges of teaching this particular topic for me as an Asian American woman for whom white space—including university and classroom space—never feels completely safe or comfortable.

After analysing the newspaper incident as a case study of the ways in which white privilege structures systemic racism in Australia, I directly addressed the students of colour and the white students separately. To the former, I said: 'You need to acknowledge the ways in which living within whiteness has made you doubt your own reality, and you need to find and create safe spaces where your difference is valued so that you can have the energy to grow and create outside the white gaze'. To the latter, I said: 'Your job is to translate this material for your white family, friends, and colleagues because no matter how brilliant, articulate, and measured the non-white students in this classroom are, they will never be heard by those in power as you will. But before you can do that, you need to acknowledge your white privilege and listen to and learn from people of colour'. The mostly first-year students in this class seemed to take this advice on board, and I was consistently impressed with the level of engagement and respect that I witnessed among them for the rest of the semester.

That said, I'm always struck by the confidence displayed by many of the white female students when discussing issues of race and racism in RRG. This is especially the case, as I will discuss later, when white women comprise the majority in a tutorial. Sara who has also experienced this phenomenon describes it below.

Sara: Throughout RRG, I have always found the white students in my classes to be highly engaged. I had expected some hesitancy on their part to discuss race yet this was rarely the case. Initially, I attributed their openness to my presence as a white teacher. I thought perhaps this made it easier for white students to talk about whiteness—a topic rarely discussed in a sustained way in Australia. However, this chattiness was not confined to the whiteness week or to my classes as I discovered in my conversations with Jane: white students are highly involved in and often dominate discussions regardless of the racial identity of the teacher.

I have come to understand that white students' approach to this class highlights Indigenous Australian scholar Aileen Moreton-Robinson (2000, p. 24) observation that '[u]niversities in Australia are 'places of whiteness'. That progressive white Australian scholars and students feel completely at ease contributing to and leading discussions on race and cultural diversity is an expression of our white privilege in educational and other public spaces: almost always our ideas are listened to and valued over those of people of colour. It also highlights the structuring force of white fragility as the Australian academy is the epitome of an 'insulated environment of racial protection [that] builds white expectations for racial comfort while at the same time lowering the ability to tolerate racial stress' (DiAngelo, 2011, p. 54). This is also bound up with the cultural allowances afforded to white people to both freely express our emotions and claim authority on a topic; an option rarely available to people of colour, especially women.

White Guilt and Whitesplaining

Sara: When I first began teaching on this course and used the McIntosh (1988/2004) list in my tutorials, I expected that feelings of white guilt would play an influential role in shaping this activity but instead found this was not something that overtly frames the conversation. On one hand, this lack of focus on white guilt was useful because, as Dyer (1997, p. 11) notes, guilt is a backwards facing or 'blocking' emotion. It is also a sign that the majority of the cohort are already progressive on issues of race and that part of our job is to critically extend their pre-existing racial literary (Warren, 2014). On the other hand, not acknowledging guilt as a structuring emotion can lead to students, particularly white progressive women, comprehending racism as something they have moved past or understand due to their gender. Moreton-Robinson (2000, p. 253) addresses this issue, stating that for some white feminist '[t]heir anti-racist practice, as an intellectual engagement, is evidence of their compassion, but racism is not a part of their interiority'.

This points to the need to push students to think through how they are implicated in and benefit from white supremacy. It also emphasises the need to adopt classroom strategies that move white students, as well as white teachers, away from performative expressions of progressiveness. As Dyer (1997, p. 11) argues, white guilt 'bears witness to the fineness of a moral spirit that can feel such guilt—the display of our guilt is our calvary'. Thus, we need to be wary of using liberal guilt to signal some sort of moral righteousness that hinders direct and frank discussions of racism.

This week is useful as it illuminates one of the central questions I continue to grapple with, as do many of the progressive white students in this course, around what it means to be an ally in the fight against racism and racist systems. Is there a place for white people in this work and if so, what should this be? I've always felt strongly that it is imperative white people are involved in racial justice work, especially when it comes to the potentially transformative space of education, although the parameters and specific aims of this involvement have been less clear.

When it comes to the university classroom, I am unsure how to balance my role as a teacher—which requires some degree of centring myself in order to facilitate a class—with the goal of decentring whiteness. My pedagogical interventions in class discussions are unavoidably bound up with my whiteness and thus, I need to be aware of the possibility or perception that I am 'whitesplaining' material to students, especially students of colour who have access to a set of experiences and perspectives I do not. That said, my whiteness also allows and requires me to intervene when white students abstract or downplay racism in favour of gender or class-based explanations. This is an example of the idea that whiteness 'should and can be challenged from within' (Gachago, 2018, p. 132).

Jane: Unlike Sara, I don't feel comfortable calling white students out when they downplay racism. I have learned I need to communicate carefully with white students about race because most have been conditioned not to see racial difference or to acknowledge their own white privilege. Getting them to the point where they can make clear arguments about racial issues using concrete examples rather than trying to win points by spouting theory takes most of the semester.

In contrast most students of colour come to the class already having lived the concepts in the readings which makes them easier to grasp intellectually.

When the tutorial consists of mostly white students, they tend to dominate discussions. In these instances, I use my authority as a woman of colour to get students of colour to speak. I'll say in a light, humorous way, 'That's great! We've heard from three white women now. What do the people of colour think'? Or I draw on my own experience of discomfort from the past: 'I remember feeling uncomfortable speaking in mostly white classrooms when I was at university—but your input is really valuable especially in a class like this'. Either way I try to high-light how the different responses from white and non-white students underscore the power dynamics of the room and exemplify the racial privilege that white students embody and students of colour have internalised. Sometimes I make students write responses to questions then call on the usually quiet ones (again, in this case, they are often non-white and sometimes international students for whom English is a second language) to read what they have written. I realise some students have anxiety about speaking in class so make it a point at the beginning of the semester to ask those students to alert me so I do not call on them.

In a tutorial with 50/50 white and nonwhite students or a group of particu-larly vocal students of colour, sometimes I have a hard time getting white stu-dents to speak because they feel they lack authority and/or they are scared to say something that might offend the radical, often angry students of colour. In this situation, while I honor and bear witness to the difficult emotions expressed by the students of colour, I also try to get them to relate these experiences of raciali-sation and racism more closely to the readings. At the same time, I attempt to create a sense of safety for white students to speak, mentioning it is important to be brave and make mistakes in order to learn—that we are all learning from each other as we come to this material with different perspectives and experiences.

Reflections and Contributions of Students of Colour

Sara: One of the reasons I find the McIntosh (1988/2004) list a useful resource is that is provides students of colour with the space to have their affective and experiential narratives of racism listened to and valued in an academic space where discussions about race are generally 'theoretical, guarded, disembodied' (Gachago, 2018 p. 133). This directly builds upon our reading of Frantz Fanon (1967) from the previous week in which personal testimony of racism as a black man in France served as the basis of his humanity and resistance.

In tutorial discussions over the years, it has always become clear quite quickly to white students that students of colour do not need a list like McIntosh's (1988/2004) to tell them things many of them have been experiencing their entire lives. This activ-ity thus helps make overt the different lived experiences which students of colour come into the classroom with—something white people are rarely encouraged to stop and consider (Croll, 2014, pp. 78–79). During this activity, I have had to be especially vigilant not to ask students of colour to perform their difference and racialised trauma as a teaching moment for the white students in the class. This is something that can very easily happen in this space, and often does, as Jane explores below.

I am keenly aware that I can't offer students, especially students of colour, what Jane or other academics of colour can. When I teach in theses spaces I am implicated in long histories and presents of colonisation and white supremacy. I recognise that I am more valuable in this class to white students as opposed to students of colour. This is a confronting idea but nonetheless something that white academics including myself must acknowledge and grapple with. Part of why the team-teaching model with Jane has been so useful is that it allows multiple perspectives and intercultural dialogue to be foundational to how the course is presented to students.

Jane: I completely agree. Discussing teaching techniques with Sara all these years and watching her in action in lectures and tutorials has given me so much insight into the different ways this material can be taught and ways I can improve my own teaching. Also it illuminates the potential and the limits of our own bodies, how they are read by the students, and how we position and perform ourselves in response.

The McIntosh exercise sharply marks these body politics. I always do the exercise with my students. I ask how many students marked yes for most of the items and how many marked no, how many were 50/50 or had another breakdown. Generally, Aboriginal and Torres Strait Islander, Arab, and black students will fall into the first category; white students in the second; and Asian and mixed-race students in the third. We discuss how this breakdown, which links our proximity to whiteness based on our phenotype, makes us feel.

We then consider which items don't apply in Australia and the current time period, and which items we would add. Almost always students bring up parallels between sexism and racism—for example, how white women can relate to people of colour through items like feeling vulnerable to attack in public space. I emphasise it is important to bring up these commonalities without collapsing experiences of marginalisation. If students don't bring up class, I will, pointing out ways in which class and cultural capital can make you conditionally white (encapsulated for instance, in the stereotype of the model minority) as well as how lack of this capital if you are white can marginalise you in a different way. For instance, I ask: 'why do we have the term "white trash" but not "yellow trash" or "black trash"'?

Sara: As I have gained more experience in terms of teaching and researching on issues of race, my clarity around the role of whiteness in these spaces is becoming more complicated and tenuous. Even as I write this, I am wary of embodying the 'good white nationalist' position that Hage (1998) critiques. In the initial years I was involved in teaching RRG, admitting to this uncertainty in any real way in the classroom seemed like a risk. Would it make students of colour feel like they didn't have a teacher committed to the cause and to them? Would I be providing white students with an incoherent model of allyship? Would it undercut the 'authority' I needed to cultivate as a young female academic at an elite university? What is the line between activism and scholarship in the classroom? This sense of riskiness was also certainly an expression of my own white fragility.

While these issues remain, as I have gained more experience I have become more comfortable with directly bringing these questions into the classroom and as Jane has taught me, being more open to using discomfort as a pedagogical tool. Gachago (2018, p. 137 emphasis in original) highlights the importance of listening to others and argues that a vital step 'towards white allyship is to learn humility, to recognise that we *don't know*, that we might not hold the knowledge, experience and skills necessary' to answer every question. I have come to understand that a key way my identity as a white woman can be useful in this space is by allowing myself to visibly sit with this discomfort and uncertainty in the classroom. It is only then I can model active listening and self-reflexivity for my students.

Jane: I often wish I were allowed to have different spaces for teaching this material to white and non-white students. I wish I didn't always have to worry about speaking 'cross-marketing' my material, and managing the feelings of my white students through what I jokingly refer to as my academic Oprah role.

I acknowledge these feelings, and when appropriate, articulate them to my students so I can model ways for them to allow themselves to be emotionally honest and vulnerable to each other. As so many feminist teachers and scholars have expressed, it is from a sense of vulnerability that genuine communication and exchange across and through difference can happen (Ahmed, 2017; Alexander, 2005; Hooks, 2003). How then do we make visible these power dynamics while ensuring the classroom is 'safe'—and for whom? Are these two things—speaking one's truth and promoting cultural safety (again, for whom?) compatible—in a class like this which often feels like one big trigger?

One strategy I am currently playing with is developing a 'mindfulness-based pedagogy' for RRG to facilitate a 'quality of openness' in the classroom space and among my students—giving students meditation tools to 'sit with their distress', to see their discomfort as 'a place where change begins' and to focus on their breath and by extension their bodies in order to cultivate moments of 'listening silence' (Wong, 2007, p. 4). This, too, comes out of personal experience: since beginning a meditation practice a few years ago, I have learned to be more present and emotionally authentic, to listen more actively, and to practice more compassion for myself and by extension for others. These are qualities that are integral to the aim of RRG, which is not only identifying and critiquing racism and the other 'isms' in which it is implicated but to go further and begin the lifelong process of decolonising our minds.

Conclusion

This paper is the result of many years of conversations between the two of us on how best to create a sense of community through (not despite) difference in our demographically mixed classrooms in RRG. Drawing on the work of Patricia Hill Collins (2000) and bell Hooks (1994), Carissa Froyum (2014, p. 81) argues that '[e]motionally connecting to each other and developing an ethic of caring . . . is critical to challenging racism'. While the increasingly corporate university space often restricts the very possibly of creating the necessary climate to engage in these complicated discussions, we have observed the capacity of this course, the material we engage, and our own energy and enthusiasm to develop a critical racial consciousness among our students that is grounded in self-reflection, openness, and compassion.

This is particularly important in light of the increasingly conservative climate around difference generally, with discrimination and hate speech targeting people of colour, Muslims, Jewish people, women, LGBTQI people, and people with disabilities. How we teach race—through constant self-reflection and intercultural dialogue in classrooms centered on an ethics of caring—speaks to students as embodied, contextualised subjects. We aim to draw on our own embodied identities and experiences in the teaching space to challenge and break down, rather than replicate, binaries of self/other. In this paper we have provided a snapshot of our teaching methodology. This methodology values and gives room to our students' and our own feelings and personal narratives alongside more theoretical discussions of racial difference and racism in order to show how concepts of race and experiences of racialisation and racism are inextricably connected.

Disclosure Statement

No potential conflict of interest was reported by the author(s).

Notes on Contributors

Dr. Jane Park is a senior lecturer in the Department of Gender and Cultural Studies at the University of Sydney. Her research examines the social impact of minority representations in popular culture and embodied aspects of racialization, focusing on Asian diasporic communities in the US and Australia. Jane has published work in a wide range of journals including Cultural Studies, World Literature Today, and Inter-Asia Cultural Studies as well as a number of anthologies on film, media, and popular culture. Her monograph, Yellow Future: Oriental Style in Hollywood Cinema (University of Minnesota Press, 2010), explored the emergence of East Asian aesthetics as technologized backdrop in Hollywood films during the late twentieth century.

Dr. Sara Tomkins completed her PhD in the Department of Gender and Cultural Studies at the University of Sydney in 2017. Her thesis analysed the ways in which the cultural and political connections between Jewish Americans and African Americans are articulated in contemporary comedy. Her research interests include transnational race-based comedy as well as diversity and inclusion in education. She is currently a research assistant and sessional instructor at the Australian Catholic University in the Faculty of Education and Arts.

References

Ahmed, S. (2017). *Living a feminist life*. Duke University Press.
Alexander, M. (2005). *Pedagogies of crossing: Meditations on feminism, sexual politics, memory and the sacred*. Duke University Press.

Bermúdez, C. M., & Camacho, R. R. (2019). Women of color in academia: Self-preservation in the face of white fragility and hegemonic masculinity. In K. Zaleski, A. Enrile, E. L. Weiss, & X. Wang (Eds), *Women's journey to empowerment in the 21st century: A transnational feminist analysis of women's lives in modern times* (pp. 105–119). Oxford University Press.

Collins, P. H. (2000). *Black feminist thought: Knowledge, consciousness, and the politics of empowerment*. Routledge.

Croll, P. R. (2014). Getting students to say what they are not supposed to say: The challenges and opportunities in teaching about race in a college classroom. In K. Haltinner (Ed.), *Teaching race and anti-racism in contemporary America: Adding context to colorblindness* (pp. 75–79). Springer.

DiAngelo, R. (2011). White fragility. *The Journal of Critical Pedagogy*, *3*(3), 54–70.

Dyer, R. (1997). *White: Essays on race and culture*. Routledge.

Evans-Winters, V. E., & Hines, D. E. (2020). Unmasking white fragility: How whiteness and white student resistance impacts anti-racist education, *5*(1), 1–16. *Whiteness and Education*. https://protect-au.mimecast.com/s/mgW_CROND2u8LJ9Dt9O1uJ?domain=doi.org

Fanon, F. (1967). *Black skin, white masks*. Grove Press.

Froyum, C. M. (2014). Managing emotions in the classroom. In K. Haltinner (Ed.), *Teaching race and anti-racism in contemporary America: Adding context to colorblindness* (pp. 81–89). Springer.

Gachago, D. (2018). Lessons on humility: White women's racial allyship in academia. In S. A. Shelton, J. E. Flynn, & T. J. Grosland (Eds.), *Feminism and intersectionality in academia: Women's narratives and experiences in higher education* (pp. 131–144). Palgrave MacMillan.

Hage, G. (1998). *White nation: Fantasies of white supremacy in a multicultural society*. Pluto Press.

Haltinner, K. (2014). Repacking the white privilege knapsack. In K. Haltinner (Ed.), *Teaching race and anti-racism in contemporary America: Adding context to colorblindness* (pp. 195–205). Springer.

Hooks, b. (1994). *Teaching to transgress: Education as the practice of freedom*. Routledge.

Hooks, b. (2003). *Teaching community: A pedagogy of hope*. Routledge.

McIntosh, P. (1988/2004). White privilege: Unpacking the invisible knapsack. In M. Anderson and P. Collins (Eds.), *Race, class and gender* (pp. 95–105). Wadsworth Press.

Moreton-Robinson, A. (2000). Duggaiban or 'place of whiteness': Australian feminist and place. In J. Docker and G. Fischer (Eds.), *Race, colour and identity* (pp. 240–255). UNSW Press.

Park, J. C. H. (2019). Embodied inter-referencing: Encounters with and among "Asian" students in the Australian classroom. *Inter-Asia Cultural Studies*, *21*(2), 271–289. https://doi.org/10.1080/14649373.2019.1613730

Warren, J. (2014). After colorblindness: Teaching antiracism to white progressives in the U.S. In K. Haltinner (Ed.), *Teaching race and anti-racism in contemporary America: Adding context to colorblindness* (pp. 109–121). Springer.

Wong, Y.-L. (2007). Knowing through discomfort: A mindfulness-based critical social work pedagogy. *Critical Social Work*, *5*(1), 1–16. www1.uwindsor.ca/criticalsocialwork/knowing-through-discomfort-a-mindfulness-based-critical-social-work-pedagogy

Wright, G., (Director), Pringle, I., & Scharf, D. (Producers). (1992). *Romper stomper [Motion Picture]*. Village Roadshow.

Chapter 12

My Journey Into the 'Heart of Whiteness' Whilst Remaining My Authentic (Black) Self

April-Louise M. O. O. Pennant

Editors' introduction

In this essay published in 2022, April-Louise M. O. O. Pennant explores her educational experiences growing up as a Black woman in England using analytic and critical autoethnography, and interweaves this account with a broader examination of her doctoral research on the educational challenges faced by Black British women more generally. While Pennant elaborates how she was encouraged by her parents to see herself as both British and shaped by the cultures of Nigeria and Jamaica, in the academically selective schools she attended she observed a lack of diversity around her, as well as in the curriculum, where the limited discussions of Black people in history focused on slavery and civil rights in the United States, rather than on the history of Black people in the United Kingdom. However, through engaging in extracurricular activities focused on empowering and centring Black identities, Pennant was still able to preserve and cultivate her sense of self despite these curricular deficiencies. In university, Pennant was able to also study Black feminism, Black British experience, and Black Caribbean women's experiences for the first time. From these intellectual foundations, Pennant pursued her doctoral research focused on Black British women's educational experiences and the intersections of their gender, race, and social class identities. This article shares first-hand and second-hand experience, showcasing the importance of intersectional theory as well as the continued challenges Black people (especially Black women) face in the United Kingdom to see themselves represented positively in society, education, and curricula.

Introduction

The pursuit of education for many Black girls and young women are considerable feats as they navigate within hostile white academic spaces, motivated by their commitment to education and the obligations they feel to themselves, their families and their wider communities to succeed (Mirza, 2006, 2008; Pennant, 2019). According to Casey (1993: 132), Black women embarking on such journeys occupy contradictory positions and thus experiences because they naively carry "expectations of mythic proportions; their odysseys, they believe . . . will

DOI: 10.4324/9781003346104-13

transform not only their lives, but also those of other black people," yet; "separated from their families, from their cultural communities, from their system of signification, from their existing black identities, these young women's passages turn out to be isolated, individual journeys into the heart of whiteness."

However, despite these difficult journeys, there is evidence to illustrate the commitment of Black women to gaining education beyond compulsory levels. Data collected by Advance HE (2019: 169, 178) reported that while all ethnic groups have higher proportions of women participating in higher education, "this gender difference was largest among UK black students." On the other hand, statistics also indicate the consequences, in terms of attainment, of such journeys into the 'heart of whiteness' where only 50% of Black British African girls and 44% of Black British Caribbean girls achieved the national average at GCSE level (Gov, 2019a); where only 5% of all Black British students achieved 3 'A' grades at A-Level (Gov, 2019b); and lastly where Black women are the second least likely, compared to other ethnic and gender groups, to attain a First or a 2:1 at the end of their degrees (Advance HE, 2019: 190). It is this discrepancy between the commitment and obligation displayed by Black girls and women for education and their academic results, that strongly warrants more understanding and exploration into this group's educational experiences and journeys. In this regard, this paper will draw upon my own educational journey into the 'heart of whiteness' as a Black British woman who has beaten the odds (O'Connor, 2002) and retained my (Black) identity, progressing to complete a PhD. It will also reference my PhD research where I explore the educational journeys and experiences of other Black British women graduates, to illustrate how they have also centred their identities.

In order to do this effectively, an autoethnography approach has been selected. While there are many kinds of autoethnography, as stated by Lake (2015: 681), the "essential components of autoethnographic work are the public exposition of personal ideas and theories to further knowledge through analysis and dialogue with 'others', including the literature." More specifically, I align with analytic and critical autoethnography styles as developed and discussed by Anderson (2006) and Boylorn and Orbe (2014) respectively. For Anderson (2006: 375) analytic autoethnography is "ethnographic work in which the researcher is (1) a full member in the research group or setting, (2) visible as such a member in the researcher's published texts, and (3) committed to an analytic research agenda focused on improving theoretical understandings of broader social phenomena." In this way and as mentioned previously, the centring of my own identity and educational journey, along with my PhD research in this paper, complements Anderson's analytic autoethnography. Additionally, Boylorn and Orbe (2014: 18–19) introduce critical autoethnography through a selection of scholarly works where they believe that it explores "the inextricable relationship between culture and communication and the influence of pre-existing potential . . . enhance[ing] existing understandings of lived experiences enacted within social locations situated within larger systems of power, oppression and social privilege." This kind of autoethnography is useful when exploring the educational journeys and experiences of Black women due to their intersectional identities positioning them in "ideological blind spots" (Mirza, 1997: 4) where they are often "falling between the cracks" (Ricks, 2014). The application of analytic and critical autoethnography also connects well with my theoretical frameworks and enables me to include my whole self in this paper. This is significant and conveyed by Lorde (2009: 182–183) when she said, "if I do not bring all of who I am to whatever I do- then I bring nothing of lasting worth, for I have withheld my essence."

This paper is structured as follows: first I introduce myself, my educational journey and my PhD research in order to provide context. Secondly, I review key literature regarding the whiteness of the education system. Lastly, the methods and theoretical frameworks employed within my PhD research will be outlined, as well as two participant narratives to illustrate the ways in which other Black British women graduates have grappled with the whiteness of the education system.

Self, Educational Journey and PhD Research

Self

I remember vividly, at the age of four, announcing to my mother that I had decided that I was going to dress up as a *Black* Barbie for a friend's costume party. When she obliged and helped me to prepare my costume, I remember at the party beaming with pride as I told anyone that would listen that I had not just come dressed up as Barbie, I had come as *Black* Barbie. I share this memory to illustrate the sense of pride in my Black identity that my parents had instilled within me, that I was displaying from a very young age and how I had used a costume to signal and perform my gendered and racial identity (Clammer, 2015). Looking back, it was this sense of pride that provided me with solace (and at times frustration) and resilience, carrying me through my educational journey regardless of how white the space was (Butler-Barnes et al., 2018). Parents play significant roles in the upbringing of a child and my parents were no exception. For as long as I can remember, they made sure that myself and my sister were exposed to different extracurricular educational, cultural and creative activities so that we quickly became familiar with children from a wide range of backgrounds as well as different spaces and places (Vincent et al., 2012a). While my parents had modest incomes, through their extensive knowledge, interests, experiences and aspirations, they prioritised providing myself and my sister with many opportunities to explore ourselves, our communities and our society so that we were able to "locate [our]selves within wider UK society, [be] comfortable in [our] own skin and alive to the individuality of the diverse people around [us]," (Ajegbo et al., 2007: 23). Despite notions that *There ain't no Black in the Union Jack* (Gilroy, 1987) I was always made aware by my parents that I was in fact British and belonged here as much as anyone else did; but, that I was not *just* British, I was also a descendant of the rich, vibrant and powerful cultures of Nigeria and Jamaica (Rattansi, 2000; Lam & Smith, 2009). The well-known phrase 'knowledge is power' underpinned the love that I had for learning, as well as how education in all its forms were central within my household and established excitement to enter into the education system.

Educational Journey

Influenced by her own educational experiences, my mother was the architect of my educational journey where she desired for me to follow an academic route at the "appropriate educational age-stage" (Hamilton, 2018: 5); and she supported me vehemently at every step of the way (Vincent et al., 2012b). She was adamant that myself and my sister would attend academically selective schools preferably private or grammar- because she was aware of the opportunities that such schools could provide and she would always explain to me that: "That is where the future leaders, managers and entrepreneurs go," (Brown, 2013). This pursuit of quality education led to my movement and participation in several different educational institutions- in both the private and state sector at primary and secondary level.

Regardless of the type of school that I attended, I recall there being a lack of diversity in the curriculum which contradicted with my socialisation at home, and I became increasingly frustrated about that (Gray et al., 2018). One of the secondary schools that I attended was situated in the suburbs surrounding London and was Roman Catholic, predominantly white and working class. Here, as a student, I often experienced racial slurs and had to defend myself against my peers and teachers alike (Chapman & Bhopal, 2019). For one of my GCSE subjects, I chose history because I craved being able to engage with other cultures, contributions and histories of people like myself, and I thought I would be able to gain this here. However, as a class, we were only taught about Black people in a limited capacity- particularly in the US, regarding slavery and the civil rights movement (Doharty, 2018). I remember challenging the teacher- who didn't have the knowledge, interest or tools to do so - about why he didn't highlight the experiences of Black British people (Alexander & Bernard-Weekes, 2017). I didn't understand why we were only learning about the 1955 Montgomery bus boycott in the U.S. and not about the 1963 Bristol bus boycott in the UK; I didn't understand why the Black Panther organisation was depicted as terrorists confined to US contexts and not about their global presence and their chapters in London (BBC, 2019).

It was not until I attended college that, at the age of seventeen, during the second year of my A-Level studies in my sociology classes, that my teacher introduced us to the canon of Black Feminism and more specifically, research that centred Black British experiences. In particular, the work of Mirza (1992) about second-generation Black Caribbean young women's experiences in schools stood out for me. It enabled me to connect because I could relate to these experiences as a young Black woman and develop deep understandings about the education system and the differences in experiences and outcomes due to the interplay of identities within it. I also remember being astonished because for the first time, I was able to see that Black British people could be both the author and subject of research, and from that moment, I wanted to be a creator of such knowledge (Rollock, 2013). Although I had not decided on pursuing a career in academia at that point, I went on to study sociology at university where I was able to strengthen my understandings, with the discovery of conceptual and theoretical tools, to articulate the mechanisms operating within society, as well as channelling and deepening my passions about Black identities in constructive ways (Maylor, 2009). It is necessary to add that alongside my formal education, from secondary school onwards, I was always actively engaged in leading, organising and participating in activities and events that empowered, enhanced or re-centred Black identities within the space. By doing these additional actions, I was able to preserve my Black identity and pride while simultaneously filling the voids and lessening the disconnect I constantly felt as a young Black British girl/woman navigating and progressing through a (white) education system (Payne & Suddler, 2014).

PhD Research

While I was happy to have knowledge of Black British literature and educational research, I began to view it as limited in that Black British girls and young women were largely invisible (Mirza, 1986; Rollock, 2007a) and there were established underachievement discourses characterising Black British students as a whole (Crozier, 2005; Rollock, 2007b; Tomlin et al., 2014). Again, I became frustrated because these narratives did not reflect my own experiences as a third-generation Black British woman of dual Caribbean and African heritage; nor did they reflect the experiences of many of my Black girl friends. Therefore, I became keen and excited to identify, explore and illustrate alternative, positive and more up-to-date narratives that highlighted the diversity within Blackness, as well as the achievements of Black British students and specifically Black girls and young women (Dei, 2018).

My PhD is a qualitative research study that centres the educational journeys and experiences of 25 Black British women graduates. It illustrates the full educational trajectory from primary school to university and explores how the participants have navigated, strategised and engaged within the English education system. In particular, it focuses on the intersections of their gender, race and social class identities and how this shapes their journeys and experiences; as well as the role of their families and extended networks in supporting their trajectories. Based upon my interest in Black identities, a significant contribution that my research makes is expanding the boundaries of Blackness through emphasising the nuances and diversity within this group through ethnicity and cultural considerations alongside race, gender and social class. My PhD research also critiques notions of academic 'success' which are limited and underpinned by meritocratic and neoliberal ideals that fail to consider the inequalities inherent in the education system that dis/advantages particular groups. Overall, my research aims to- by foregrounding the experiences of a range of Black British women- highlight the transformative power of education- but only if the education system is understood and navigated effectively.

As is evident from the brief overview of myself, my educational journey, and my PhD research, throughout my life and particularly within my education, my Black identity has played a significant role. It has provided me with confidence and resilience, motivating me in ways that have enabled me to carve out spaces within the 'heart of whiteness' to insert my own Blackness and those of others. In this regard, my reflections and story emphasises that 'pro-black doesn't mean anti-white' (Herring et al., 1999) precisely because, I can love all of who I am and coexist, without hating others.

The next section will review the relevant literature regarding the whiteness of the education system, particularly the role of the curriculum, before discussing the methods, theoretical frameworks and some participant narratives from my PhD research.

Literature Review

Why Is My Curriculum White?

Particularly within university settings, there has been outrage to and opposition of the overwhelming whiteness of the curriculum (Ajegbo et al., 2007; Arday & Mirza, 2018; Bain, 2018). Gaining momentum as a largely student-led movement in 2015, universities were increasingly being held accountable and asked, "Why is my curriculum white?" by students exerting pressure for the curriculum to be diversified (UCL, 2015; Swain, 2019). However, the whiteness of the curriculum can be viewed as one manifestation of the whiteness of the entire education system. According to Gillborn (2005: 498), this whiteness is upheld by education polices that "assumes and defends white supremacy through the priorities it sets, the beneficiaries that it privileges, and the outcomes that it produces." In this way, the education system symbolises 'institutionalised whiteness' (Puwar, 2004; Shilliam, 2015), positioning Black bodies as out of place- particularly within elite institutions- where microaggressions consistently marginalise them through "every day, interpersonal manifestation[s] of institutional whiteness and structural white supremacy . . . creating and maintaining white space," (Joseph-Salisbury, 2019: 12). Therefore, the curriculum should be viewed as a "culturally specific artefact designed to maintain a White supremacist master script" (Ladson-Billings, 1998: 18); a master script that "silences multiple voices and perspectives, primarily legitimising dominant, white, upper-class, mail voicings as the "standard" knowledge students need to know," (Swartz, 1992: 341).

Black Bodies in White Spaces: Implications and Surviving Within White Spaces

For Dumas (2014), the education system is a 'site of black suffering' which is echoed within the work of Givens (2016). The established differences in experiences and outcomes at key stages in the education system (Gov, 2019a, 2019b);

the higher exclusion and dropout rates (Social Market Foundation, 2017), as well as the consistent Black and Minority ethnic (BME) attainment gap at universities (UUK & NUS, 2019) can be used to indicate the implications of Black bodies within hostile white academic spaces (Cabinet office, 2017; Sian, 2017). Additionally, Carter (2007: 52) highlights the psychological aspects of young Black women in her study who she notes "were constantly negotiating Whiteness to survive, or in their words, to pass the course." Carter proceeds to explain that "I use the term survive to capture the intellectual and mental struggles that these young women had to endure as they believed that their identities were constantly challenged," (ibid: 52). In fact, similarly, one of the salient points that was made within the National Union of Students' (NUS) participation in the 'Why is my curriculum white?' campaign was that "Black British students are psychologically damaged by a white curriculum," (Osborne, 2016).

On the other hand, the deep commitment and obligation to gaining education has meant that Black students (particularly Black girls and young women) and Black communities have developed many strategies to survive within these hostile, white academic spaces (Fuller, 1980; Chigwada, 1987; Mac an Ghaill, 1988; Coultas, 1989; Andrews, 2013, 2016). These include creating safe spaces and social networks to affirm Black identities and offer emotional support (Rollock et al., 1992; Guiffrida, 2003; Weekes, 2003; Carter, 2007; Ojo, 2009; Greyerbiehl and Mitchell, 2014; Cook and Williams, 2015), as well as utilising additional resources (Yosso, 2005; Kynard, 2010; Kelly, 2018) and creating ideologies like 'achievement as resistance' (Carter, 2008). While such strategies support Black girls and young women in navigating, resisting and disrupting white spaces; they are also underpinned by the maintenance and assertion of pride in their Black identities which become "a 'suit of armour' against hostilities of the environment" (Miller and MacIntosh, 1999: 161); and asserted in opposition to the erasure and/or negative portrayals of Black identities in the white educational space (Rollock, 2007a, 2007b).

Having discussed some of the literature regarding the whiteness of the education system by highlighting the role of the curriculum and the implications on Black students, along with the ways they have resisted to survive in these spaces; the next section of this paper addresses the methods, theoretical frameworks and introduces some findings from my PhD research.

Methods

As a qualitative research study, face-to-face semi-structured interviews were the method of choice in order to gain in-depth insights about the educational experiences and journeys of the Black British women graduates. With the permission of participants, all interviews were audio recorded and transcribed verbatim after each interview. Using the computer software NVivo, interview transcriptions were uploaded, and a process of thematic analysis occurred. Ethical considerations were made such as informed consent, confidentiality, limiting harm and informing participants of their right to withdraw at any given time. Accordingly, participants were given information sheets and consent forms before interviews; pseudonyms were used to uphold confidentiality in the final work; signposting to relevant support was given in order to limit psychological harm that recounting educational experiences and journeys may trigger; lastly, participants were provided with my contact details if they wished to withdraw.

This research is underpinned by a theoretical amalgam of Black feminist epistemology, Critical Race Theory (CRT) and Bourdieu's theory of practice (BTP) in order to articulate the intersectional identities of the sample. While Black feminist epistemology privileges and centres the lived experiences and knowledge production of Black women specifically (Collins, 2000); CRT illuminates the central role of race and racism within society and its educational institutions which deliberately disadvantages Black and minority ethnic students (Ladson-Billings, 1998; Chadderton, 2013). BTP supplies the social class dimensions in order to show how resources are acquired and utilised in order to navigate within educational fields, as well as, with the support of CRT, the underlining whiteness of such fields in which these resources operate and are given power (Rollock et al., 2015).

I was able to interview 25 Black British women graduates in the Midlands and the South East of England. These graduates came from a diverse range of ages, ethnicities, cultural backgrounds and socio-economic statuses, as well as an array of educational institutions, pathways and degree subjects which provided insightful and varied narratives. For the purposes of this paper, I will share the reflections of two of these participants: La'Shay and Deja.

Discussion

Within interviews, both La'Shay and Deja expressed similar sentiments to my own reflections of my education, namely their awareness of the whiteness of the space and the internal contractions they encountered as they navigated within it. In this way, I assert that for many young Black women, gaining an education within the English education system becomes a personal site of struggle (Pennant, 2019). In the following extract, La'Shay demonstrates how her Jamaican heritage and culture means that she feels that it is inevitable that she will be marginalised in the space because of what she perceives it to represent:

> "I think Jamaican culture has this legacy of challenging the system, I just think of Marcus Garvey and like Rastafarianism and it's very much like {Jamaican accent} "Bun Babylon and me nah waan . . ." Do you know what I mean? And I think there's that spirit of rebellion that makes- or in my opinion- made me very aware of what systems were at play and also gave me an understanding that not everything in Britain is for me. Even though uni was encouraged, I was already- whenever I enrolled- was thinking about middle-class white values and colonialism and these were things that I'd learnt from before, and race and how that might play into things. Just having that awareness was almost like when

you're . . . I think what's it, double consciousness from W.E.B. Du Bois, so it was already having an experience but being an observer myself. I think that kinda made it harder for me cos whether it was true or not, I still had a perception that maybe there were some people in this institution that would rather not have me be here and maybe would rather that I did fail."

(La'Shay)

By way of her interpretation of Jamaican culture's "legacy of challenging the system" and "spirit of rebellion," La'Shay illustrates the way, using a Bourdieusian lens, "a field consists of a set of objectives, historical relations between positions anchored in certain forms of power (or capital), while habitus consists of a set of historical relations "deposited" within individual bodies in the form of mental and corporeal schemata of perception, appreciation, and action," (Bourdieu and Wacquant, 1992: 16). Based on this, La'Shay embodies Jamaican culture in her habitus and her presence within the education field as well as her awareness of the power dynamics in which middle-class whiteness dominates. Therefore, through previous racial and cultural socialisation, she has been able to "create spheres of influence that are separate from but engaged with existing structures of oppression," (Mirza, 1997: 276). Within a study about how Caribbean young women negotiate their racialised and gendered identities within education (Phoenix, 2009), the notion of education as a site of struggle is carried forward by Pratt (1991: 6) who writes that classrooms become "contact zones" as well as "social spaces where cultures meet, clash, and grapple with each other, often in contexts of highly asymmetrical relations of power, such as colonialism, slavery, or their aftermaths as they are lived out in many parts of the world today." Through her reference to W.E.B Du Bois's (1989) 'double consciousness', La'Shay is also calling out the internal contradictions and the struggles she encounters as a British *and* Jamaican young woman venturing through an education system which she feels does not and will never fully accept her. Yet, she still pursues education as a means to an end. Additionally, this resistance invoked by Jamaican culture and carried forward by La'Shay demonstrates the nuances of her Black identity and the ways in which she feels it is positioned within whiteness. By centring her experiential knowledge, she uses counter-storytelling to critically analyse the space (Solorzano & Yosso, 2002).

For Deja, she responds to her awareness of the whiteness of the space by actively resisting and navigating it as her authentic (Black) self:

"I don't want to conform; I want the things that make me different to stand out so that you can see it. I think that's why I have my nails as long as I want or I have my hair as natural as I want it to be and I wear bright colours in corporate colour environments, because it is becoming more ok for you to be yourself. But I'm also seeing it as being unapologetic about being who I am and being authentically me, because there's more value in that and it's more sustainable. In the education system, in terms of at university you don't have a uniform so you can see it from the things people wear and me coming to lectures . . . I'll wear my Afrocentric earrings without thinking about it because that's the style I want to wear, and seeing other Black girls who act in the same way . . . So I think it is about becoming, because they are doing it independently themselves, then the things and the environments that they are going to such as the education sector, they will bring themselves with them. I think that there is an integration between the two because that accepting of yourself allows you to then move into different environments and then be yourself."

(Deja)

Deja's belief that it is important that Black girls "bring themselves with them" throughout their educational journey is similar to the strategy I employed which enabled me to survive and thrive throughout my education. Deja's desire to make her differences stand out, as well as seeing value in doing so contributes to "a specialised knowledge produced by black women that clarifies a particular standpoint of and about black women," (Reynolds, 2002: 596). From this standpoint, Black women are able to use the strength of marginal positions by using innovative ways or in the case of Deja, disruptive ways to challenge the perceived norm about who should be in that space, what they should look like and what they should wear. In fact, Deja employs her style of dress in this process, comparable to how I used my Black Barbie costume, to redefine herself by boldly wearing 'Afrocentric earrings' noting that other Black girls are also taking similar steps. This and similar acts "emerge from a different location . . . fundamental to the process of decentering the oppressive other and claiming our right to subjectivity and is the insistence that we must determine how we will be and not rely on colonising responses to determine our legitimacy," (hooks, 1990: 22).

Both La'Shay and Deja also illustrate the importance of understanding the operations of whiteness in academic educational spaces as well as the power that such understanding can provide. Additionally, both draw upon their Black identities- Jamaican culture for La'Shay and clothing for Deja- as a way to gain power and to survive within the whiteness. This resonates with previous research (Carter, 2003; Modood, 2004; Yosso, 2005; Wallace, 2017, 2018) which contends that ethnicity, cultural background and race can provide additional resources within educational experiences and journeys for Black and minority ethnic students.

Conclusion and Recommendations

To conclude, it is evident that Black British women are committed to education but have unique experiences within the English education system based upon their intersectional identities. The overwhelming whiteness embedded within the education system means that young Black women have to constantly find energy and develop strategies that enable them to navigate within it. This will inevitably make it more difficult to concentrate on working towards achieving academic 'success' and statistical evidence suggests that for many Black girls and young women, doing so has proved to be quite a challenge. Therefore, moving forward, it is imperative that research about this group should employ intersectional approaches that consider all of their identities and how they impact upon their educational journeys. Moreover, attention needs to be paid to the diversity within this group such as differing social class positions as well as ethnicities and cultural backgrounds which further affect how they engage and journey within the education system. Lastly, as asserted by Evans-Winters and Esposito (2010: 22), Black girls' "existence at the margins presents both constraints and possibilities for all educational reform efforts and overall societal transformation. Therefore, research with and on behalf of Black girls benefit the whole of society," (Evans-Winters & Esposito, 2010: 22).

Disclosure Statement

No potential conflict of interest was reported by the author(s).

Notes on Contributor

April-Louise M. O. O. Pennant is an award-winning doctoral researcher, funded by the Economic and Social Research Council (ESRC) in the Department of Education and Social Justice at the School of Education, University of Birmingham. She just passed her viva and is currently working in education policy in the Welsh Government.

ORCID

April-Louise M. O. O. Pennant http://orcid.org/0000-0002-1963-7832

References

Advance, H.E. (2019). *Equality þ higher education: Students statistical report 2018.* www.advance-he.ac.uk/knowledge-hub/equality-higher-education-statistical-report-2019

Ajegbo, K., Kiwan, D., & Sharma, S. (2007). *Diversity and citizenship curriculum review.* www.educationengland. org.uk/documents/pdfs/2007-ajegbo-report-citizenship.pdf

Alexander, C., & Bernard-Weekes, D. (2017). History lessons: Inequality, diversity and the national curriculum. *Race Ethnicity and Education, 20*(4), 478–494. https://doi.org/10.1080/13613324.2017.1294571

Anderson, L. (2006). Analytic autoethnography. *Journal of Contemporary Ethnography, 35*(4), 373–395. https://doi. org/10.1177/0891241605280449

Andrews, K. (2013). *Resisting racism: Race, inequality, and the Black supplementary school movement.* Trentham Books.

Andrews, K. (2016). The problem with political blackness: Lessons from the Black supplementary school movement. *Ethnic and Racial Studies, 39*(11), 2060–2078. https://doi.org/10.1080/01419870.2015.1131314

Arday, J., & Mirza, S. J. (Eds). (2018). *Dismantling race in higher education: Racism, whiteness and decolonising the academy.* Palgrave Macmillan.

Bain, Z. (2018). Is there such a thing as 'white ignorance' in British education? *Ethics and Education, 13*(1), 4–21. https://doi.org/10.1080/17449642.2018.1428716

BBC. (2019). *The British Black Panthers.* www.bbc.co.uk/mediacentre/proginfo/2019/32/the-british-black-panthers

Boylorn, R. M., & Orbe, M. P. (Eds.). (2014). *Critical autoethnography: intersecting cultural identities in everyday life.* Left Coast Press.

Brown, P. (2013). Education, opportunity and the prospects for social mobility. *British Journal of Sociology of Education, 34*(5–6), 678–700. https://doi.org/10.1080/01425692.2013.816036

Butler-Barnes, S. T., Leath, S., Williams, A., Byrd, C., Carter, R., & Chavous, T. M. (2018). Promoting resilience among African American girls: Racial identity as a protective factor. *Child development, 89*(6), e552–e571. https://doi.org/10.1111/cdev.12995

Cabinet office. (2017). *Race disparity audit: Summary findings from the ethnicity facts and figures website.* https://assets.publishing.service.gov.uk/government/uploads/system/uploads/attachment_data/file/686071/Revised_RDA_ report_March_2018.pdf

Carter, D. J. (2007). Why the black kids sit together at the stairs: The role of identity-affirming counter-spaces in a predominantly white high school. *Journal of Negro Education, 76*(4), 542–554.

Carter, D. J. (2008). Achievement as resistance: The development of a critical race achievement ideology among black achievers. *Harvard Educational Review, 78*(3), 466–497. https://doi.org/10.17763/haer.78.3. 83138829847hw844

Carter, P. L. (2003). "Black" cultural capital, status positioning, and schooling conflicts for low-income African American youth. *Social Problems, 50*(1), 136–155. https://doi.org/10.1525/sp.2003.50.1.136

Casey, K. (1993). *I Answer with my Life: Life histories of Women Teachers working for social change.* Routledge.

Chadderton, C. (2013). Towards a research framework for race in education: Critical race theory and Judith Butler. *International Journal of Qualitative Studies in Education, 26*(1), 39–55. https://doi.org/10.1080/09518398.2011. 650001

Chapman, T. K., & Bhopal, K. (2019). The perils of integration: Exploring the experiences of African American and black Caribbean students in predominately white secondary schools. *Ethnic and Racial Studies, 42*(7), 1110–1120. https://doi.org/10.1080/01419870.2018.1478110

Chigwada, R. (1987). Not victims- not superwomen. *Spare Rib, 183*, 14–18.

Clammer, J. (2015). Performing ethnicity: performance, gender, body and belief in the construction and signalling of identity. *Ethnic and Racial Studies, 38*(13), 2159–2166. https://doi.org/10.1080/01419870.2015.1045305

Collins, P. (2000). *Black feminist thought: Knowledge, Consciousness and the Politics of Empowerment* (2nd ed.). Routledge.

Cook, A. D. & Williams, T. (2015). Expanding intersectionality: Fictive kinship networks as supports for the educational aspirations of black women. *Western Journal of Black Studies, 39*(2), 157–166.

Coultas, V. (1989). Black girls and self-esteem. *Gender and Education, 1*(3), 283–294. https://doi.org/10.1080/0954025890010306

Crozier, G. (2005). There's a war against our children': Black educational under-achievement revisited. *British Journal of Sociology of Education, 26*(5), 585–598. https://doi.org/10.1080/01425690500293520

Dei, G. J. S. (2018). Black like me: Reframing blackness for decolonial politics. *A Journal of the American Educational Studies Association, 54*(2), 117–142. https://doi.org/10.1080/00131946.2018.1427586

Doharty, N. (2018). I FELT DEAD': applying a racial microaggressions framework to black students' experiences of black history month and black history. *Race Ethnicity and Education*, 1–20.

Du Bois, W. E. B. (1989). *The souls of black folk*. Penguin.

Dumas, M. J. (2014). Losing an arm': schooling as a site of black suffering. *Race Ethnicity and Education, 17*(1), 1–29. https://doi.org/10.1080/13613324.2013.850412

Evans-Winters, V. E., & Esposito, J. (2010). Other people's daughters: Critical race feminism and black girls' education. *Educational Foundations*, 11–24.

Fuller, M. (1980). Black Girls in a London Comprehensive. In R. Deem (Eds), *Schooling for women's work* (pp. 52–66). Routledge & Kegan Paul Ltd.

Gillborn, D. (2005). Education policy as an act of white supremacy whiteness: Critical race theory and education reform. *Journal of Education Policy, 20*(4), 485–505.

Gilroy, P. (1987). *There ain't no black in the union jack: The cultural politics of race and nation*. Routledge.

Givens, J. R. (2016). A grammar for black education beyond borders: exploring technologies of schooling in the African diaspora. *Race Ethnicity and Education, 19*(6), 1288–1302. https://doi.org/10.1080/13613324.2015.1103724

Gov.uk. (2019a). *GCSE results ('Attainment 8') for children aged 14 to 16 (key stage 4)*. www.ethnicity-facts-figures.service.gov.uk/education-skills-and-training/11-to-16-years-old/gcse-results-attainment-8-for-children-aged-14-to-16-key-stage-4/latest#by-ethnicity-and-gender

Gov.uk. (2019b). *Students aged 16 to 18 achieving at least 3 A grades at A level*. www.ethnicity-facts-figures. service.gov.uk/education-skills-and-training/a-levels/students-aged-16-to-18-achieving-3-a-grades-or-better-at-a-level/latest

Gray, D. L., Hope, E. C., & Matthews, J. S. (2018). Black and Belonging at School: A Case for Interpersonal, Instructional, and Institutional Opportunity Structures. *Educational Psychologist, 53*(2), 97–113. https://doi.org/10. 1080/00461520. 2017.1421466

Greyerbiehl, L. & Mitchell, D. (2014). An intersectional social capital analysis of the influence of historically black sororities on African American women's college experiences at a predominantly white institution. *Journal of Diversity in Higher Education, 7*(4), 282–294. https://doi.org/10.1037/a0037605

Guiffrida, D. A. (2003). African American student organizations as agents of social integration. *Journal of College Student Development, 44*(3), 304–319. https://doi.org/10.1353/csd.2003.0024

Hamilton, D. G. (2018). Too hot to handle: African Caribbean pupils and students as toxic consumers and commodities in the educational market. *Race Ethnicity and Education, 21*(5), 573–592. https://doi.org/10.1080/13613324. 2017.1376635

Herring, M., Jankowski, T. B., & Brown, R. E. (1999). Pro-black doesn't mean anti-white: The structure of African-American Group Identity. *The Journal of Politics, 61*(2), 363–386. https://doi.org/10.2307/2647508

hooks, B. (1990). *Yearning: Race, gender and cultural politics.* South End Press.

Joseph-Salisbury, R. (2019). Institutionalised whiteness, racial microaggressions and black bodies out of place in higher education. *Whiteness and Education*, 4(1), 1–17. https://doi.org/10.1080/23793406.2019.1620629

Kelly, L. L. (2018). A snapchat story: How black girls develop strategies for critical resistance in school. *Learning, Media and Technology*, 43(4), 374–389. https://doi.org/10.1080/17439884.2018.1498352

Kynard, C. (2010). From candy girls to cyber sista-cipher: Narrating black females' color-consciousness and counter- stories in and out of school. *Harvard Educational Review*, 80(1), 30–141. https://doi.org/10.17763/haer.80.1. 4611255014427701

Ladson-Billings, G. (1998). Just what is critical race theory and what's it doing in a nice field like education? *International Journal of Qualitative Studies in Education*, 11(1), 7–24. https://doi.org/10.1080/095183998236863

Lake, J. (2015). Autoethnography and reflective practice: reconstructing the doctoral thesis experience. *Reflective Practice*, 16(5), 677–687. https://doi.org/10.1080/14623943.2015.1071247

Lam, V., & Smith, G. (2009). African and Caribbean adolescents in Britain: ethnic identity and Britishness. *Ethnic and Racial Studies*, 32(7), 1248–1270. https://doi.org/10.1080/01419870802298421

Lorde, A. (2009). Poet as teacher—Human as poet—Teacher as human. In R. P. Byrd, J. B. Cole, & B. Guy-Sheftall (Eds), *I am your sister: Collected and unpublished writings of Audre Lorde* (pp. 182–183). Oxford University Press.

Mac an Ghaill, M. (1988). *Young, gifted and black.* Open University Press.

Maylor, U. (2009). Is It because I'm Black? A Black research experience. *Race Ethnicity and Education*, 12(1), 53–64. https://doi.org/10.1080/13613320802650949

Miller, D. B. & MacIntosh, R. (1999). Promoting resilience in urban African American adolescents: Racial socialisation and identity as protective factors. *Social Work Research*, 23(3), 159–169. https://doi.org/10.1093/swr/23.3.159

Mirza, H. (2008). *Race, gender and educational desire: Why Black women succeed and fail.* Routledge.

Mirza, H. S. (1986). Absent again? No excuses!: Black girls and the Swann Report. *Ethnic and Racial Studies*, 9(2), 247–249. https://doi.org/10.1080/01419870. 1986.9993526

Mirza, H. S. (1992). *Young, female and black.* Routledge.

Mirza, H. S. (2006). Transcendence over Diversity: black women in the academy. *Policy Futures in Education*, 4(2), 101–103. pp https://doi.org/10.2304/pfie.2006.4.2.101

Mirza, H., ed. (1997). *Black British Feminism: A reader.* Routledge.

Modood, T. (2004). Capitals, ethnic identity and educational qualifications. *Cultural Trends*, 13(2), 87–105. https://doi. org/10.1080/0954896042000267170

O'Connor, C. (2002). Black women beating the odds from one generation to the next: How the changing dynamics of constraint and opportunity affect the process of educational resilience. *American Educational Research Journal*, 39(4), 855–903. https://doi.org/10.3102/00028312039004855

Ojo, E. (2009). Support systems and women of the diaspora. *New Directions for Adult and Continuing Education*, 122, 73–82. https://doi.org/10.1002/ace.336

Osborne, S. (2016). *Black British students 'psychologically damaged by white curriculum' says, NUS president.* www.express.co.uk/news/uk/713043/Malia-Bouattia-National-Union-Students-black-British-students-psychologically-damaged

Payne, Y. A., & Suddler, C. (2014). Cope, conform, or resist? Functions of a Black American identity at a predominantly white university. *Equity & Excellence in Education*, *47*(3), 385–403. https://doi.org/10.1080/10665684.2014.933756

Pennant, A.-L. (2019). *"Look, I have gone through the education system and I have tried damn hard to get to where I am, so no one is gonna stop me!": The educational journeys and experiences of Black British women graduates* [Unpublished PhD thesis]. University of Birmingham.

Phoenix, A. (2009). De-colonising practices: Negotiating narratives from racialised and gendered experiences of education. *Race Ethnicity and Education*, *12*(1), 101–114. https://doi.org/10.1080/13613320802651053

Pratt, M. L. (1991). Arts of the contact zone. *Profession*, *91*, 33–40.

Puwar, N. (2004). *Space invaders: Race, gender and bodies out of place*. Berg Publishers.

Rattansi, A. (2000). On being and not being Brown/Black/Black-British: Racism, class, sexuality and ethnicity in post- imperial Britain. *Interventions*, *2*(1), 118–134. https://doi.org/10.1080/136980100360832

Reynolds, T. (2002). Rethinking a black feminist standpoint. *Ethnic and Racial Studies*, *25*(4), 591–606. https://doi.org/10.1080/01419870220136709

Ricks, S. A. (2014). Falling through the Cracks: Black girls and education. *Interdisciplinary Journal of Teaching and Learning*, *4*(1), 10–21.

Rollock, N. (2007a). Why Black girls don't matter: Exploring how race and gender shape academic success in an inner city school. *Support for Learning*, *22*(4), 197–202. https://doi.org/10.1111/j.1467-9604.2007.00471.x

Rollock, N. (2007b). Legitimizing Black academic failure: deconstructing staff discourses on academic success, appearance and behaviour. *International Studies in Sociology of Education*, *17*(3), 275–287. https://doi.org/10.1080/09620210701543924

Rollock, N. (2013). A political investment: revisiting race and racism in the research process. *Discourse: Studies in the Cultural Politics of Education*, *34*(4), 492–509.

Rollock, N., Gillborn, D., Vincent, C., & Ball, S. J. (2015). *The colour of class: The educational strategies of the Black middle classes*. Routledge.

Rollock, D. A., Westman, J. S. & Johnson, C. (1992). A black student support group on a predominantly white university campus: Issues for counselors and therapists. *The Journal for Specialists in Group Work*, *17*(4), 243–252. https://doi.org/10.1080/01933929208414356

Shilliam, R. (2015). Black academia: The doors have been opened but the architecture remains the same. In C. Alexander, & J. Arday (Eds), *Aiming higher: Race, inequality and diversity in the academy* (pp. 32–34). The Runnymede Trust.

Sian, K. (2017). Being black in a white world: Understanding racism in British universities. *Papeles del CEIC*, *2017*(2), 1–26. https://doi.org/10.1387/pceic.17625

Social Market Foundation (2017). *On course for success? Student retention at university*. www.smf. co.uk/wp-content/uploads/2017/07/UPP-final-report.pdf (accessed on 30th April 2019).

Solorzano, D. G., & Yosso, T. J. (2002). Critical race methodology: Counter-storytelling as an analytical framework for education research. *Qualitative Inquiry*, *8*(1), 23–44. https://doi.org/10.1177/107780040200800103

Swain, H. (2019). *Students want their curriculums decolonised. Are universities listening?* www.theguardian. com/education/2019/jan/30/students-want-their-curriculums-decolonised-are-universities-listening

Swartz, E. (1992). Emancipatory narratives: Rewriting the master script in the school curriculum. *Journal of Negro Education*, *61*(3), 341–355. https://doi.org/10.2307/2295252

Tomlin, C., Wright, C., & Mocombe, P. (2014). A structural approach to understanding Black British Caribbean Academic Underachievement in the United Kingdom. *Journal of Social Science for Policy Implications*, *2*(2), 37–58.

UCL. (2015). *Why is my curriculum white?* www.dtmh.ucl.ac.uk/videos/curriculum-white/

UUK and NUS. (2019). *#ClosingTheGap Black, Asian and Minority Ethnic Student attainment at UK Universities: Case Studies*. www.universitiesuk.ac.uk/policy-and-analysis/reports/Documents/2019/bame-student-attainment-uk-universities-case-studies.pdf

Vincent, C., Rollock, N., Ball, S., & Gillborn, D. (2012a). Raising middle-class Black children: Parenting priorities, actions and strategies. *Sociology*, *47*(3), 427–442. https://doi.org/10.1177/0038038512454244

Vincent, C., Rollock, N., Ball., & Gillborn, D. (2012b). Being strategic, being watchful, being determined: Black middle-class parents and schooling. *British Journal of Sociology of Education*, *33*(3), 337–354. https://doi.org/10.1080/01425692.2012.668833

Wallace, D. (2017). Reading 'race' in bourdieu? Examining Black cultural capital among Black Caribbean youth in South London. *Sociology*, *51*(5), 907–923. https://doi.org/10.1177/0038038516643478

Wallace, D. (2018). Cultural capital as whiteness? Examining logics of ethno-racial representation and resistance. *British Journal of Sociology of Education*, *39*(4), 466–482. https://doi.org/10.1080/01425692.2017.1355228

Weekes, D. (2003). Keeping it in the community: creating safe spaces for black girlhood. Community, *Work & Family*, *6*(1), 47–61. https://doi.org/10.1080/1366880032000063897

Yosso, T. J. (2005). Whose culture has capital? A critical race theory discussion of community cultural wealth. *Race Ethnicity and Education*, *8*(1), 69–91.

Index

abolition 86–88
affective approaches in education
189–199
Afrocentricity 51–53; Afrocentric
education 53–54; critical comparative
analysis of CRT and 54–55
ambivalence, race 77–79, 86–91; post-
race as an opportunity 92–97; from
racial to post-imaginary 79; the
stubborn significance of race and
racism 79–86anti-Blackness 165–166;
and Lacanian psychoanalysis
167–172, 175–176; and No Child
Left Behind 172–175; and race in
education 166–167
Asian-American children 147–149;
education 149–159; institutionalized
discourses 157–159; and power
relations 159–161; and racializing
discourses 149–155; and segregated
schooling 155–157
attendance, qualification for 149–155, 160
audience 124–139
authority 104–108, 116–119; and
ethnography and hospitality 109–112;
and *le français parisien* 112–116; and
migration to Canada 108–109

Big Bang race theory 88–90
Black bodies 170–172, 187–188,
206–207
blackness 130, 135, 137, 201–203,
206–211; and educational journey
204–205; literature; and PhD research
205–206; and self 203–204

California, education in 147–149;
institutionalized discourses

constituting childhood 157–159;
and power relations 159–161; and
racializing discourses 149–155; and
segregated schooling 155–157
California School Law: 1864 150;
1866 151
Canada 108–109
class: critical race theory class narrative
60–63
color-blind ideology 63–67, 81–82
comparative analysis: of CRT and
Afrocentricity 54–55
critical comparative analysis: of CRT and
Afrocentricity 54–55
critical pedagogy 46–48, 71–72; and
Afrocentric education 53–54; and
Afrocentricity 51–55; and the centrality
of racism in education 63–67; and
CRT 48–51, 60–63, 67–70; and points
of connections 55–57; and teacher
education and educational leadership
70–71
critical race theory (CRT) 48–50, 71–72,
165–166; and the centrality of racism in
education 63–67; class narrative 60–63;
critical comparative analysis 54–55; and
Lacanian psychoanalysis 167–172,
175–176; links to critical pedagogy
67–70; links to education 50–51; and
No Child Left Behind 172–175; race
in education 166–167; and teacher
education and educational leadership
70–71
curriculum 206

Derrida, Jacques 8, 39, 78, 83, 105,
107, 109, 116, 119n3, 121n15
desire 14, 18–26